WITHDRAWN BY THE
UNIVERSITY OF MICHIGAN

THE KNESSET

SARA F. YOSELOFF MEMORIAL PUBLICATIONS
In Judaism and Jewish Affairs

This volume is one in a series established in memory
of Sara F. Yoseloff,
who devoted her life to the making of books.

THE KNESSET

Parliament in the Israeli
Political System

Gregory S. Mahler

RUTHERFORD • MADISON • TEANECK
FAIRLEIGH DICKENSON UNIVERSITY PRESS
LONDON AND TORONTO: ASSOCIATED UNIVERSITY PRESSES

© 1981 by Associated University Presses, Inc.

Associated University Presses, Inc.
4 Cornwall Drive
East Brunswick, N.J. 08816

Associated University Presses Ltd
69 Fleet Street
London EC4Y 1EU, England

Associated University Presses
Toronto M5E 1A7, Canada

Library of Congress Cataloging in Publication Data

Mahler, Gregory S., 1950-
   The Knesset: Parliament in the Israeli political system.

   Bibliography: p.
   Includes index.
   1. Israel. **Knesset**. I. Title.
JQ1825.P35M34   328.5694   80-67633
ISBN 0-8386-3071-5   AACR2

Printed in the United States of America

For Marjorie and Alden

Contents

List of Tables		9
List of Figures		11
Preface		13
Acknowledgments		17

Part I: The Israeli Political System

1	Introduction: The Study of Legislatures	23
2	The Israeli Political System	34
	The Constitutional Framework. The Political Party System. The Electoral System. Ideology. Implications of the Political System for Legislative Behavior.	
3	Government Coalitions and The Knesset	54
	Introduction. Theories of Coalition Formation. Parties in the Knesset and Political Coalitions. Knesset Coalitions and Cabinet Formation. Inhibitors of Minimum Winning Size. Returns to Knesset Parties for Coalition Membership.	

Part II: The Legislative System

4	The Knesset in the Israeli Political System	85
	The Knesset as a Parliamentary System. The Member of Knesset. Summary.	
5	The Member of Knesset	106
	Demographic Characteristics. Political Socialization. Political Awareness. Political Interest. Party Identification. Summary.	

6	The Recruitment of Members of Knesset Early Patterns of Recruitment. Patterns of Later Recruitment to Party Activity. Patterns of Officeholding and Candidacies. Summary.	138

Part III: Legislative Attitudes and Behavior

7	Legislators' Perceptions of the Israeli Political System Perceptions of the Job. Legislative Roles. The Legislators and Knesset Procedure. Legislative Expertise and Cabinet Membership. "Influentials" in the Knesset. Summary and Conclusions.	163
8	Legislative Behavior in the Knesset: Intralegislative Frustration and Extralegislative Effectiveness. Legislators and the Government. Legislators and Committees. Legislators and the Knesset. Legislators and Constituencies. Summary and Conclusions.	186
9	The Knesset in the Eighties Introduction. Some Comparative Observations. The Ascendancy of Menachem Begin. Reforms in the Knesset.	210
Appendix 1	A Note on the Interviews	226
Appendix 2	The Interview Schedule	229
Bibliography		242
Index		249

List of Tables

1.1	Party Distribution in the Sample	31
3.1	Party Membership in the Knesset through 1974	59
3.2	Parties Represented in Cabinets	62
3.3	Ministries and Occupants	72
3.4	"Keys" to the Cabinet	76
5.1	General Descriptive Characteristics of MKs	107
5.2	Geographic Backgrounds of MKs	110
5.3	Jewish/Zionist Organization Membership prior to Migration	111
5.4	Education of MKs	112
5.5	Occupational Backgrounds of MKs	114
5.6	Average Ages of First Political Awareness of Four Cohorts of Israeli Legislators	117
5.7	Average Ages of First Political Awareness of Israeli Legislators by Location of Birth	119
5.8	Average Ages of First Political Awareness of Israeli Legislators and Parental Politics	120
5.9	Correlation Analysis of Family Environments of MKs: Political Awareness	122
5.10	Subjects of Initial Political Awareness of Israeli Legislators	123
5.11	Averages Ages of First Political Interest and Awareness of Four Cohorts of Israeli Legislators	125
5.12	Correlation Analysis of Family Environments of MKs: Political Interest	127
5.13	Average Ages of First Political Interest of Israeli Legislators by Location of Birth	128
5.14	Subjects of Initial Political Interest of Israeli Legislators	129
5.15	Average Ages of Initial Party Identification of Israeli Legislators and Parental Politics	132

5.16	Correlation Analysis of Family Environments of MKs: Party Identification	134
5.17	Average Ages of Initial Party Identification of MKs and Why They Identified with the Party	135
6.1	"Early" Recruitment Patterns of Israeli Legislators	143
6.2	Correlation Analysis of Variables in the Early Recruitment of Israeli Legislators	146
6.3	Average Ages of First Party Activity and Group Membership of Israeli Legislators	149
6.4	Patterns of Party Officeholding of Israeli Legislators Prior to Legislative Candidacy	150
6.5	Types of Preparliamentary Offices Held by Israeli Legislators	152
6.6	Levels of Preparliamentary Offices Held by Israeli Legislators	153
6.7	Recruitment to Candidacy of MKs	155
6.8	Reasons Offered by MKs for Their Receiving Legislative Nominations	157
7.1	Gratifying Characteristics of the MK's Job	165
7.2	Burdensome Characteristics of the MK's Job	166
7.3	Areas of Indicated Expertise of Members of Knesset	173
7.4	Criteria Applied for the Selection of Cabinet Members	174
7.5	Cabinet Opportunities for MKs	176
7.6	Likelihood of Cabinet Membership for MKs	177
7.7	"Influentials" in the Knesset	180
7.8	Influential Government Ministries and Knesset Committees	183
8.1	Which Ministers Are Contacted Most Often	191
8.2	Committee Membership and Committee Interest	195
8.3	Committee Work and Committee Preparation	197
8.4	Perceived Functions of Legislative Committees	198
8.5	Factors That Could Affect MK Committee Influence	199
8.6	Areas Other Than Committees through Which MKs Could Influence the Work of the Knesset	201
8.7	Things MKs Would Miss Not Being in Knesset	206
8.8	How MKs Feel Their Time Should Be Spent	207
9.1	Final Results of Elections to the Ninth Knesset May 17, 1977	215

List of Figures

1.1	Factors in the Political System Affecting Legislative Behavior	30
2.1	The Evolution of Israel's Political Parties	40
2.2	Party Ideologies	49
4.1	A Schematic Representation of Individual Legislative Behavior in the Political System	100
5.1	Average Ages of First Political Awareness and First Political Interest of Four Cohorts of Israeli Legislators	126
6.1	Prelegislative Political Experiences of Israeli Legislators: Pathways to Parliamentary Office	141
8.1	A Schematic Representation of Individual Legislative Behavior in the Political System	188

Preface

This is a study of legislative behavior in one of the world's most unique political settings. Every nation-state can be referred to as being unique, strictly speaking, because of a number of idiosyncratic characteristics it may be said to possess. Many attributes of politics in Israel and the Israeli Knesset, however, make the Knesset more than simply different from other legislatures and make it an excellent subject of study. Any one or two of these attributes would be interesting to study; when all of these special aspects are found in one setting, as they are in the Knesset, the study is especially interesting.

Israel is a study in contrasts. It can be characterized as a Western democracy in a non-Western setting in which democracies do not traditionally fare well. Israel is a new nation that faces some of the problems that are characteristic of developing nations and, at the same time, has many of the problems of industrialized and developed states. It has a system of government without a fully written constitution and in which many of the most basic principles of the state have not yet been fully resolved. It is a country in which the observer may witness debates over the role of religion in the political process and whether Zionism as a concept has any further role in society, and in which immigration has played a more important role than in perhaps any other country in the world.

In most countries it is possible to talk about a single political culture in which political values are passed down from generation to generation. However, because of the nature and amount of immigration to Israel this process can be an extraordinarily difficult one. Only 36 percent of our sample of legislators were born in Israel, and only 14 percent had parents who were born in Israel; the rest are immigrants. In many respects, it is surprising that

Israel as a nation exists—individuals from Poland, South Africa, the Soviet Union, the United States, Germany, France, and many other settings have been able to come together to create a new country and develop a new political culture.

This book addresses these topics and controversies through a discussion of the Knesset, Israel's parliament. Because of the representative nature of Israel's Knesset, all of the issues that divide the society at large can be found to be divisive in the legislature. The legislature is a "mirror" of the public, and a study of the legislature tells us a great deal about the society.

The primary focus of this book is upon legislative behavior and the role of the individual legislator in the political system. After an introduction dealing with the study of legislatures in contemporary political science, the Israeli political system is described in a chapter discussing the constitutional framework of Israeli politics, political parties, elections, and ideologies. A discussion of coalition governments and their role in Israeli politics is then presented, laying the framework for a thorough understanding of the environment within which the individual member of Knesset (MK) operates.

The second section of the book begins with a chapter on the legislative system (chapter 4), which discusses the Knesset as a parliamentary system and explains patterns of behavior and the role of the individual MK in the Knesset. The individual himself is the focus of chapter 5, which deals not only with the demographic characteristics of the MKs—where they were born, their parents' backgrounds, their educations, and so on—but also with the political socialization of the MKs and the process by which they developed their political awareness, political interest, and party identification. Political recruitment, a continuation of the political socialization process, drawing individuals into the political arena, is the subject of chapter 6, which covers childhood political activities, later party activity, and patterns of officeholding and candidacies prior to Knesset membership.

The third section of the book deals with contemporary legislative attitudes and behavior. Chapter 7 deals with the legislators' perceptions of the Israeli political system and presents data dealing with MKs' perceptions of many issues: their jobs, the roles of legislators, current Knesset procedures, cabinet membership, and the nature and impact of influence in the

Knesset. Chapter 8 focuses on behavior itself, discussing relationships between legislators and the Government, legislators and committees, legislators and the Knesset, and legislators and their constituencies. The last chapter is an introduction to the Begin era, tracing his rise to the prime minister's office and discussing the implications his ascendancy may have for Israeli policy as well as for legislative behavior in the Knesset.

Acknowledgments

One of the rewards associated with the completion of a project such as the writing of this book is that one is afforded the opportunity to thank those who have provided support, assistance, and encouragement along the way. Some of these individuals have been less directly related to this project than others, but I nonetheless feel grateful to them for their overall guidance and encouragement. John D. Lewis and Jere Bruner of Oberlin College have consistently encouraged and supported me since my departure from that institution. R. Taylor Cole, Allan Kornberg, and Richard Trilling (formerly) of Duke University all provided a great deal of advice and support in the research phase of this project. I owe a special debt of gratitude to Allan Kornberg, whose work on Canadian legislative behavior served as a model for my research and whose comments and critiques contributed greatly to this study.

My year abroad was made possible by a Fulbright-Hays Research Grant, for which I am grateful to the U.S. Department of Health, Education, and Welfare. Duke University provided funds for the initial phase of compilation and analysis of this data.

In Israel, eighty-six members of Knesset took time out from their busy schedules to talk with me, patiently explaining some of the more complex aspects of Israeli political life to me. Emanuel Gutmann of the Political Science Department of Hebrew University in Jerusalem provided me with advice, a point of orientation, and some initial contacts in the Knesset. Itzik Mazon, a page in the Knesset, was invaluable to me by reminding MKs of their appointments with me—which they forgot all too often—and by helping me to arrange meetings with other MKs.

On more occasions than I can remember I received support and encouragement from my parents and parents-in-law, Irwin and Eleanor Mahler and Max and Grace Ward, support that was very important to me. Finally, for the support she provided in the course of this research and writing I thank my wife, Marjorie. Without her help and encouragement, in all phases of this project, this book might never have been written.

THE KNESSET

Part I

The Israeli Political System

1

Introduction: The Study of Legislatures

The study of legislatures and their component parts—legislators—has been among the most popular subjects of scrutiny for political scientists in recent years for a number of reasons, not the least of which is that the national legislature is usually an important structure in national governmental systems.[1] Legislatures are among the oldest political institutions known to man as well. Although their functions and powers within particular political systems have varied and continue to vary greatly today on a country-by-country basis, the assumption that legislative institutions are representative, if not embodiments of the public will, continues to be widely shared.

Many reasons have been suggested as providing a rationale for the study of legislatures, including the facts that "the generic function of a legislature is to make the values, goals, and attitudes of a social system authoritative in the form of legislative decisions," that the legislators serve as role models for the public and in this way serve an educative function for society generally, and that legislatures "often perform the function of facilitating a catharsis of societal grievances by allowing for the expression of grievances in a public forum."[2] As a very general rationale, "the very prevalence of legislative institutions . . . may be construed as affording *prima facie* evidence of their relevance for inquiry."[3]

It has been suggested that legislatures may be more important in some contexts than in others, as, for example, the central role that parliaments play in promoting the stability of a regime.[4] Another example of such a context is the process of modernization: legislatures are important to study in this regard "because of their affinity to aspects of modernization itself."[5] Sisson points out that "legislatures, although relatively impotent at one point in time, may assume new and more powerful functions as modernization proceeds."[6] Although legislatures may have more direct impact upon some subjects or processes (e.g., regularizing and helping to make individual and group interaction predictable) than others (e.g., land reform), it is not difficult to imagine ways in which legislatures can affect wide areas of human concern. The universal acceptance in contemporary politics of the existence of legislatures should afford, in itself, a sufficient rationale for their study.

Approaches to the study of legislatures and legislators have varied greatly in recent years. Some political scientists have approached legislatures with a "structural-functional" framework of analysis in mind,[7] whereas others have used a systems approach.[8] Still others have emphasized role theory in their conceptual frameworks.[9] Some researchers have used more than one approach finding, for example, that role theory could fruitfully be applied within a "systems" approach to politics.[10] The several approaches that have been used to study legislatures have been a cause of concern to some scholars. Thus, Patterson and Wahlke have noted the ". . . lack of a common framework, common focus, and common agreement upon what problems are important and what questions most need answering."[11]

This concern over a lack of a common framework of analysis in the discipline, as well as a lack of agreement over which problems should be the focus of study, is certainly nothing new; social scientists have been decrying the situation for years. The problem is a significant one in that because of its existence, political scientists often talk past each other, defining similar concepts differently and challenging each other to prove that what each is studying is of relevance for a greater understanding of the system at large.

Although the quest for a general macro-level theory of the political system may be futile, a greater amount of middle-range theorizing about politics and political causation is certainly a worthy goal. Better developed middle-range theories of the political system, the way it operates, and the interrelationships between and among processes and variables active within it may lead to the point at which there is no lack of a common framework, common focus, or common agreement upon what problems are important and what questions most need answering.

Introduction: The Study of Legislatures

In spite of the general lack of agreement on how to approach the study of legislatures, or upon which are the most important questions to ask, there is a surprising degree of consensus as to the structures and functions of legislatures, as well as their common attributes.

> Manifestations of parliament do share at least two identifying structural characteristics ... (1) their members are formally equal to one another in status, distinguishing parliaments from hierarchically organized organizations; and (2) the authority of their members depends upon their claim to be representing the rest of the community.[12]

In general, five broad functions that legislatures perform for political systems may be derived from the literature. These are, not necessarily in order of importance: (a) criticism and control of other branches of government, most notably the executive; (b) debate; (c) legislation or lawmaking; (d) communication, representation, and legitimation; and (e) recruitment, education, and socialization.

Not all legislatures can be said to perform all of these functions, nor, if they do, can it be said that they perform them all equally well. On the other hand, some legislatures, because of idiosyncratic characteristics of the systems in which they can be found, may be said to perform functions in addition to the five discussed here. Because a legislature fails to perform *all* of these functions does not mean that it performs none of them. As Riggs suggests, "if an assembly exists, it must serve some function in its polity, or it would not be able to survive."[13]

Much research on legislatures mentions the *criticism and control* function as being necessary for the maintenance of a stable political system. Such phrases as "criticizing and checking executive powers"[14] may frequently be found in the literature. This function of the legislative branch of government has its roots in seventeenth- and eighteenth-century democratic political theory, when the role of the legislature as a check upon the arbitrary power of monarchs was first practiced. An outgrowth of this function has been the recent "decline of legislatures" literature,[15] which suggests that legislatures have, in modern times, been increasingly less able to satisfactorily perform this very important function.

A second function ascribed to legislatures is that of *debate*, or discussion of values and rules for the political system. This has been variously described in the literature as "proposing, deliberating, and deciding about public policy,"[16] or as "providing a forum for discussion and criticism of government policies,"[17] to cite but two examples. Although this function is closely related both to the lawmaking/legislating and criticizing functions, it is easy to imagine situations in which it would *not* fit within those functional categories. For example, in many nations the role of the legislature in the legislative process is rather modest. The legislature might discuss a bill proposed by the executive or the bureaucracy, but the bill may become law even if it is never actually voted on and passed by the legislature. Alternatively, a legislature might have the power to vote on a bill *in toto*, but not to amend it, or it may vote to reject a bill and the bill still might become law by executive decree. In such instances, a legislature may appear to be performing both a debating and a legislating function, but *de facto* its function is limited to debate.

The function that is most frequently ascribed to legislatures in Western countries is that of *lawmaking*. "From the theorists of the 17th Century to those of the contemporary world, it has been held as axiomatic. . . that the function of legislatures was to make laws."[18] This legislative function is one that is almost universally attributed to legislative bodies—even if they only ratify or "rubber stamp" legislation introduced from outside the legislature. Increasingly, however, the lawmaking function is no longer being considered the litmus test by which a legislature is judged. Singhvi observes that "in formal terms the principal function of the Parliament . . . is to pass legislation. But, legislation is only a part of the Parliament's business,"[19] Ultimately, the question of *how much* of a legislative function a legislature plays in a given political system is an empirical question.

The fourth function suggested is that of *communication, representation, and legitimation*. Included in this function are actions such as appraising and explaining to constituents actions taken within the legislature, answering mail and other forms of communication, interceding with members of a bureaucratic agency on behalf of individuals or groups, and having resources allocated to a constituency. Much of the legislator's individual authority derives from his or her ability to undertake these activities,[20] and to successfully perform them. The collective actions of legislators in these matters help build support not only for the legislature as an institution but also for the regime itself. By so doing the legislature also helps clothe the actions of a regime's leaders with legitimacy.[21]

A chain of three interconnected concepts is at work here. First, legislators are necessarily aware of communications, both supportive and demanding, from their constituents. Second, by performing actions in response to these communications, the legislators can be said to be acting in a representative manner. Finally, by acting in a representative manner, the legislator can contribute significantly to the legitimacy of the governmental structure.

The fifth function that has been attributed to legislatures is that of *recruitment, education, and socialization*. Through the process of attracting individuals to politics, giving them political experience, and enabling them to attain higher office, legislatures engage in the recruitment process. By engaging in open and publicized debates, investigations, and well-reported discussions, legislatures help to educate the public both as to issues that are important and to possible positions they can take on issues. By serving as role models and by developing and maintaining political norms, legislatures actively participate in the process of political socialization. In some circumstances legislatures are invested with special functions as a result of a particular constitutional framework or historical background. For example, in addition to the other functions it performs, the British Parliament (and many parliaments like it) also has an elective function, that of selecting the Prime Minister. The U.S. House of Representatives has a similar elective function, but because of the nature of the Electoral College and historical factors it has only rarely been called upon to perform this task.

In addition to a consensus related to the functions just described, there is also some degree of consensus as to structures and other common attributes of legislatures. Although legislatures may vary greatly in size ("from between 24 and 30 national lawmakers in such nations as Barbados, Botswana, and Swaziland, to 888 members in China's unicameral assembly"[22]), and type (some unicameral and some bicameral[23]), legislatures share many characteristics.

Legislatures are assemblies of individuals—elected or appointed—who come together to perform some or all of the functions discussed. These assemblies are governed by rules, either written or unwritten, perhaps encoded in a national constitution or encoded elsewhere, regarding the method of selection of legislators, their rights and duties, their roles in the political system, and their relationship with other branches of the government. These assemblies may have many or few officers, and may have greater or lesser degrees of individual opportunities for action, such as introducing legislation.

Legislative behavior is important to study because of the nature of the legislature itself, and because of the functions that the legislature serves in the polity of which it is a part. The nature of the legislature in virtually all political systems dictates that the output of the legislative body will be a function, to greater and lesser degrees, of the interaction between and among individual legislators, as well as between and among individual legislators and bureaucracies, societal needs and demands, and other extralegislative factors.

The role that individual legislators play in the generation of legislative output varies in different political systems. According to many theorists, the manner in which a legislator perceives his or her roles in different subsystems of the political world will influence the way he or she behaves politically. A political role, as the term is used here, consists of "... a pattern of expected behavior for individuals holding particular positions in a system."[24]

> Legislative role orientation, and hence behavior, is thus a product of both initial expectations held by an individual for the legislative position, and attitudes and perspectives subsequently developed in response to the expectations and requirements of significant others interacting with him in the legislative system.[25]

Much research has been done that indicates that in those situations in which legislators perceive their role in the legislative process as being of minimal importance or significance for the political system, they will behave accordingly and will be much more likely to become alienated, apathetic, or cynical than legislators who feel highly efficacious. Mezey's examination of the behavior of legislators in Thailand in a "minimal" legislative setting illustrates this pattern.[26]

Various lists, typologies, and frameworks of legislative roles have appeared in the literature. One author lists seventeen possible roles; others list twenty-three.[27] Rather than debate the exact number of roles that a political actor, in our case a legislator, could assume—if, indeed, such a list is even possible—we simply state that the possibilities are numerous. The literature seems to be in agreement that variations in role perceptions can affect role behavior, which, in turn, can affect legislative behavior.

All legislative behavior, and thereby legislative output, is influenced by many factors in the legislative system, including the constitutional system in which the legislator acts;[28] formal substructures within the legislative system, including committees;[29] legislative staff and services;[30] legislative buildings and facilities;[31] party organization inside the legislature;[32] legislators' backgrounds and socialization;[33] legislative recruitment;[34] constituency and interest group pressures;[35] and party organization outside the legislature.[36]

All these structures and subsystems of the "legislative system" influence legislative action, which, in turn, affects the larger political system. These structures and subsystems are of two types, those that are included within or are related to the legislative assembly itself, and those which are found outside of the legislative assembly itself. These factors are represented in Figure 1.1.

This book presents a study of legislative behavior in a specific legislature in a specific national setting: the Knesset in Israel. More specifically, this study focuses upon legislative behavior in the Eighth Knesset (1973–77), the last Knesset controlled by the Labor party prior to the ascendency of Menachem Begin's Likud coalition. The study describes and documents, as thoroughly as possible, those political structures, institutions, and behaviors that are of significance in Israel's legislative system and that affect behavior in the Knesset.

Many of the structures and systems described in this chapter are shown in the course of this book to be of great significance in determining legislative behavior in the Knesset—both within and outside the legislature. Some of these structures, because of the idiosyncratic characteristics of the Israeli political system, will be

INTRA-LEGISLATIVE FACTORS	EXTRA-LEGISLATIVE FACTORS
Constitutional System	Socialization
Formal Substructures	Recruitment
Staff and Services	Background
Physical Plant	Groups
Party	Party

Legislative Behavior

Figure 1.1

Factors in the Political System
Affecting Legislative Behavior

seen to have very little, if any, impact upon legislative behavior.

The Knesset has occupied a critical place in the Israeli political system. The creation of a new state places great demands upon all existing political institutions, and many very difficult decisions have had to be resolved by the Knesset in its first thirty years of existence. There was never any doubt that a legislature should exist in the new political system; Israel was from the outset committed to democratic political structures, and the 120-member Knesset (literally "assembly") was an obvious political structure.[37]

The study of Israel's Knesset affords the opportunity to observe the heart of Israeli politics. Very little that goes on in Israeli politics is not reflected in the behavior of the Knesset or in the behavior of individual members of Knesset (hereafter MKs). The Israeli situation is a fascinating study of legislative behavior in a multiparty parliamentary system in which legislative structures and processes are both imported and native, much as are the people of Israel themselves.

Introduction: The Study of Legislatures

Data used in this study, unless otherwise indicated, come from extensive and prolonged interviews with the members of Knesset.[38] Altogether, 86 of the 120 members of Knesset were interviewed, or 72 percent of the total membership. Generally, the sample interviewed was highly representative of the overall membership of the Knesset, as indicated in Table 1.1. As might be expected, the party with the lowest percent of its membership interviewed in this study was the Labor party, the party of the Government, because so many of its members were occupied in cabinet/administrative tasks and were unavailable for interview.

Table 1.1

Party Distribution in the Sample

Party	Number in Knesset	Number Interviewed	Percent of Party
Agudah	5	4	80
Citizens' Rights Movement	3	3	100
Independents	2	1	-
Independent Liberals	5	5	100
Labor (Mapai, Mapam, Rafi, Ahdut HaAvodah)	51	30	59
Likud (Herut, Liberals, Free Center, State List, Greater Israel Movement)	39	31	79
Moked	1	1	100
National Religious Party	10	8	80
Rakah	4	3	75
	120	86	

Notes

1. Jean Blondel writes that "of the 138 countries which exist in the world today, only five, all in the Middle East, have never had a legislature." See Jean Blondel, *Comparative Legislatures* (Englewood Cliffs, N.J.: Prentice-Hall, 1973), p. 7.
2. Allan Kornberg, *Canadian Legislative Behavior* (New York: Holt, Rinehart and Winston, 1967), p. 2.
3. Allan Kornberg, Harold Clarke, and George Watson, "Toward a Model of

Parliamentary Recruitment in Canada," in *Legislatures in Comparative Perspective*, ed. Allan Kornberg (New York: David McKay, 1973), p. 271.

4. Joseph LaPalombara, *Politics within Nations* (Englewood Cliffs, N.J.: Prentice-Hall, 1974), p. 177.

5. Kornberg, Clarke, and Watson, "Toward a Model of Parliamentary Recuitment," p. 276.

6. Richard Sisson, "Comparative Legislative Institutionalization: A Theoretical Explanation," in *Legislatures in Comparative Perspective*, ed. Allan Kornberg, p. 20.

7. Two contemporary examples of this are Blondel, *Comparative Legislatures*, and LaPalombara, *Politics within Nations*.

8. Probably the most often cited source of this school is the study by John Wahlke and others, *The Legislative System* (New York: John Wiley, 1962).

9. Included in this category would be such work as Kornberg, *Canadian Legislative Behavior*.

10. For example, Malcolm Jewell and Samuel Patterson, *The Legislative Process in the United States* (New York: Random House, 1973).

11. Samuel Patterson and John Wahlke, *Comparative Legislative Behavior: Frontiers of Research* (New York: John Wiley, 1972), p. 289.

12. Gerhard Loewenberg, *Modern Parliaments: Change or Decline?* (Chicago: Atherton, 1971), p. 3.

13. Fred Riggs, "Legislative Structures: Some Thoughts on Elected National Assemblies," in *Legislatures in Comparative Perspective*, ed. Allan Kornberg, p. 74.

14. Kornberg, *Canadian Legislative Behavior*, p. 1. Similar descriptions of the function may be found in K. C. Wheare, *Legislatures* (New York: Oxford University Press, 1968), p. 1; or LaPalombara, *Politics within Nations*, p. 161.

15. See among other studies Loewenberg, *Modern Parliaments*.

16. John Wahlke and others, *The Legislative System*, p. 3.

17. Michael Mezey, "The Functions of a Minimal Legislature: Role Perceptions of Thai Legislators," *Western Political Quarterly* 25 (1972):700.

18. Jean Blondel, *Comparative Legislatures*, p. 4.

19. Laxmi Singhvi, "Parliament in the Indian Political System," in *Legislatures in Developmental Perspective*, ed. Allan Kornberg and Lloyd Musolf (Durham, N.C.: Duke University Press, 1970), p. 217.

20. Gerhard Loewenberg, *Modern Parliaments*, p. 3.

21. David Easton, "A Re-assessment of the Concept of Political Support," *British Journal of Political Science* 5 (1975):435-57.

22. Joseph LaPalombara, *Politics within Nations*, p. 118.

23. "In 1970 there were 108 nations with national legislatures. Fifty-six of these were unicameral (single-chamber) bodies; the remainder, being two chambers, were bicameral." Ibid., p. 114.

24. Raymond Hopkins, "The Role of the MP in Tanzania," *American Political Science Review* 64 (1970):754.

25. Kornberg, *Canadian Legislative Behavior*, p. 8. For an example of a diagrammatic depiction of role orientations, see Jewell and Patterson, *The Legislative Process in the United States*, p. 408.

26. Michael Mezey, "Thai Legislators."

27. LaPalombara, *Politics within Nations*, pp. 180-82, and Jewell and Patterson, *The Legislative Process in the United States*, respectively.

Introduction: The Study of Legislatures

28. See M. Cormack, "The Australian Senate," *Parliamentarian* 53 (1972):175–85; J. Lynsky, "The Role of the British Backbenchers in the Modification of Government Policy," *Western Political Quarterly* 23 (1970):333–47; and Sheva Weiss and Avraham Brichta, "Private Members' Bills in Israel's Knesset," *Parliamentary Affairs* 23 (1969):21–33.

29. See J. Pettifer, "Privilege in the Parliament of the Commonwealth of Australia," *Parliamentarian* 53 (1972):288.

30. See M. Limaye, "On Private Members' Bills," *Journal of Constitutional and Parliamentary Studies* 3 (1969):110–13; J. Ley, "Strengthening the Position of the Backbencher in Papua, New Guinea," *Parliamentarian* 53 (1972):303–8; or J. Robinson, "Staffing the Legislature," in *Legislatures in Developmental Perspective*, ed. Allan Kornberg and Lloyd Musolf, pp. 367–90.

31. See A. McMullin, "Proposed New and Permanent Parliament Houses for the Australian Parliament," *Parliamentarian* 51 (1970):263–69; or Kenneth Wheare, *Legislatures*, pp. 4–5.

32. See Valerie Herman and James Pope, "Minority Governments in Western Democracies," *British Journal of Political Science* 3 (1973):191–212; or W. Swanson, "Voting Behavior in a Nonpartisan Legislative Setting," *Western Political Quarterly* 25 (1972):39–50.

33. See Kornberg, *Canadian Legislative Behavior*, pp. 43–52.

34. See Samuel Patterson and G. Robert Boynton, "Legislative Recruitment in a Civic Culture," *Social Science Quarterly* 50 (1969):254; or R. Wences, "Electoral Participation and the Occupational Composition of Cabinets and Parliaments," *American Journal of Sociology* 75 (1969):181–92.

35. See Laxmi Singhvi, "Parliament in the Indian Political System."

36. See Malcolm Jewell, "Linkages between Legislative Parties and External Parties," in *Legislatures in Comparative Perspective*, ed. Allan Kornberg, p. 210.

37. The question of size of the Knesset was one of the subjects debated in the provisional Council of State prior to the creation of the State. The number of 120 seats was decided upon because of "the historical fact that the Great Assembly, the first supreme legislative authority to be elected by the Jews in the era of the Second Commonwealth, had had 120 members." Asher Zidon, *Knesset* (New York: Herzl Press, 1967), p. 27.

38. Data used in this analysis, unless otherwise indicated, were gathered over a ten-month period in 1974–75 while the author was in Israel funded by a Fulbright-Hays Dissertation Research Grant.

2

The Israeli Political System

Although politicians in Israel consider themselves a part of the Western European family of parliamentary nations, many aspects of politics in Israel are distinctly different from those of Western Europe. This chapter begins with a discussion of Israel's constitutional makeup and the structure of political parties and their importance for the Israeli political system. We then turn our attention to related concepts, the nature of the electoral system, and the role of ideology in the Israeli political world. The chapter ends with a brief discussion of the manner in which the Knesset operates in the Israeli political system.

The Constitutional Framework

Members of the Knesset in Israel, if asked, will not hesitate to proudly point out that the Israeli political system is modeled after that of Britain. Israelis consider themselves members of the European family of nations, and of the British family at that. One example that is frequently cited is Israel's lack of a written constitution. It is argued that Israel's "Founding Fathers," following the British model, consciously decided not to have a single written document for a constitution, but instead decided to build the constitutional framework of the country as they went along. One recent study of the Israeli political system had, as part of its purpose, "to demonstrate the profound influence which British constitutional ideas, traditions, and doctrines, and the laws, conventions, and practices implementing them have exercised in the shaping of Israel's constitutional law."[1]

Many students of Israeli politics are not in agreement with the theory that Israel's heritage is predominately British. One well-known student of Israeli politics has totally rejected the comparison made between Israel's constitutional system and the "Westminster Model."[2] Others argue that upon closer examination, the Israeli system may be seen to combine aspects of *many* constitutional systems, including the American, Russian, German, French, and Yugoslavian systems, to name but a few.[3]

The Provisional Council of Government in 1948 decided, for various reasons,[4] against the idea of writing a constitution for the newly formed State of Israel. In place of a single written document, a system has emerged in which a constitution is slowly being written, chapter by chapter. Thus far, six "chapters" have been written, each of which is called a Fundamental Law. Fundamental Laws are acts of the Knesset that are passed by a simple majority. The Fundamental Laws do not require extraordinary majorities, and are deemed to have a preferred position to "regular" legislation. Since the Fundamental Laws are simple decisions of a majority of the Knesset—"preferred position" or not—they can, in principle, be modified or done away with by a majority of the Knesset as well.

To date six Fundamental Laws have been passed by the Knesset: "Fundamental Law: The Knesset" (1958); "Fundamental Law: Israel Lands" (1960); "Fundamental Law: The President of the State" (1964); "Fundamental Law: The Government" (1968); "Fundamental Law: The Economy" (1973); and "Fundamental Law: The Army" (1975).[5] A "Fundamental Law: Human Rights" is currently being considered by the Knesset.

In addition to these Fundamental Laws, several other pieces of legislation passed by the Knesset have appeared to surface over the years as what might be called "para-constitutional" doctrines, laws that are not designated as Fundamental Laws, yet which are perceived by many to be equally broad and fundamental in scope. Included among these Major Statutes are the Law and Administration Ordinance of 1948, the Law of Return (1950), the Equal Rights for Women Law (1951), the Nationality Law (1952) regulating among other things the naturalization of non-Jews, the Judges Law (1953), the Courts Law (1969), and the Contracts Law (1970). Since the policy of judicial review has already been established in Israel,[6] the Israeli constitution will undoubtedly be a mixture of Fundamental Laws, Major Statutes, and judicial interpretation of law, rather than solely a product of the Knesset.

One result of having a constitutional framework of this type is that the Knesset is sovereign in the political system. The Knesset elects the president; the Government takes office only with its formal approval and must resign if it loses the confidence of the Knesset. Although the principle of judicial review has been established for "constitutional" issues, the acts of the Knesset are generally immune from challenge in the courts. Theoretically a majority of members of Knesset could legally pass any bill they desired; there are virtually no limits on the power of the legislature.

The first of the Fundamental Laws to be passed, which dealt with the Knesset, described the relationship between and among the various branches of the government. The Knesset elects the head of state, the president, for a five-year term. The president is responsible to the Knesset and can be removed from office by the Knesset for misconduct or incapacity. Special majorities are required in the Knesset for the election and removal of a president. One of the duties of the president is to sign legislation; he cannot refuse to sign an act of the Knesset. That is, the president has no veto power, although the situation has never arisen in which a president has refused to sign an act of the Knesset. Presumably this would precipitate a constitutional crisis of major proportion, since the "Fundamental Law: The Knesset" is ambiguous and vague in this matter.

The president plays a role in the formation of the Government. The "Fundamental Law: The Government" states that the president ". . . shall entrust to one of the Members of the Knesset the duty of forming a Government." This made formal what had been prior to 1968 only a convention, that the prime minister would have to be a member of Knesset himself. Prior to 1968, when the "Fundamental Law: The Government" was passed, there was considerable debate as to whether the president could invite a nonmember of Knesset to be prime minister. The question is now moot. (Currently, with the exception of the prime minister, cabinet members do not have to be members of Knesset, and many MKs resign from the Knesset after being named to the cabinet to allow party colleagues to inherit their seats in the legislature.)

As the head of state is chosen by the Knesset, so too is the head of Government, the prime minister. The president asks the appropriate party leader in the Knesset to assume the task of forming a Government, and the Knesset invests that Government with power. The president cannot dissolve the Government; the Knesset may do so if it so wishes. With the leader of the Government being the leader of the Knesset, there is a notable lack of separation of powers between the executive and legislative branches of government, which is characteristic of parliamentary systems of government.

The Knesset-Government relationship is based on the constitutional concept that it is the duty of the Knesset to "bring forth" an effective government. Upon its formation, a Government presents itself before the Knesset with its programme. When its composition and its programme are approved by the Knesset, the Government becomes "established," and it continues as such so long as it enjoys the confidence of the Knesset. Throughout its existence it is subject to Knesset control. . . . The ultimate sanction possessed by the Knesset against the Government is the vote of no-confidence, but this is a double-edged sword, and not to be employed too hastily—at least if the Knesset is not sure that it can produce an alternative Government.[7]

This practice implies the principle of legal continuity of government that is practiced in Israel: One Knesset does not dissolve nor does a Government fall until its successor has been installed. A Government is always in existence. If a Government fails to win a vote of confidence, it stays in power as an "interim Government" until some other coalition, or perhaps the same one, can show that it has the necessary support to maintain a majority in the Knesset. If no new coalition can be formed with a majority supporting it, new elections are ordered, but the interim Government remains until the new Government is installed.

The cabinet draws its power directly from the Knesset. Several links exist between the Knesset and the cabinet, all of which help to blur the separation of powers between the executive and legislative branches of government. First, the person chosen to form the new Government must be a Member of Knesset. Second, the new Government must secure a vote of confidence before assuming office. Third, the Government is collectively responsible to the Knesset. Finally, the Knesset may at any time move a vote of no confidence in the Government.[8] The cabinet has traditionally tended to occupy a position of power in relation to the Knesset, even to the point of supervising the agenda and introducing private members' bills. This, one author suggests, is for good reason:

> Cabinet members, as leaders of their respective parties, and as directors of continuing programs of government, are authoritative spokesmen of policy. Knesset control or supervision over public administration has been decidedly weak, and the same can be said concerning security affairs and the conduct of foreign policy.[9]

The Political Party System

The underlying factor in contemporary Israeli politics that can be seen to explain most actions in the political system is that of the political party. Israel has been referred to as a *"parteienstaat par excellence,"*[10] and the description is appropriate. Political parties played an important role in Israel's achieving statehood; one could say that the State of Israel "was actually brought into existence by political parties, which were organized and developed entities . . . years before the coming of statehood."[11] Indeed, contemporary Israeli political parties are a direct link to the past; virtually all parties in Israel today have roots in some prestate political organization or party.[12]

The political party system could almost be classified as "overdeveloped" in Israel. Twenty-one different party lists were presented to the voters of Israel in the elections of the Eighth Knesset,[13] and many of these lists represented temporary electoral coalitions of up to five separate political party organizations. Many members of Knesset believe that the system would be better off with only three or four parties and see no real need for so many party organizations.[14] They argue, for example, that there is no need for four "religious" parties in Israel today. (These four parties are merged into two "blocs" in the Knesset; the National

Religious party, composed of the Mizrahi and the HaPoel HaMizrahi parties, and Agudah party, composed of the Agudat Israel Movement and the Poale Agudat Israel Movement.)

The tendency toward preelection coalitions of the many political parties is an interesting one, and on the surface would lead an observer to believe that a merging of the many political parties is finally occurring, so that, for example, instead of four "labor" parties currently in the Labor alignment, there might be only one party,. Similarly, on the "right," the aligning of five "nonlabor" parties might indicate a major consolidation there. This unfortunately is not the case. Although the Labor Alignment functions most of the time within the Knesset as one party, with party discipline strong and often applied, there is no doubt in the Knesset of the true party allegiance of every member there: MKs do not refer to each other as "Labor" members, but rather as members of Mapai, Rafi, Ahdut HaAvodah, or Mapam, as the case may be. Similarly on the "right," members who belong to the Likud bloc do not lose their primary allegiance to their parties, either the State List Movement, the Greater Israel Movement, the Free Center party, the Liberal party, or the Herut party.

There are, of course, reasons why the independent party organizations continue to function and thrive in spite of the fact that they are losing their autonomy of action within the legislature. These reasons are, simply put, that party organizations are engaged in considerably wider ranges of activity than legislative behavior; they do not confine their activity only to the political. Parties "occupy in Israel a place more prominent and exercise an influence more pervasive than in any other state with the sole exception of some one-party states."[15] In Israel, parties work for their members in order to maintain their support. Akzin has described the party-member relationship beautifully:

> A person who subscribes to the party's daily newspaper, is given medical care in a party-sponsored clinic, hospital, or convalescent home, spends his evenings in a party club, plays athletic games in the party's sports league, gets his books from the party's publishing house, lives in a village or in an urban development inhabited solely by other adherents of the party, and is accustomed to look to the party for the solution of many

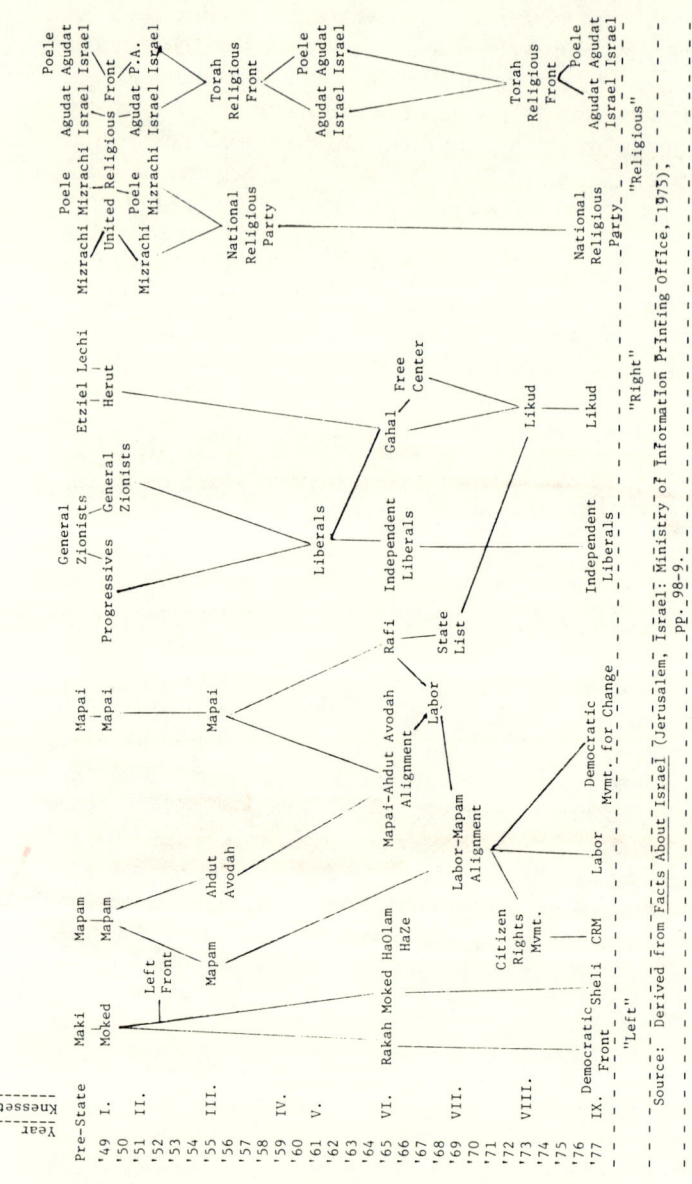

Figure 2.1
The Evolution of
Israel's Political Parties

of his daily troubles—is naturally surrounded and enveloped by an all-pervasive partisan atmosphere.[16]

At the same time that one makes the argument that parties are active in so many spheres of daily life, the disclaimer must be added that the *degree to which* parties are active in Israel today is less than it was several years ago. Whereas many in Israel applaud the decline of the political party and its power of patronage, many decry the situation and worry about the implications of the situation: the increased governmental control of daily life.

One high-ranking Likud party official explained the decline of party strength, and the subsequent equalization of parties in the Knesset over the years, as a function of governmental activity in the economy.[17] In 1949 when the State of Israel was created, this official explained, people were entirely dependent upon their parties for housing, education, medical-care clinics and hospitals, sports activities,[18] newspapers, labor unions, and the like. Over the years, more of these functions have been "nationalized," in that nonparty organizations of similar natures have been established, usually by the government, and these functions have been taken out of the position of being party gifts to supporters. For example, there is now a national welfare institute, a Ministry of Housing, and national health insurance. As each of these, and further, steps were reached, people became that much more independent of their political parties.

This explains, the argument goes, the gradual decline in the electoral strength of Mapai, the largest political party in Israel and the keystone of all government coalitions in Israel until 1977. Since Mapai had always been the largest party, it traditionally had the most "plums" to give out to its supporters in the way of patronage, so many people who might not have ideologically supported Mapai did so out of a knowledge that it would make them eligible for more benefits than would supporting a smaller party that couldn't afford to equal the level of benefits of Mapai. Now that more of these "plums" are being distributed equally by the government ministries, Mapai is losing the advantages it used to hold over the other, smaller parties and consequently voters have felt freer in recent years to support smaller parties, knowing that the perquisites of party membership would be theirs in any case. Thus, parties have become more equal in strength over the last several elections in Israel.

Political parties in Israel are organized on both a national and local level, and as the following example of the Agudat Israel Movement indicates, are active organizations.[19] Every four years 301 delegates are elected from among the local party chapters—this number is larger with larger parties—to attend the national convention. This convention elects a 151-person congress. Twice a year this 151-person congress meets and elects a new 36-member Central Committee. The Central Committee meets six times a year to discuss party business; from among its own members it elects an eleven-member Executive, which meets twice a month to discuss party business. One person is elected from the eleven-member Executive to be the Director-General (sometimes called Secretary-General) of the party.

At the same time that national parties function so actively, so too do the local party organizations. Local parties do not have as many levels of organization as do the national parties, but consist of a general membership, a central committee, an executive, and a secretary-general. They may meet as often as every two weeks, which, considering the vast range of party concerns previously detailed, is not too frequently. Local parties, as national parties, discuss issues including the housing of party members, taxes, and employment. Local parties also run newspapers, sports leagues, and health clinics, and they are constantly sponsoring demonstrations and rallies pertaining to a varied assortment of issues.

Parties play very important roles in the socialization and recruitment of individuals to politics in Israel. Children join youth groups in Israel any time after they begin school (and occasionally earlier), from about the age of six years onward. Once the children join a youth group they are very likely to stay within that party and be active within that party for the rest of their lives. In a recent study,[20] Gutmann and Landau pointed out that "The Israeli case is striking in that the political elites are entirely party based or affiliated, and most leaders have risen through the ranks of their respective parties."[21]

Many members of Knesset attribute their first political activity and/or memory to membership in a youth group, and also cite this membership as the reason for their initial party identification. Members of Knesset join the party through the youth group at an early age, are taken to rallies whose issues they do not always understand, but which the party's group leader explains, and are recruited to a new level of activity through the party.

At the same time the members of Knesset generally bemoan the great number of political parties in Israel—60 percent of the members of Knesset interviewed in this study indicated that there were too many parties today—they pride the Israeli system for its democratic nature in *permitting* so many political parties to exist and to survive.

It has been argued, as in the classic argument put forth by Duverger,[22] that there is a relationship between party numbers and structure and the electoral system of the nation within which the party is to be found. A good deal of the credit for Israel's multiplicity of parties can be given to the electoral system, which also explains why parties in Israel have such strong control over their members of Knesset.

The Electoral System

The Israeli electoral system employs a single-ballot, national constituency, proportional representation electoral framework.[23] That is, the whole country is one electoral district, and each voter casts his or her single vote for the party whose platform and candidates he or she most prefers. The percentage of votes received by each party in the national election determines the percentage of seats the party will receive in the Knesset. Any party that receives at least 1 percent of the national vote is entitled to representation in the Knesset. The total number of votes cast in the election is divided by 120, the total number of seats in the Knesset, thereby establishing a "key." Seats remaining in the Knesset after the initial assignment of seats on the basis of keys are then distributed, in order, among the parties with the highest number of "surplus votes."[24]

Most of the serious parties submit lists to the electorate with 120 names on them, one for each possible seat in the Knesset, even though the parties can be sure that they will not each win 100 percent of the vote. Smaller parties and the "unrealistic" parties often submit smaller lists, knowing that there is no point in listing 120 names. In one surprise result, in the elections for the Eighth Knesset in 1973, the Citizens' Rights Movement, which was started by a former Mapai member of Knesset, submitted a list of only five names to the electorate for the election, not really expecting that the party would win enough votes for even the first name on the list to be given a seat. To everyone's surprise, the party won enough votes for the first three names on the party list to be given seats in the Knesset.

The assignment of seats in the Knesset is determined purely by position on the party list. If a party wins 26 percent of the national vote, and is alloted thirty-one seats in the Knesset on the basis of that result (26% x 120 seats = 31), the seats are awarded to the first thirty-one names on the party list. If a member of Knesset dies during a Knesset term, or if a member resigns for some reason, his or her seat is simply passed along to the next name on the party list, and so on. Two years after the elections for the Eighth Knesset, halfway through the Knesset's term of office, three nonelected members of the Labor party list had advanced to the Knesset by this method of succession.

The importance of rank order on the party list immediately becomes clear. Since a party will put a great number of names on its list that have no chance whatsoever of being elected (because the party will not win 100 percent of the vote), it is of crucial importance to a serious candidate that he or she be placed in a realistic position on the party list. This positioning has a great deal of significance in the recruitment process in Israel, a point that is further developed later. It also has a great deal of significance in terms of intraparty and interfactional argument over which individual is placed in which position on the party list. In a coalition of parties, in which one electoral list is submitted for a number of parties, such as the Likud alignment composed of the Herut, Liberal, Free Center, State List, and Greater Israel parties, the position on the list is of crucial importance for the parties as well as for the individuals concerned. This position is determined in a conference of party leaders, the most important party in the alignment receiving the best positions, and so on. In the case of the Labor alignment composed of Mapai, Ahdut HaAvodah, Mapam, and Rafi, the distribution of the first eight places on the joint list for the Eighth Knesset was as follows:

1. Mapai	5. Ahdut HaAvodah
2. Mapai	6. Mapai
3. Mapai	7. Mapai
4. Rafi	8. Mapam

There is no overall formula for the placement of party factions in order on the list, such as 3:1:1:1 and then repeat. Each position is argued over individually until some consensus is reached.

The argument can be carried to extremes, as illustrated by the Likud alignment. When the party leaders were meeting to determine the order of candidates on the joint list, the alignment almost fell apart because of fighting between the State List and Free Center parties over which would receive the thirty-sixth position on the party list and which would receive the thirty-seventh place.[25]

Some parties reach a compromise on list positions by determining that there shall be a rotation of office; this is especially frequent in the smaller parties which can only elect a few members. In the middle of the term of the Eighth Knesset a member of the Agudah bloc resigned because a preelection compact within his party had determined that he would give up his seat halfway through the Knesset's term of office so that a member of an opposing party faction, who was in the next position on the party list, could assume his position in the Knesset.[26]

Party lists can analytically be broken down into three sections: (a) "safe" positions, which are those positions on the party list corresponding to the number of seats won in the previous election, minus about 10 percent; (b) "marginal" positions, which are those positions corresponding to the number of seats won in the previous election plus or minus about 10 percent; and (c) "symbolic" or "unrealistic" positions, those positions on the party list that are virtually assured of not being elected. The most heated debate between party factions, as one might imagine, comes over those seats in the "safe" and "marginal" positions, hence the Likud argument over positions thirty-six and thirty-seven—the Likud ended up winning thirty-nine seats in the Eighth Knesset. There would not have been similar argument over positions ninety-eight and ninety-nine.

A position on the party list, which is important to the leaders of party factions who desire maximum representation in the Knesset, is likewise critical for serious candidates. On the Labor alignment list, which won fifty-one seats in the election for the Eighth Knesset, positions forty-five through fifty-five were in the maximum risk area. A higher position was considered "safe" since it was virtually assured that the party would win that share of the vote, and a lower position was considered "unrealistic" since it was equally virtually assured that the party would *not* win *that* much of the vote.

Since their position on the list is so critical for individuals who want to advance their political careers, the individual members of Knesset are extremely vulnerable to the party leaders and list makers. The member who is elected from a "safe" position on the party list who is too much of a maverick during the Knesset term, may find his or her position on the next electoral list lowered, perhaps by only one or two positions as a warning, or perhaps more. This ability to lower a member's position on the list puts a real lever in the hands of those who demand party discipline in the Knesset.

Since the assignment of a "safe" position on the party list, or even the assignment of a "marginal" position, is entirely up to the discretion of the party leaders, a safe position is usually awarded as a prize or a reward for a history of good work for, and loyalty to, the party. The work may involve living on a party kibbutz, working at the party's headquarters in one of many possible full-time positions, or merely being active in campaign activities. Even being placed in a "symbolic" position can be seen as an honor for a political neophyte, for it implies that with continued good work and loyalty a higher list rank and possibly a Knesset seat may eventually be forthcoming. The party list thus becomes a prime tool for recruiting new members in the hands of the party leaders. If leaders see an individual whom they would like to nurture and encourage to become active in the party, they can place him or her in the "marginal" zone, or slightly below that, with the implicit understanding that better things are to come.

In addition to recruiting individuals with the Knesset list, the party can also use the list strategically to attract groups. Czudnowski has developed a model of the recruitment process in Israeli politics which uses the group as the focal point. He argues that there are two major types of Israeli legislators, the national party leaders and those who were recruited by these party leaders and their corresponding party organizations. The recruitees are broken down by Czudnowski into three main groups, those who are candidates for executive offices, those who are "group representatives," and those who are "symbolic representatives."[26]

The distinction between "group representative" and "symbolic representative" is an important one, because this factor will determine to whom the member of Knesset will feel responsible. "Group representatives" are defined as those candidates who have been formally elected or chosen by their organized group to be the group's representative on the party Knesset list. "Symbolic representatives," on the other hand, are members of certain occupational, ethnic, or demographic groups who are selected by the party leaders to draw support from that group to the party list.

Certain groups in the Israeli political system have sufficient power to be able to demand and receive "safe" places on the major parties' lists. For example, the Tel Aviv Women's Association demanded a "safe" place, and chose as its candidate Mrs. Ora Namir, who had no previous political experience at all. She was given position number fifty on the Labor party list for the Eighth Knesset and was subsequently elected to the Knesset. The Jerusalem Women's Association similarly demanded a "safe" place on the Labor list, but since its electoral influence was not as great as the Tel Aviv group, the Jerusalem group was given a position in the low eighties—a symbolic reward only.

All types of groups are "represented" on the party list, irrespective of how the *group candidates* are chosen. Local party organizations vie for "safe" places as well as union organizations, professional associations, ethnic groups, and the like. In the setting of the "smoke-filled room" the party leaders must decide which groups' support is most important to them, and they must consequently provide some groups with more than simply symbolic rewards (i.e., a "safe" position on the list), whereas other groups must be content with merely a symbolic position on the party list and the hope that with continued party work and support a better position will be forthcoming for them on future electoral lists.

Ideology

The political parties represented in the Knesset are of various types, ideological stands, and characters.[28] One study done over twenty years ago, the results of which are still applicable today, identified five major issue continua that were active in Israeli party platforms:

1. Private enterprise (a) vs. socialism (b);
2. "Activist" Arab policy (c) vs. restraint (d);
3. Torah-oriented life (e) vs. secularism (f);

4. Pro-Soviet Union (g) vs. pro-West (h);
5. Zionist (i) vs. non-Zionist (j).[29]

Based upon these five issues, Goodland constructed thirty-two party platforms, of which nineteen were logically impossible or ideologically incompatible (such as a pro-Soviet Union, private enterprise, Torah-oriented, non-Zionist platform). Ten party platforms corresponded with political parties of the time, and three were logically possible but hadn't yet been offered as political alternatives. With the exception of the Soviet question (4) which is not really a matter of contention in Israel today (with the exception of the Moscow-oriented Communist party), the other four issues remain active and central in Israeli politics and continue to be the cause of further party fragmentation and more political parties. The approximate party positions in the Eighth Knesset on the major issues, as depicted by the MKs themselves, are represented in Figure 2.2.

One of the real problems with political ideology in Israel is the number of cross pressures that individuals face. For example, members of the National Religious party (NRP) and the Agudah bloc are agreed on the importance of the role of the Torah and Zionism, but disagree on Arab policy and economic policy. Members of the Likud alignment are in agreement that a strong national security policy is necessary, especially against the Arab states, but are more divided over the role of the Torah. The large number of "major" issues causes a great deal of disharmony in the political system and helps to promote the formation of more political parties with more specific combinations of policy positions.

More parties are needed, some say, because of the great number of possible issue positions that can be taken. Although the total number of positions on four bipositional issues is only sixteen, some of which are logically contradictory or incompatible, the various degrees of opinion and intensity of belief for each issue leave the possibility open for more competing party organizations to form. The NRP and Agudah agree that the Torah should become more central in day-to-day life and that Zionism is a good and worthy goal, but they differ greatly over the latter issue as to degree. The Agudah bloc is willing to annex any territory that is currently occupied and is indeed anxious to conquer more territory in the quest to establish a greater State of Israel, whereas some of the more moderate NRP members are more inclined to recognize the exigencies of contemporary politics.

Abbreviations of Party Names

Herut	H	Agudat Israel	AI	Mapai		Ma
Liberals	L	Independent Liberals	ILP	Mapam		Mp
State List	SL	Citizens' Rights	CRM	Ahdut HaAvodah		Ah
Free Center	FC	National Religious Party	NRP	Rafi		Ra
Moked	M			Rakah		R

"Economic Policy"

R M Mp Ah Ra Ma SL CRM ILP NRP AI FC   L   H

Socialism   Private Enterprise

"National Security"

R M Mp Ah Ma Ra CRM ILP   NRP AI L FC SL H

Negotiate/   Hard Line
Compromise

"Religion"

            CRM ILP L SL
R M Mp Ah Ra Ma FC   H   NRP   AI

Secular   Religious

"Zionism"

    Ma Ra Ah
 AI NRP FC Mp
H L ILP SL CRM   M   R

Zionist   Anti-Zionist

Figure 2.2

Party Ideologies

Implications of the Political System for Legislative Behavior

Israel's parliamentary type of government is the first characteristic that has major implications for individual legislative behavior. Because of the parliamentary model, power in Israeli politics can be perceived as flowing from the top down. That is, as in any parliamentary system, which is characterized by the existence of party discipline, the prime minister is the prime minister *precisely because* he or she is able to keep his or her followers "in line." Were he or she not able to do so, the prime minister would not command a parliamentary majority and would not, in fact, be prime minister. The same is true for leadership and party discipline in the opposition parties.

One important characteristic of the Israeli political system is thus the existence of strong party discipline. The obvious implication of this for individual legislative behavior is discussed in detail in Chapter 8. The opportunities for autonomous and independent legislative behavior are few, especially within the legislature, and legislators therefore are limited in the scope of their potential behavior. Parties exist in virtually all facets of "nonpolitical" life, as well as in the clearly political processes, and as such are the central framework around which the Israeli individual, and member of Knesset, will orient his or her political actions.

Because of the many different issues that are all perceived as "central" to the public, the several parties have been able not only to survive but also to thrive, and with new parties continually being created in Israel, the party system seems to be more than surviving modern life, in spite of the fact that many critics claim that parties offer no new positions or policy alternatives when they come into being. Some parties key their orientation to religious matters, others to economic matters, and still others to security matters, although all parties recognize the existence of the various "central" issues.

Parties appear to be the central socializing, educating, and recruiting organizational frameworks in the political system. The structures of youth groups, party-sponsored private schools, and other party activities all make it extremely easy for a child to be caught up in a party's organizational framework somewhere along the line. Once a child is within the party structure, it is rare that he or she will leave, even if the party whose youth group the child has joined is not the same as that of his or her parents. Parties are the prime means by which individuals are recruited to politics, initially to a lower degree of party activity, such as attending party meetings or rallies, then to party activity on a local level, and then national electoral activity. Parties use their electoral lists as "plums" with which to draw individuals to activity, these lures appear to be effective, since there is no dearth of candidates for elective office.

Much of the parties' significant impact upon the legislative process can be attributed to the electoral system, under which an individual is entirely dependent upon the party leaders in determining his or her position on the party electoral list. The difference in a few positions on the list may be crucial, especially in the "marginal" portion of the party list. Many individuals in Israel have been in "unrealistic" or "symbolic" positions since the First Knesset elections, and have no desire or ambition to be further advanced; to them the party list is merely a structural way for the party to thank them for loyalty and good work.

Because Israel is a single national electoral district, with proportional representation and the kind of electoral list system that it has, opportunities for independent legislative behavior are seriously restricted. These restrictions do not come from the many formal limits on, or prohibitions against, individual legislative behavior, but come instead from informal pressures. Individual legislators know how important rank order on the party electoral list is. They therefore know that if they want to stay in the Knesset, to develop greater seniority and more power, and to ultimately possibly serve in the cabinet, they must follow the line of their leaders. Imaginative, autonomous, and independent legislators are not the model for success.

Thus, some characteristics of the Israeli political system can be seen to have direct and immediate implications for *how* the legislators will behave once they reach the legislature. Other characteristics of the system, such as constitutional idiosyncracies, patterns of voting, the role of interest groups, and the general structures of political parties, all have varying degrees of impact upon legislative behavior as we progress in our examination of the Knesset. One other significant structural factor is the fact that Israel has always had coalition governments, of varying degrees of stability. This has determined to a great degree whether the legislature could feel free as an institution to take action in certain areas of concern, or whether it was forced into a state of "immobilisme," in which it could not act upon certain areas of concern because any action would result in the dissolution of the government coalition of the day. We now turn to an examination of the impact of the existence of coalition governments upon legislative behavior.

Notes

1. Emmanuel Likhovski, *Israel's Parliament* (Oxford: Clarendon Press, 1971), p. 191.
2. Steven Sager, "Pre-State Influences on Israel's Parliamentary System," *Parliamentary Affairs* 25 (1971):29-49.
3. See, for example, Leslie Wolf-Phillips, "The Westminster Model in Israel," *Parliamentary Affairs* 26 (1973):415-39.
4. Ibid., pp. 418-21. See Also David Ben-Gurion, *Israel: A Personal History* (New York: Funk and Wagnalls, 1971), pp. 331-34. For discussions of the Israeli constitution generally, see Joseph Badi, *The Government of the State of Israel* (New York: Twayne, 1963); Yehuda Freudenheim, *Government in Israel* (New York: Oceana Press, 1967); Leonard Fein, *Israel: Politics and People* (Boston: Little, Brown, 1966), ch 1; or Asher Zidon, *Knesset: The Parliament of Israel* (New York: Herzl Press, 1967), ch. 24.
5. Michael Rossetti, "Israel's Parliament," *Parliamentary Affairs* 8 (1955):451.
6. Wolf-Phillips, "The Westminster Model," pp. 421-23.
7. Likhovski, *Israel's Parliament*, p. 125.
8. Zidon, *Knesset*, p. 245.
9. Scott Johnston, "Party Politics and Coalition Cabinets in the Knesset," *Middle Eastern Affairs* 13 (1962):130-38.
10. Emanuel Gutmann, "Israel," *Journal of Politics* 25 (1963):703-17.
11. Scott Johnston, "Politics of the Right in Israel," *Social Science* 40 (1965):104-13.
12. For a description of the history of parties in Israel, see Benjamin Akzin, "The Role of Parties in Israeli Democracy," *Journal of Politics* 17 (1955):507-45.
13. Twenty-four parties presented themselves for the First Knesset election; in the 1969 elections for the Seventh Knesset there were sixteen party lists, of which thirteen won seats. See Alan Arian, "Stability and Change in Israeli Public Opinion and Politics," *Public Opinion Quarterly* 35 (1971):19-35.
14. This suggests a "left" party, a "right" party, a "religious" party, with perhaps a Communist party as a fourth party.
15. Akzin, "The Role of Parties," p. 509.
16. Ibid., p. 520.
17. Yechiel Kadashai, secretary and first assistant to Likud party leader Menachem Begin. Information was gathered in an interview that was held April 3, 1975, in the Knesset in Jerusalem.
18. Although today, Kadashai mutters, athletic competition is so extreme that players are recruited for the Beytar (Herut) team "who aren't even Herutnicks!"

19. This description of the Agudat Israel party was furnished by Israel Katzover, the secretary general of its Jerusalem branch, in an interview held February 15, 1975. Since this party is representative of other party organizations, it is used as an example here.
20. Emanuel Gutmann and Haim Landau, "The Political Elite and National Leadership in Israel," in *Political Elites in the Middle East* ed. George Lenczowski (Washington, D.C.: American Enterprise Institute, 1975), p. 163.
21. Patterns of political advancement through party activity are discussed in Chapter 7.
22. Maurice Duverger, *Political Parties* (New York: John Wiley, 1963).
23. For further discussion, see Zidon, *Knesset*, pp. 21–29.
24. For a fuller explanation of this complicated process, see Freudenheim, *Government in Israel*, p. 126, or the *Jerusalem Post: Overseas Edition* May 24, 1977, p. 7.
25. This specific event was covered in the *Jerusalem Post*, September 10, 1973, p. 1.
26. See the *Jerusalem Post: Overseas Edition*, November 12, 1975, p. 3.
27. See Moshe Czudnowski, "Legislative Recruitment under Proportional Representation in Israel: A Model and a Case Study," *Midwest Journal of Political Science* 14 (1970):216–48; and Moshe Czudnowski, "Socio-Cultural Variables and Legislative Recruitment," *Comparative Politics* 4 (1972):561–87.
28. For discussions of the ideological character of Israeli parties, see the following: Alan Arian, *Ideological Change in Israel* (Clevelend: Press of Case Western Reserve University, 1968); Emanuel Gutmann, "Some Observations on Politics and Parties in Israel," *India Quarterly* 17 (1961):3–29; A. Etzioni, "Kulturkampf ou Coalition: Le Cas de Israel," *Revue Francais de Science Politique* 8 (1958):311–31.
29. Thomas Goodland, "A Mathematical Presentation of Israel's Political Parties," *British Journal of Sociology* 8 (1957): 263–66.

3

Government Coalitions and the Knesset*

Introduction

As was indicated in chapter 1, the Israeli government is a parliamentary-based structure. That is, as with any of the "Westminster model" systems, the prime minister and his or her cabinet derive their authority and power from the Parliament, the Knesset. Only after he or she has received a vote of confidence from the Knesset does the prime minister take office, and the prime minister can be turned out of office at any time by a vote of no confidence by the legislature. Ostensibly, then, as is the model in parliamentary systems, the principle of "legislative supremacy" is characteristic of the Israeli political system, with the legislature doing the hiring and the firing of the executive branch.

In recent years there has been a great deal of discussion in the literature dealing with legislative institutions of the tendency toward a "decline of legislatures."[1] The argument presented is that the increasing growth of executive government around the world, which occurs for a variety of reasons,[2] is matched by a corresponding decreasing share of power given to the legislature. Power in the political system is seen as a zero-sum quantity, and every unit of growth in the executive's power is said to be matched

---

* Portions of this chapter originally appeared under the title "Coalition Behavior and Cabinet Formation: The Case of Israel" by Gregory S. Mahler and Richard J. Trilling published in *Comparative Political Studies* 8, no. 2 (July 1975):200–233 and are reprinted herewith by permission of the publisher, Sage Publications, Inc.

by a unit of decline in the legislature's power. This situation, it has been suggested, has given rise to the *de facto* existence in parliamentary governments of "cabinet supremacy" rather than the *de jure* principle of "legislative supremacy."

The principle of "cabinet supremacy" is relatively easy to express in its basic form. Party discipline exists in parliamentary systems; the individual member of parliament is expected to follow the instructions of his or her party leaders. Because the party leaders of the majority party or the majority coalition in the Knesset also happen to be members of the cabinet, we find a situation in which the legislature, which is supposedly in command in the governmental structure, actually takes its orders from the leaders of the executive branch, the cabinet, hence "cabinet supremacy."

This principle of "cabinet supremacy" has a great deal of significance for individual legislative behavior in the Knesset, because it means that individual MKs are expected *not* to engage in individual behavior; they are expected to do what they are told to do by their leaders. Members of opposition parties are expected to follow their party leaders, and members of government coalition parties are expected to follow their party leaders, who also happen to be members of the cabinet.

Because of the many political parties that are active in the Israeli political system, no single party has ever had an outright majority in the Knesset. It has always been the case in Israeli politics that several political parties have banded together in the Knesset after elections have been held and created a government coalition, in essence pooling their respective seats in the Knesset to create a parliamentary majority. The least number of parties that has participated in a coalition in Israel's history has been three; the greatest number of parties participating in a coalition has been six.

The existence of government coalitions is significant in a study of legislative behavior in Israel. Because it has traditionally been necessary for a number of political parties in the Knesset to band together to form a coalition, there has been less opportunity for individual party behavior and individual legislative behavior in the Knesset than there otherwise might have been. Party discipline is extremely tight, and coalition lines are rigidly enforced. In this chapter we investigate the nature of coalition governments in Israel and study Knesset behavior in relation to these coalitions, discussing which parties in the Knesset have joined coalitions, why they join, and what demands they make in return for their support of the coalition. However, before we begin this examination, a brief discussion of the nature of coalition government is in order.

Theories of Coalition Formation

Politics has been defined by many as the process of coalition building,[3] and from this perception has been developed what we now call *coalition theory*. The essential concept in this theory is that of the minimal winning coalition (W_m)[4], the idea that a winning coalition includes no unnecessary partners. Among all possible winning coalitions some are "minimal winning, i.e., coalitions where the subtraction of a single member reduces them to (nonwinning) protocoalitions."[5] Many variations on the "minimum winning coalition" theory have been suggested in the literature.[6] Herman and Pope have suggested a serious challenge to all of these theories because they are all based on the idea of minimal *winning* coalitions:

> All the theories of coalition formation known to us incorporate an assumption (or a set of assumptions which imply) that coalitions which are formed must be "winning" . . . yet out of the total of 207 governments which have formed in twelve western democracies since the war, 74 of them [35.7%] have not been winning.[7]

There are several problems with broad theories of coalition formation. First, the theories may be more or less valid in one political system than in another. Second, as much of Leiserson's work on the Liberal Democratic party in Japan indicates, many political actions in a governmental system may be idiosyncratic to that system. That is, much of the explanation of why the political system works as effectively as it does in Japan may be explained by the personalistic style of politics in Japan; that which explains patronage in Japan may not explain patronage in Iceland.[8] Finally, the distribution of cabinet positions may be explained by many different theories, including the number of seats a party can claim

Government Coalitions and the Knesset

to control, patronage, loyalty, payment for future support, and a variety of other reasons. As we turn our attention to coalition behavior in Israel, we should keep these several points in mind.

Parties in the Knesset and Political Coalitions

Several themes must be kept in mind in an analysis of the formations of coalitions among Israeli political parties. First, political parties play an overwhelming role in not only the "political" but also the social and economic life of Israel. Parties publish newspapers, run medical clinics, sponsor athletic and social events, and, in short, permeate every aspect of life in Israel.[9] Second, one must note the number of parties that are active in the Israeli political system. As many as twenty-four parties presented themselves at elections for the First and Second Knessets;[10] in the 1969 election for the Seventh Knesset there were sixteen party lists, of which thirteen won seats. In the election for the Eighth Knesset, seventeen parties won seats, although several of these parties ran together in preelectoral coalitions; thirteen parties won seats in the 1977 elections for the Ninth Knesset.

The mere number of political parties that are active in the political system may affect our ability to theorize about coalition formation. It has been noted that whereas twelve cabinets had actually formed through 1965 in Israel since its independence, in those twelve cabinet-forming periods, there were 7,873 possible winning coalitions.[11] This is the number of coalitions that contained enough Knesset members to support a government, and it does not count the number of near-winning or minority coalitions that were possible. To provide a comparison, in Belgium since World War II, there have been fourteen actual coalitions with 463 possible winning coalitions.[12]

Third, the military situation, the idea of national security, has always been of paramount importance in Israeli politics. We shall see that war situations, especially in 1967, greatly influence the size of the coalitions that are formed.

Fourth, the concept of a minimal winning coalition must be treated carefully in this analysis. With the Knesset membership of 120, a majority would be 61 seats. However, on several occasions blocs of MKs abstained on all parliamentary votes. This had the effect of lowering the active population of the Knesset from 120 to 100 on the one occasion in which 20 members abstained, which, in turn, lowered the effective minimal winning coalition from 61 to 51.

Fifth, imperfect information may increase the size of a coalition. The Israeli party system contains strong and highly disciplined parties—many political scientists argue that the Israeli system is second to none in the relative impotence of the individual members and in the strength of the party leaders.[13] A certain amount of imperfect information remains, however, because of the large number of parties and because of the fact that even though the parties may run for office together in a grand alliance, they will not necessarily be in agreement in all policy spheres. This means that the party that forms the governmental coalition cannot automatically count on any party's vote, but also means that the issues and positions are clearly understood. One illustration that is not at all unusual is the elaborate "contract" among members of the eighteenth cabinet-governing coalition, which defined precisely the conditions under which party members and coalition members could "vote their consciences"; a similar "contract" was developed for the first Begin cabinet in 1977.[14]

Finally, the history and ideological nature of the Israeli party system must be considered. The party system in Israel has been called overdeveloped by many, and several political scientists have written that the large number of political parties is not really necessary in the nation. The abundance of political parties is usually attributed to the fact that most parties existed before the state did; "every one of the political parties represented in the Fifth Knesset (August, 1961), with the exception of two small Arab lists, had roots in and at least some organizational history going back to the pre-state period."[15] This history, combined with the proportional representation electoral system that encourages new parties to form by making representation in the Knesset relatively easy, has encouraged the expansion of parties.

Table 3.1 presents party membership in the Knesset in the eight elections for the Knesset from Israeli independence in 1949 through 1974. The data reveal a trend toward consolidation and alignments of the major parties; the preelection grand alliance now appears to be an accepted phenomenon. This trend is especially clear in the 1973 election, in which four left-of-center

Government Coalitions and the Knesset

Table 3.1

Party Membership in the Knesset through 1974

PARTY/Knesset #	1	2	3	4	5	6	7	8
Israel Communist party (MAKI)	4	5	6	3	5	1	1	1
New Communist List (RAKAH)						3	3	4
United Workers party (MAPAM)	19	15	9	9	9	8		
Labor Unity (AHDUT HA'AVODA)			10	7	8			
Israel Labor party (MAPAI)	46	45	40	47	42	45[a]	56[b]	51[c]
Israel Worker's List (RAFI)						10		
Progressives (Ind. Liberals)	5	4	5	6		5[e]	4	4
General Zionists (Liberals)	7	20	13	8	17[d]			
GAHAL						26[f]	26	
HERUT	14	8	15	17	17			
Free Center							2	39[g]
State List							4	
Ha'Olam Ha'Ze						1		
Mizrahi (Religious Zionist Mvmt)		2						
(together called NRP)	16[h]		11	12	12	11	12	10
HaPoel HazMizrahi		8						
Agudat Yisrael (orthodox)		3	6	6	4	4	6	5
Labor Mvmt of Agudat Yisrael		2			2	2		
Sephardim	4	2						
Citizen's Right								3
WIZO (Women's Int'l Zionist Org.)	1							
Fighters	1							
Yemenites	1	1						
Arab Democrats	1	3	2					
Progress and Labor (Arab)		1	2	2	2	2	[i]	2
Agriculture and Development (Arab)		1	1	1				
Cooperation and Brotherhood (Arab)					2	2		
Beduin and Villagers (Arab)								1

[a] In the elections for the Sixth Knesset, Mapai and Ahdut Ha'Avoda ran together as the Alignment.
[b] In the elections for the Seventh Knesset, the Alignment was expanded to include Mapam, and its name was changed to Labor.
[c] In the elections for the Seventh Knesset, the Labor alignment remained the same.
[d] In the elections for the Fifth Knesset, the Progressive and General Zionist parties joined together to become the Liberals.
[e] The Independent Liberals split away from the Liberal party when the Liberals joined with Herut to form Gahal.
[g] In the elections for the Eighth Knesset, Gahal (Liberals plus Herut) joined with the Free Center and State List to form the Likud (unification) party.
[h] In the elections for the First Knesset, all religious parties ran together as the United Religious Front.
[i] In the elections for the Seventh Knesset, six Arab seats were won; their precise distribution has been impossible to determine.

parties formed an alliance as did five right-of-center parties. Old party labels are to some degree still intact, but the consolidation process appears to be making headway.

After every election since independence, through 1977, the Mapai party has formed a governing coalition; the Likud formed a government coalition in 1977. There has never been in Israel what Herman and Pope have called a "majority situation,"[16] that is, one in which the party organizing the government had more than 50 percent of the seats in parliament. Israel has always been an illustration of a "minority situation, majority government," one in which a party with less than a majority of parliamentary seats joins with other minority parties to form a majority government.[17] This situation has resulted in coalitions being formed not only after elections of the Knesset but also often between Knesset elections. In fact, during the first seven Knessot (the plural of Knesset), there were seventeen cabinets.[18] The makeup of these cabinets through the eighteenth cabinet in 1974, as reflected in Tables 3.2 and 3.3, is the subject of the following analysis.

Knesset Coalitions and Cabinet Formation

Table 3.2 shows those parties belonging to governmental coalitions (specifically, those holding ministries) in the eighteen cabinets, and the number of seats in the Knesset held by each party in the cabinet. By summing the number of seats held by each party "represented" in each cabinet, it is possible to get some idea of the "size" of the coalition and how nearly it proximates a minimum winning coalition. By examining this pattern over time, we are able to identify factors of some general significance that seem to cause the size and nature of governing coalitions to differ from the predictions of theories of coalition formation.

The first two cabinets, as indicated in Table 3.2, both exceeded an absolute minimal winning coalition of sixty-one seats. The numbers of seats represented were ten and eleven greater than "minimal winning" size, or 8.3 percent and 9.1 percent larger, respectively. These cabinets were not ideologically "wall-to-wall" coalitions, but were composed of labor and religious parties. Considering the number of parties with seats in the First Knesset, the high "imperfect information" factor resulting from the newness of the political state, and the need faced by Israel at the time (as in all new states) for establishing political legitimacy and political integration, these initial coalition governments were surprisingly small.

The third cabinet actually represented a "minority situation, minority government" in the terms of Herman and Pope; only fifty-six seats were represented in cabinet. The "parties in the Government were Mapai, HaPoel Ha-Mizrahi-Mizrahi, Agudat Israel, and Arabs."[19] The Arabs were not represented in this cabinet, but if we add the six Knesset seats held by Arab parties supporting the government to those represented in the cabinet, we find a total of sixty-two seats, remarkably near a minimal winning coalition size. It can be assumed that Arab payoffs for support were in terms of policy positions of the new government.

The fourth and fifth cabinets were larger than their predecessors; each represented seventy-seven seats in the Knesset, 13 percent more than a strict minimal size. These cabinets were the first in the nation's history to include the General Zionist party, and as such can be seen to be broadening the range of political support possessed by the government. These cabinets also were larger than their predecessors, containing sixteen ministries instead of twelve and thirteen. In Israeli politics it appears that parties were often carried along in a coalition even when the parties were not necesssary to form a governing coalition. This was especially true for the religious parties, HaPoel HaMizrahi and Mizrahi (together called the National Religious party, the NRP) in the fourth, fifth, seventh, eighth, and fourteenth through seventeenth cabinets. If we subtract the NRP's eight-seat total from the seventy-seven seats represented by the governing coalition in the fourth and fifth cabinets, the number of seats represented in the cabinet drops to sixty-nine, much nearer the minimal size.

We cannot be sure, but all evidence points to the conclusion that, as Leiserson suggested, "posts may be given to factions simply to keep them from stirring up trouble."[20] Certain fundamental and highly controversial religious questions have long existed in a semidormant state in Israeli politics, and the religious parties may have been given the ministries they held in return for their agreement not to "stir up trouble." Support for this theory may be found in more recent events. The support of the religious

Table 3.2

Parties Represented in Cabinets

Party	Cabinet #	1 1949-50	2 1950-51	3 1951-52	4 1952-54	5 1954-55	6 1955	7 1955-58	8 1958-59	9 1959-61
Mapam								9	9	9
Ahdut Ha'Avodah								10	10	7
Mapai		46	46	45	45	45	45	40	40	47
Rafi										
N.R.P.		16 (as United Religious Front)	16	8	8	8	8	11	11	12
Agudat Yisrael				3						
Sephardim		4	4							
Progressives		5	5		4	4	4	5	5	6
General Zionist					20	20				
Gahal										
Independent			1							1
Total Seats Represented		71	72	56	77	77	57	75	75	82
# Ministries		12	13	13	16	16	16	16	16	16

Table 3.2 (continued)

Party	Cabinet #	10 1961–63	11 1963–64	12 1964–65	13 1965–67	14 1967–69	15 1969	16 1969–71	17 1971–74	18 1974
Mapam					8	8	8			
Ahdut Ha'Avodah			8	8						
Mapai		42	42	42	45[a]	45	45	56[d]	56	51
Rafi						10[c]	10			
N.R.P.		12	12	12	12	12	12	12	12	10
Agudat Yisrael										
Sephardim										
Progressives/Independent Liberals					5[b]	5	5	4	4	4
General Zionist										
Gahal						26	26	26		
Independent										
Total Seats Represented		62	62	62	70	106	106	98	72	65
# Ministries		16	16	16	16	21	21	22	18	23

[a] In 1965 Ahdut Ha'Avoda and Mapai ran together as the Alignment.
[b] Name change to Independent Liberals.
[c] Rafi was a dissident wing of the Mapai party.
[d] The enlarged Alignment changed its name to the Labor party.

parties was crucial to the formation of the eighteenth cabinet; finding themselves in the powerful position of being pivotal to the formation of a new government, the religious parties revived the semidormant but still highly volatile question of "Who is a Jew?"[21]

At the same time, the payoffs to the NRP in the fourth and fifth cabinets may have been of much less value to other potential recipients of these payoffs than to the NRP. That is, the ministries of religious affairs and of social welfare are more salient for the NRP than for other parties. If most parties in Israel compete along a socialism-nonsocialism ideological dimension, we can perhaps assume that ministries and other potential rewards to parties that relate to the socialism-nonsocialism dimension will have greater utility for these competing parties than will ministries and rewards that do not relate to this dimension. In a sense, then, the payoffs made to the NRP in the fourth and fifth cabinets may have cost other coalition members very little in the short run since they did not relate to this dimension. And in the long run, the payoffs may have helped to induce the NRP's support that Mapai would eventually find essential.

That the payoffs to the NRP in the fourth and fifth cabinets may have cost other coalition partners very little is also suggested by the fact that the number of ministerial posts in the fourth and fifth cabinets, sixteen, exceeded the number for earlier cabinets. In other words, in the fourth and fifth cabinets, even after rewarding the ministries of religious affairs and of social welfare to the NRP, Mapai still had as many or more ministries as in the third cabinet to award as payoffs to other coalition partners. If ministries constitute (some of) the payoffs in the government-formation "game," then the Israeli experience suggests that such a game occasionally may become a nonconstant sum.

The sixth cabinet was a minority government. It was, however, only a caretaker government since its main task was to make preparations for elections to be held for the Third Knesset. With a life expectancy of one month, any analysis of the implications or significance of coalition members in the sixth cabinet would be highly suspect.

The seventh and eighth cabinets, constituting the term of the Third Knesset, were both in excess of minimal winning coalitions. They included two parties to the left of Mapai, as well as

Mapai's earlier allies. As indicated previously, if we theorize that the ministries of religious affairs and posts were given to the religious parties to "keep them quiet," and if we then subtract the eleven seats represented by the religious parties from those represented in the cabinet, we are left with a cabinet representation of sixty-four seats, not a great deal above a minimal winning coalition.

The ninth cabinet, whose life corresponded to that of the Fourth Knesset, was the same size (sixteen ministers) as its predecessors, but more seats in the Knesset were represented in it (eighty-two) than in any of its predecessors. The parties represented in the ninth cabinet were the same as those of its immediate predecessor with the exception of the addition of one independent MK. In the elections for the Fourth Knesset, several of the old coalition partners gained votes and consequently picked up seats in the Knesset. In order to maintain a minimal winning coalition, the Mapai party would have had to expel some of its former allies from the coalition. This cabinet seems to show that although minimal size is important, certain political considerations, such as loyalty, are clearly not enduring considerations. This can be seen by comparing the ninth cabinet with the tenth, eleventh, and twelfth cabinets.

The tenth, eleventh, and twelfth cabinets all correspond surprisingly well to predicted minimal winning size. The Mapam and Progressive parties had been sheared from the alliance, and the coalitions became minimal winning not only in the sense of a minimal number of seats in excess of majority but also in the sense of minimal number of parties. There was no single party whose seats could have combined with those of Mapai to yield a majority in the Knesset, so a three-party coalition was necessary.

The interesting question is, why did Mapai shear the governing coalition in the tenth cabinet but not in the ninth? The tenth, eleventh, and twelfth cabinets all belong to the same Knesset, the Fifth, but to a Knesset that was different from that of the ninth cabinet. This timing suggests that the election for the Fifth Knesset affected Mapai's strategy. Either Mapai retained a greater-than-minimal winning coalition before the election in order to improve its own electoral chances or it simply realized after the election that the extra coalitional support was no longer necessary. It may simply be that coalitions tend toward minimal winning size in the long run. The timing of the election, however, suggests that coalition strategy may affect future electoral strategy.

In the thirteenth cabinet, we can see the beginnings of a trend toward preelection grand alliances. In the Sixth Knesset (thirteenth through fifteenth cabinets), Mapai and Ahdut Ha'Avoda ran together as the alignment; a dissident Mapai wing, Rafi, split off the majority party and was not represented in the cabinet. A preelectoral alliance was also struck on the right, with Herut and the General Zionists running together as Gahal. This movement toward electoral alliances is indirect support for the argument that electoral and coalition strategies are intertwined.

In the thirteenth cabinet, a strict minimal winning coalition could have been achieved without the eight seats represented by the Mapam ministers in the cabinet; the expansion of the voting base of support to the left may be seen as another attempt during a period of tension in the Middle East to broaden the popular base of support in the cabinet. This trend is clearly reflected in the fourteenth cabinet in which the number of seats represented in the cabinet soared to 106, and the number of ministries expanded from its fifteen-year level of 16 to a new level of 21. This figure of 106 seats, representing 88.3 percent of the Knesset membership, may clearly be seen to be a result of the 1967 war: it was a government of national unity, including the right-wing Gahal alliance as well as the left-wing Mapam party. Following the 1967 war, a major attempt was made to have the government portrayed as a "government of unanimity" in its goal of national security. Certainly, wartime grand alliances are not uncommon; the British Labour-Conservative coalition in World War II is but one other example. For Israel, the security question was just as salient even after the cessation of the fighting in the six-day 1967 war, so the grand alliance that persisted after the cessation of fighting is not surprising.

In 1969, on the death of Premier Levi Eshkol, a new cabinet officially came into being when Golda Meir took over the reins of government. There was some rearrangement of ministries, but the parties represented in the fifteenth cabinet remained the same as in the Knesset. The fifteenth cabinet lasted only nine months before the election of a new Knesset.

The Seventh Knesset saw the trend to preelection alliances continue, with the expansion of the 1965 Mapai-Ahdut Ha'Avoda alignment to include Mapam (and a consequent renaming of the alliance to "Labor"). The Gahal alliance remained intact on the right. The left-of-center coalition continued to lose votes, and its loss in votes corresponded to its attempt to broaden the alliance: in the Fifth Knesset, Mapai and Ahdut Ha'Avoda together had fifty seats and when they ran together in 1965 they won forty-five seats. The Rafi, Alignment, and Mapam seat total in the Sixth Knesset was sixty-three; when all three parties ran together as Labor for the Seventh Knesset, they won fifty-six seats (for a net loss of seven seats). The only reasonable interpretation of these figures is that the preelectoral alliance was utilized in order to stave off some of the losses that were anticipated, although it is certainly possible that expansion increased these losses. The election returns show a slow increase of seats won by center and right-of-center parties at the expense of the left parties.

The continued loss of electoral support may have forced the left-of-center coalition to bring Gahal into the sixteenth cabinet, even though this raised the number of seats represented there to ninety-eight, much more than a minimal winning coalition. After two years of this wall-to-wall cabinet, Gahal encountered a governmental policy that it opposed so strongly that it withdrew from the coalition. In April 1971, the cabinet was reshuffled; the number of ministries was reduced from twenty-two in the sixteenth cabinet to eighteen in the seventeenth cabinet and the number of Knesset seats represented in the cabinet declined from ninety-eight to seventy-two. This is further evidence that the parliamentary coalition game is not constant sum, since the size of the cabinet and the number of ministries available as payoffs can be varied to meet the particular coalition situation.

The Gahal alliance no longer was a part of the coalition; the only parties in the coalition were Labor, the NRP, and the Independent Liberals. In April 1972, the cabinet was enlarged slightly when the portfolios for finance, commerce, and industry were given to two Labor ministers, whereas previously they had been held by one Labor minister, but still no Gahal members were part of the cabinet.

At the end of 1973, elections for seats in the Eighth Knesset were held, and again witnessed a loss of seats on the left (from fifty-six to fifty-one) and a gain on the right (from thirty-two to thirty-nine). A grand alliance of the right evolved out of the old Gahal alliance, composed of two parties, into the new Likud alliance, containing five parties. Mapai, as the party with the most seats, was again asked to form the government. The Labor alignment held only fifty-one seats, and with promised Arab support it commanded only fifty-four seats in the Knesset. The Independent Liberals added four seats to this total, raising the new total to fifty-eight votes. The ten seats of the NRP became crucial to Golda Meir as she attempted to form her government. Finding themselves in the powerful position of cabinet maker-or-breaker, the NRP again rolled out the highly controversial issue of "Who is a Jew?" and was determined that the new Government adopt the NRP's policy stance in return for its support. Several people suggested to Meir that she forsake NRP support and instead invite the Likud into the cabinet, but she declined, stating that a wall-to-wall cabinet (the phrase is hers) could not accomplish necessary goals.

Sixty-five seats in the Knesset were represented in the cabinet, belonging to the Labor-Mapam alignment, the NRP, and the Independent Liberals (Arab support, again, was not represented in the cabinet). The NRP did not succeed in getting the Government to promise to adopt its position on the who-is-a-Jew question, but the "coalition contract" referred to earlier, permitted the NRP to vote on its own will on that question, independent of the rest of the coalition, and the Government did set up a commission to study the implications of this policy position.[22] These two actions were departures from past positions of the Meir government, and as such are a clear indication of the power that the NRP wielded in the coalition-formation stage, by virtue of its occupying a pivotal position.

Menachem Begin, the leader of Likud, attacked the manner in which cabinet ministries were given out in the eighteenth cabinet. He said that the manner of the distribution of ministries amounted to a "depreciation of the status of minister." Begin indicated in a speech attacking the Meir cabinet that the Independent Liberal party had been awarded one ministry for each two MKs, and the NRP had been awarded one ministry for each two-and-one-half MKs. He stated that "This is nothing more than political bribery."[23]

In a speech defining the cabinet's formation, Aharon Yadlin

(secretary general of the Labor party) stated that a broad-based, wall-to-wall coalition including the Likud, for which many people had lobbied, "was inappropriate to present political circumstances and would have induced paralysis in practice, for all its attraction in principle."[24] Yadlin continued, apologizing that the Labor alignment could not adopt the NRP position on the who-is-a-Jew question, saying that adopting as governmental policy the more narrowly defined answer to this question, favored by the NRP, would have offended millions of Jews abroad, whose support (including financial assistance) was essential for Israeli security. The NRP had also argued that the Likud ("unification") party be accepted into the coalition as well, but Meir had opposed this move, knowing that the right-wing Likud would have opposed some of the territorial compromises she favored.[25]

Inhibitors of Minimum Winning Size

As we look back on the history of cabinet formation in Israel through 1974, we can identify factors of general significance that seemed to prevent closer attainment of minimum winning size. First, as Riker theorized, imperfect information serves to increase the size of the winning coalition.[26] Mapai has always controlled a majority of the cabinet, but imperfect information has led Mapai to add to the cabinet enough parties such that if one party dropped out of the coalition there would still be enough seats represented in the cabinet to maintain a government. Imperfect information would seem to result from the immature nature of the party system and from the political tension that engulfs the Israeli state. More stable politics in which coalition stakes are not so high might lead to more explicit expectations and better information.

Second, ideological considerations serve to constrain the number and kind of viable coalition partners. Thus, Axelrod's notion of connectedness seems appropriate.[27] Israeli political history suggests that Mapai has built governing coalitions by adding a sufficient number of ideologically "close" parties, along the socialism-nonsocialism dimension that underlies Israeli politics. The NRP and Arab lists are notable exceptions, whose support is discussed later. Nevertheless, connectedness is most evident in Mapai's avoidance of Likud, in the eventual departure of Gahal, and in Mapai's rejection of wall-to-wall cabinets. These strategies occasionally could be explained in terms of minimal winningness rather than in terms of ideological disconnectedness, and the general, more significant tendency is toward minimal winningness. Nevertheless, ideological considerations can also be seen in the rhetoric of Mapai party leaders and in the rejection of parties on the right when these right-wing parties were not the only potential coalition partners.

Third, throughout Israel's existence, until the 1977 election, Mapai has been asked to form a government. Leiserson[28] seems to be correct, then, when he states that the largest actor will enter the governing coalition, especially in a dominant party system, in which "one party possesses less than half the parliamentary seats . . . (but) outdistances its rivals over a period of time."[29] That the largest party assumes or acquires responsibility for forming the government suggests that some special significance accompanies placing first electorally, beyond the mere differences in numbers, even in a state with proportional representation.[30]

Fourth, at several times Israeli coalition formation may involve a nonconstant game, or perhaps may convert a constant-sum situation into a nonconstant-sum one in order to facilitate coalition formation or coalition maintenance. The number of ministries that are available as payoffs is itself a variable, and a more sophisticated theory of political coalition formation might provide us with an understanding of why and how this number varies.

Fifth, the available evidence suggests that the payoffs given to the NRP for supporting the governing coalition had very little value for other potential recipients. Consequently, coalition formation processes may be constrained by payoff valuations that are peculiar to some political players. In general, this constraint served to provide Mapai with NRP support, which was not essential, because what Mapai paid to receive NRP support meant very little to Mapai or to other potential recipients. In the Israeli case, this constraint stems from the distinctive ideological issue that motivates the NRP, but which operates obliquely to the dominant Israeli political dimension, socialism-nonsocialism.

Evidence also exists to suggest that coalition strategy not only has the short-run objectives of achieving and maintaining governing status and implementing policy but also has certain long-run objectives. A sixth force that serves to cause winning coalitions to be greater than minimal size is the considerations of future electoral consequences. It is obvious that electoral outcomes will affect the process of coalition formation. What perhaps may be less obvious is that the coalition formation process may affect future electoral success. A left-wing party may find it hard to maintain its credibility in parliamentary alliance with a right-wing party against an opposition center alliance. A possible explanation for the greater than minimal winning size in the ninth Israeli cabinet, but not in the tenth, is that Mapai was concerned about its electoral chances in the election for the Fifth Knesset (tenth cabinet). Furthermore, electoral alliances have become more common in Israel, again connecting campaign strategy with coalition strategy.

The ninth cabinet suggests a seventh factor that may affect coalition size, loyalty to old coalition partners. Mapai did retain Mapam or Progressive support in the ninth cabinet when such support was not necessary. This may have been done out of loyalty to, and in appreciation for, support in the eighth cabinet, or in the hopes of inducing support for Mapai in future cabinets. We are less persuaded by this argument than by the explanation of differences between the ninth and tenth cabinets based on electoral considerations. However, the loyalty factor deserves consideration, since under conditions of imperfect information, it may be quite rational for Mapai to have sought and accepted the support of a known quantity, Mapam or the Progressives.

The ninth cabinet also suggests that ideological connectedness may make it difficult to shear partners from a coalition. Electoral considerations and loyalty have been offered as possible explanations of the greater than minimal winning size of the ninth cabinet, but a third possibility is that Mapai simply could not easily shear its ideological neighbors, Mapam and the Progressives.

These factors all take on peculiar colorations in the Israeli case, but we believe that they have general significance outside of Israel. Together they suggest that current theories of coalition formation are not inherently defective; rather, to the extent that these theories are descriptively inadequate, this inadequacy derives from parsimony and not from internal inconsistency or poor logic.

Table 3.3

Ministries and Occupants

Cabinet #	1	2	3	4	5	6	7	8	9	10	11	12	13	14	15	16	17	18
Knesset #	1	2	2	2	2	2	3	3	4	5	5	5	6	6	6	7	7	8
MINISTRY																		
Prime Minister	MA	MA	MA	MA	MA	MA	MA	MA	MA	MA	MA	MA	MA	MA	MA	L	L	L
Deputy Prime Minister	•	-	•	-	-	-	-	-	-	-	MA	MA	-	-	-	-	L	L
Defense	MA	MA	MA	MA	MA	MA	MA	MA	MA	MA	MA	•	•	RA	RA	L	L	L
Foreign Affairs	MA	MA	MA	MA	•	N*	MA	MA	MA	MA	MA	MA	MA	MA	MA	L	L	L
Finance	MA	MA	MA	GZ	MA	MA	MA	MA	MA	MA	MA	MA	MA	MA	MA	L	L	L
Commerce & Industry	•	(ind)	MA	PR	PR	PR	PR	PR	PR	MA	MA	•	MA	MA	MA	G	•	L
Justice	PR	PR	•	MA	MA	MA	MA	MA	MA	MA	MA	MA	MA	MA	MA	L	L	L
Labor	MA	MA	MA	GZ	GZ	MA	MA	MA	MA	AH	AH	AH	AH	AH	AH	L	L	L
Health	URF	URF	NRP	GZ	GZ	MA	MP	MP	MP	NRP	NRP	NRP	MP	MP	MP	-	-	L
Immigration	•	•	-	-	-	-	-	-	-	-	-	-	-	-	-	-	MP	LIB
Interior	•	•	NRP	GZ	GZ	NRP	AH	AH	NRP	•	•	•	NRP	NRP	NRP	-	NRP	NRP
Religious Affairs	URF	URF	•	NRP	NRP	NRP	NRP	NRP	(ind)	NRP	NRP	NRP	NRP	NRP	NRP	NRP	NRP	NRP
Social Welfare	URF	URF	A	MA	NRP	NRP	•	•	NRP	NRP	NRP	NRP	NRP	NRP	NRP	NRP	NRP	NRP
Police	SE	SE	MA	MA	MA	MA	MA	MA	MA	MA	MA	MA	MA	MA	MA	MA	MA	MA
Posts	-	-	-	NRP	NRP	NRP	NRP	NRP	•	MA	MA	•	-	MA	MA	G	-	-
Education	MA	MA	MA	MA	MA	MA	MA	MA	MA	MA	MA	MA	MA	MA	MA	MA	L	L
Agriculture	MA	MA	MA	MA	MA	MA	MA	MA	MA	MA	AH	AH	MA	MA	MA	MA	IL	IL
Tourism	-	-	-	-	-	-	-	MP	MP	MP	MA	MA	MA	MA	•	IL	IL	-
Development	-	-	•	•	MA	MA	MP	•	•	•	•	•	IL	IL	IL	NRP	-	-
Housing	-	-	-	-	-	-	-	-	AH	AH	AH	AH	MP	MP	MP	L	L	L
Transportation	-	-	-	-	-	-	-	AH	•	•	-	-	AH	AH	AH	G	L	L
Communications	MA	MA	MA	GZ	GZ	MA	AH	AH	•	MA	-	-	-	-	•	-	•	L
W/O Portfolio	•	•	MA-2	MA	MA	MA	MA	MA	MA	MA	-	-	AH	AH	AH	L-3	L	L-3
															H	G-2		NRP
													G-2		AH			
															L			
TOTAL	12	13	13	16	16	16	16	16	16	16	16	16	17	21	21	22	18	23

Party Abbreviations for Table 3.3

A	Agudat Yisreal
AH	Ahdut Ha'Avoda
G	Gahal: alignment of Herut + General Zionist + Liberal
GZ	General Zionist
IL	Independent Liberal, post-1965 name of Progressives
(ind)	independent minister
L	Labor: alignment of Mapai + Ahdut Ha'Avoda + Mapam + Rafi
LIB	Liberal, new name of General Zionist party
MA	Mapai
MP	Mapam
NRP	National Religious Party
PR	Progressives
SE	Sephardim, party disappeared after 2nd Knesset
URF	United Religious Front, early form of NRP

Note: a dash (-) indicates that that portfolio did not exist in that cabinet. An asterisk (*) indicates that that ministry was combined with another ministry in that cabinet.

Returns to Knesset Parties for Coalition Membership

Rewards to political parties for giving their support to governing coalitions come in two forms: policy and cabinet ministries. Since policy payoffs would be extremely difficult to analyze, to determine whether government action is something it would have done in any case or something it does only because it is paying off a political debt, the focus here is upon the distribution of cabinet ministries, a clear indication of the coalition-forming party "giving" something to another party in return for that party's support in the Knesset.

Table 3.3 illustrates the distribution of ministries in the eighteen Israeli cabinets through 1974. This table provides information of several types of payoff distribution that may be used in evaluating some of the theories that have been thus far discussed. First, although the ministries have not been broken down into several categories, even a brief examination of the table will indicate which ministries have been the most important to the various parties participating in the governments. The government-forming party, Mapai, has traditionally held the positions of prime minister and deputy prime minister, and the ministries of Defense, Foreign Relations, Finance, Agriculture, Police, and Education and Culture.[31] Since the beginning of the Seventh Knesset it has often been difficult to tell which party held which ministry, since old party labels were superseded by those of the new alliance. The religious parties have traditionally held the ministries of Religious Affairs and Social Welfare. The ministries of Commerce and Industry, Justice, Labor, Health, Immigration, Interior, Posts, Tourism, Development, Housing, Transportation, and Communication have passed from party to party over the years and in some cases have either existed or ceased to exist depending upon the political situation of the moment.

A second point to note is that some of the ministries appear to serve more of a bartering function than others. Tourism, Development, Housing, and Transportation have been combined with each other, dissolved, and re-created more than all other ministries combined.

It cannot be stated with certainty that in order to keep, for example, the Progressive party active in the coalition in the ninth cabinet, the prime minister had to offer it the Ministry of Justice,

Government Coalitions and the Knesset 75

but it can be stated with some confidence that all indications point to the fact that the NRP had demanded the ministries of Religious Affairs and Social Welfare as its "share of the pie" in return for its support (or its "keeping quiet"). In recent cabinets the NRP's demand has extended to the Ministry of the Interior, as well. Overall, however, once the ministries that Mapai keeps for itself are excluded, there does not appear to be a major and significant (in the sense of causing resignations) hierarchy of ministries.

Table 3.4 allows us to begin to evaluate explanations for why parties receive the payoffs that they do. Table 3.4 shows the parties represented in coalitions, the number of ministries they held, the number of seats in the Knesset they represented, and their "key" to the cabinet, the ratio of the number of ministries they received to the number of seats they controlled.

What is evident from this table is the validity of the statement of Browne and Franklin that "the number of ministries reviewed by partners in a governing coalition is indeed explained, almost on a one-to-one basis, by their contribution of seats to that coalition."[32] In only a few cases was there a marked difference between keys (ratios). Excluding the two instances (the second and ninth cabinets) in which an independent received a ministry and consequently had a key of 1.0 (the party had one seat in the Knesset and received one ministry), in only five cases did the range among parties of the ratio of number of ministries to number of seats controlled exceed 0.10, and in only three cases did it exceed 0.125.

The three cases of greatest inequality (the fourteenth, fifteenth, and eighteenth cabinets) are revealing. The fourteenth and fifteenth cabinets, both of which had differences in keys of 0.17 points, were the two cabinets following the 1967 war that attempted to portray the government of unanimity by including the right-wing Gahal party in the cabinet. The greatest variation in these cases was the participation of the Gahal coalition that received two ministries in each cabinet. This reward of two ministries for a support return of twenty-six Knesset seats was far lower than for any other keys in those coalitions (0.08), and well below the average (0.18). The dissident Mapai group, Rafi, also had a greatly lower-than-usual key (0.10). The 36 seats represented by Rafi and Gahal in these coalitions were not at all necessary for the government's life; since 106 seats in the Knesset were represented by

Table 3.4
"Keys" to the Cabinet

Knesset	Cabinet		Mapam	Ahdut HaAvodah	Mapai	Rafi	NRP	Agudat Yisrael	Party Progressive/ I.L.	Gen Zionist/L	Gahal	Sephardim	Other	Σ	Mean Key	Max Δ
1	1	# Seats			46		16		5			4		71		
		# Min's			7		3		1			1		12		
		Key			.15		.19		.20			.25			.197	.105[d]
	2	# Seats			46		16		5			4	1	72		
		# Min's			7		3		1			1	1	13		
		Key			.15		.19		.20			.25	1.0		.358	.10[a]
	3	# Seat			45		8	3						56		
		# Min's			10		2	1						13		
		Key			.22		.25	.33							.267	.11
2	4	# Seats			45		8		4	20				77		
		# Min's			10		2		1	3				16		
		Key			.22		.25		.25	.15					.218	.10
	5	# Seats			45		8		4	20				77		
		# Min's			9		2		1	4				16		
		Key			.20		.25		.25	.20					.225	.05

Table 3.4 (Continued)

Knesset	Cabinet		Party												
			Mapam	Ahdut HaAvodah	Mapai	Rafi	NRP	Agudat Yisrael	Progressive/ I.L.	Gen Zionist/L	Gahal	Sephardim	Other	Σ	Mean Key	Max Δ
2	6	# Seats			45		8		4					57		
		# Min's			12		3		1					16		
		Key			.27		.38		.25						.298	.125[d]
3	7	# Seats	9	10	40		11		5					75		
		# Min's	2	2	9		2		1					16		
		Key	.22	.20	.23		.18		.20						.205	.05
	8	# Seat	9	10	40		11		5					75		
		# Min's	2	2	9		2		1					16		
		Key	.22	.20	.23		.18		.20						.205	.05
4	9	# Seats	9	7	47		12		6		1			82		
		# Min's	2	1	9		2		1		1			16		
		Key	.22	.14	.19		.17		.17		1.0				.178	.08[a]
5	10	# Seats		8	42		12							62		
		# Min's		2	11		3							16		
		Key		.25	.26		.25								.253	.01

Table 3.4 (Continued)

Knesset	Cabinet		Mapam	Ahdut HaAvodah	Mapai	Rafi	NRP	Agudat Yisrael	Progressive/ I.L.	Gen Zionist/L	Gahal	Sephardim	Other	Σ	Mean Key	Max Δ
5	11	# Seats	8	8	42		12							62		
		# Min's	2	2	11		3							16		
		Key	.25	.25	.26		.25								.253	.01
	12	# Seats	8	8	42		12							62		
		# Min's	2	2	11		3							16		
		Key	.25	.25	.26		.25								.253	.01
6	13	# Seat	8	[b]	45[b]		12		5					70		
		# Min's	2		11		3		1					17		
		Key	.25		.18		.25		.20						.219[d]	.08[d]
	14	# Seats	8	8	45	10	12		5		26			106		
		# Min's	2	2	12	1	3		1		2			21		
		Key	.25	.25	.20	.10	.25		.20		.08				.180	.17
	15	# Seats	8	8	45	10	12		5		26			106		
		# Min's	2	2	12	1	3		1		2			21		
		Key	.25	.25	.20	.10	.25		.20		.08				.180	.17

Table 3.4 (Continued)

Knesset	Cabinet		Party											Σ	Mean Key	Max Δ
		Mapam	Ahdut HaAvodah	Mapai	Rafi	NRP	Agudat Yisrael	Progressive/ I.L.	Gen Zionist/L	Gahal	Sephardim	Other				
6	16 # Seats	c		56[c]	c	12		4		26			98		
	# Min's			13		3		1		5			22	.230	.06
7	Key			.23		.25		.25		.19					
	17 # Seats			56		12		4					72		
	# Min's			14/15		3		1					18/19	.250	.02
	Key			.25/.27		.25		.25							
	18 # Seat			51		10		4					65		
8	# Min's			17		4		2					23	.410	.17
	Key			.33		.40		.50							

[a] Excluding the single key of 1.0.
[b] In the elections for the Sixth Knesset, Mapai and Ahdut HaAvodah ran together as the Alignment. Numbers are listed in the Mapai column for convenience.
[c] In the elections for the Seventh Knesset, Mapam joined the Alignment. Numbers are listed in the Mapai column for convenience.
[d] Apparent discrepancies are due to rounding errors.

these alliances, the loss of these 36 seats would have left the government with nine seats to spare over a minimal-winning size coalition. The inclusion of Rafi and Gahal, and their lower number of ministries, were apparently the result of public opinion, which forced the government to give the Ministry of Defense to Moshe Dayan, the leader of Rafi. The only other major difference in ministerial keys exists in the eighteenth cabinet. The Labor and NRP blocs each have one minister for every three seats they possess in the Knesset, whereas the Independent Liberals have one ministry for every two seats they possess in the Knesset.

The evidence seems to show conclusively that the number of ministries that parties receive as rewards for belonging to coalitions is a direct function of the number of seats (of support for the Government) that they control. It appears that in a political system such as the one in Israel, in which a minority party must ally itself with other minority parties to attempt to form a majority government, the parceling out of the rewards must be on an egalitarian basis. That is, the dominant party (the one forming the Government) may have a right to claim certain ministries for itself, but the ratio of ministers to seats is one that must be, in most instances, consistently maintained. In most cases in which there is a large difference in party keys to the cabinet, it is the smaller parties that receive the "bonus" ministries, and not the larger, Government-forming party.

Notes

1. See, for instance, Gerhard Loewenberg, *Modern Parliaments: Change or Decline?* (Chicago: Atherton, 1971), p. 3.
2. See Joseph LaPalombara, *Politics within Nations* (Englewood Cliffs, N.J.: Prentice-Hall, 1974), pp. 221–25.
3. William Riker and Peter Ordeshook, *Introduction to Positive Political Theory* (Englewood Cliffs, N.J.: Prentice-Hall, 1973), p. 124.
4. J. Von Neumann and O. Morgenstern, *Theory of Games and Economic Behavior* (Princeton, N.J.: Princeton University Press, 1944).
5. Steven Brams and William Riker, "Models of Coalition Formation in Voting Bodies," in *Mathematical Applications in Political Science VI*, ed. J. F. Herndon and J. L. Bernd (Charlottesville, Va.: University Press of Virginia, 1972), p. 80.
6. See William Riker, *Theory of Political Coalitions* (New Haven: Yale University

Press, 1962); M. Leiserson, "Factions and Coalitions in One Party Japan," *American Political Science Review* 62 (1968):770–87; R. Axelrod, *Conflict of Interest* (Chicago: Markham, 1970); W. Gamson, "A Theory of Coalition Formation," *American Sociological Review* 26 (1961):373-82; Abraham DeSwann, *Coalition Theories and Cabinet Formations* (San Francisco: Jossey-Bass, 1973).

7. Valerie Herman and John Pope, "Minority Governments in Western Democracies," *British Journal of Political Science* 3 (1973):191.

8. Leiserson, "Factions and Coalitions."

9. See Akzin, "The Role of Parties in Israeli Democracy," *Journal of Politics* 17 (1955).

10. Ibid., p. 532.

11. Eric Browne, "Testing Theories of Coalition Formation in the European Context," *Comparative Political Studies* 3 (1971):400.

12. Ibid., p. 402.

13. Leonard Fein, *Israel: Politics and People* (Boston: Little, Brown, and Co., 1966), p. 222.

14. See the *Jerusalem Post*, March 12, 1974, p. 2; and the *Jerusalem Post: Overseas Edition*, May 24, 1977, respectively.

15. Scott Johnston, "Party Politics and Coalition Cabinets in the Knesset," *Middle Eastern Affairs* 13 (1962):130.

16. Herman and Pope, "*Minority Governments,*" p. 192.

17. Ibid.

18. The numberings of the cabinets vary from source to source. Most sources are agreed that the fourteenth cabinet served from 1967 to February, 1969; we have counted the nine-month cabinet following the death of Eshkol in 1969 as the fifteenth cabinet. Another cabinet formed after the elections for the Seventh Knesset in December 1969 lasted until April 1971, at which time there were changes in portfolios. We number these two cabinets within the duration of the Seventh Knesset as the sixteenth and seventeenth cabinets. In April 1972, the ministries of finance and of commerce and industry were given to two ministers, both Labor members, rather than to one (as they had been); this we have included in the seventeenth cabinet. The eighteenth cabinet was formed after the elections of the Eighth Knesset.

19. Asher Zidon, *Knesset: The Parliament of Israel* (New York: Herzl Press, 1967), p. 109.

20. Leiserson, p. 779.

21. The question of "Who is a Jew?" is a highly complex and intricate issue. Suffice it to say here that the NRP position was one of making the process by which non-Jews could convert to Judaism more strict and difficult. The NRP wanted the law to specify that one could convert to Judaism only under the supervision of an Orthodox Rabbi, whereas the law at the time implied, and still implies today, that conversion under the supervision of a Conservative Rabbi is acceptable for recognition as a Jew in Israel.

22. *Jerusalem Post*, March 12, 1974, p. 2.

23. Ibid.

24. Ibid.

25. *New York Times*, March 11, 1974, p. 1.

26. Riker, *Theory of Political Coalitions*, p. 77.

27. Axelrod, *Conflict of Interest*.

28. Leiserson, *Factions and Coalitions*.

29. David Nachmias, "Coalition Politics in Israel," *Comparative Political Studies* 7 (1974):331.
30. Fein, *Israel*, p. 232.
31. Eric Browne and Michael Franklin, "Aspects of Coalition Payoffs in European Parliamentary Democracies," *American Political Science Review* 67 (1973):458.
32. Ibid.

Part II

The Legislative System

4

The Knesset in the Israeli Political System

The Israeli legislature must operate within the political system already described, and it is within this system, with its idiosyncratic qualities, that the Knesset tries to perform its duties and functions in the Israeli political world. Certain aspects of the Knesset's operation, such as its organization; the immunities, rights, and duties of its members; and the legislative process itself are discussed in this chapter, as are other aspects of Knesset life, such as the influence of political parties, committee behavior, and opportunities for the individual member of Knesset to participate in the legislative process.

The Knesset as a Parliamentary System

Most parliaments of the world have some degree of parliamentary immunity and inviolability. That is, members of legislatures are "permitted to do and say what they wish in their role as lawmakers, without fear of interference from the executive or the military, of arbitrary arrest or physical harm, or of harassment in the courts."[1] These two characteristics of parliamentary membership are rarely absolute—that is, there are many instances in which freedom of speech is not absolute or in which freedom from arrest may be lost, such as in capital crimes. Since 1949, members of Knesset have been accorded parliamentary immunity, but as indicated shortly, this immunity is not absolute and may be revoked under certain circumstances.

As is the case in other nations, the reason behind parliamentary immunity for members of Knesset is to assure them freedom to perform their duties as members of the national legislature without fear of possible governmental persecution. The immunity of MKs is discussed in the "Immunity, Rights, and Duties of Members of the Knesset" Law passed in 1951, which was based on an ordinance dating back to 1949. The protection afforded MKs is extremely broad. The law states that

> A member of the Knesset shall not be held civilly or criminally responsible, and shall be immune from legal action, with regard to any vote cast, any oral or written expression of opinion, or any other act performed in or out of the Knesset, provided that such vote, opinion, or act pertains to, or has as its purpose, the fulfillment of his mandate as a Member of the Knesset.[2]

Phrases such as "or any other act performed in or out of the Knesset" and "mandate as a Member of the Knesset" are so broad and undefined that they give the individual MK a great deal of latitude in terms of the behavior in which he or she might wish to engage.

In order to further protect the individual legislators, the act protects the MKs beyond their specific legislative behavior. Neither the members of Knesset themselves nor their property may be searched, except by customs officials. While they hold office, members of Knesset are absolutely immune from arrest, unless they are caught committing a crime themselves or committing an act of treason. If an MK is arrested, the Speaker of the Knesset must be notified immediately by the authorities, and the MK may not be kept under arrest for more than ten days unless the Knesset has revoked his or her immunity.

This revocation of immunity only applies to personal immunity, not "parliamentary" immunity; a member's immunity for things he or she does or says as a member, in the "fulfillment of his mandate," can never be revoked by any authority. The member's immunity is as close to absolute as can be found in any legislature in the world. Personal immunity, however, is a different matter. The principle behind parliamentary immunity is that an individual should be able to represent his or her constituency without fear of reprisal; it is not that the individual should be beyond the reach of the law. Accordingly, an individual's personal immunity may be revoked; this revocation does not mean that the Knesset feels the individual concerned is guilty, simply that the Knesset is of the opinion that the courts should have access to the individual. A petition for revocation of immunity may be filed by any MK or by the attorney general, specifying the charges made against the MK involved. The Speaker receives the petition and refers it to the Knesset committee for consideration. The MK involved is called to testify at the meeting of the Knesset committee. If the committee feels that immunity should be lifted, it prepares a resolution to that effect, and the entire Knesset must vote on the matter. At least twenty-four hours must pass between the introduction of the committee resolution and the Knesset vote.

As with many other national legislatures, the Knesset Building itself has immunity. Under the Knesset Buildings Law of 1952, the Knesset building and grounds are under the control of the Speaker and sergeant at arms. This, too, is designed to free MKs from extralegislative pressures, such as demonstrations and other interruptions that might prove distracting to them.

Internally, the Knesset is a party assembly. ("Knesset" means assembly.) That is, as with the rest of the political world in Israel, parties organize and control activities in the Knesset to a remarkable degree. Because of party discipline the opportunities for individual legislative action in the Knesset are few, and only occur when the party leaders specifically state that the party will take no stand on a given issue.

Zidon writes that

> To date, the Speaker of the Knesset in each instance has been elected unanimously ... at the opening session of the Knesset. This indicated the aim of the political parties represented in the Knesset to remove the Speakership from the area of inter-party contention and to place it above interests. The individual who holds this position enjoys the confidence of the entire Knesset, irrespective of political party.[3]

This statement, although technically correct, is questionable in daily practice. The position of Speaker is a highly partisan one, which draws a considerable amount of partisan conflict. Although the parties symbolically make the election for Speaker unanimous, this does not make the position of Speaker any less partisan. Only after it becomes clear who will be chosen is the election made unanimous. Each of the two major parties has traditionally put forward a candidate, and voting for Speaker is always under the tightest of party discipline, with the larger party's candidate being chosen. Shortly after the opening of the Eighth Knesset there was a great deal of opposition to the reelection of the previous Speaker on the grounds that he had been overly partisan during the previous session.[4]

The office of Deputy Speaker is equally partisan, with the number of deputies to be chosen varying with party distributions in the Knesset. "Deputy Speakerships have come to be regarded as one of those Knesset posts which, like committee chairmanships, are distributed as 'plums' among the major parties when a new Knesset is organized."[5] The Eighth Knesset had five deputy speakerships, with two belonging to the Labor alignment, two to the Likud alignment, and one to the NRP.

In the same manner that the positions of Speaker and Deputy Speaker are highly partisan, so too are the committee chairmanships. Unlike a system such as that found in the United States in which the largest party receives all committee chairmanships, in the Knesset chairmanships are apportioned much as are the Deputy Speakerships. The Eighth Knesset easily decided to have ten standing committees when it first met to organize,[6] but the decision of how to apportion the chairs of the respective committees was not so easily reached. Unofficially an arrangements committee is established at the beginning of each Knesset to make this kind of decision, but at the beginning of the Eighth Knesset the committee was unable to resolve the conflict.[7] The solution was finally resolved by a compromise giving the Likud bloc control over an important subcommittee in addition to the chairmanship of a minor committee.

Seats on the committees are given to parties, not individuals, and the parties then assign their own members to the committee seats. For example, in the Eighth Knesset the State Control Committee had fifteen members, representing only the three large "parties": Labor, Likud, and NRP. The smaller parties were not represented on this committee; a decision was made that only parties with five members or more in the Knesset (four parties) would be allowed to choose on which committees they would sit—smaller parties would be at the mercy of the larger parties for their committee assignments.

Here, again, not only is there interparty competition for positions but there is *intra*party competition as well. Even though it had been decided that the Labor alignment would receive two Deputy Speakerships, the manner in which the four parties factions would divide up the two chairs remained in dispute. The decision was finally reached to rotate the chairs at the half term. Similarly, within the Likud, there was a tremendous amount of infighting as to how to divide up four committee chairmanships among five separate factions in the alignment.

Committee meetings are all closed to the press and public, so that all information about what happens within the committee meetings must come from the committee members themselves. Committee members are divided over what the true role of the committee is, as they see it, in terms of Knesset action generally. This is a subject to which we return in chapter 8. Many say that the committee's role depends upon the particular legislation that is before a given committee at a given time. Most are agreed, however, that committee action is generally "meaningless" because the Government as a general rule takes no notice of committee recommendations, and although committees may spend a good deal of time modifying Government legislation, or drafting their own legislation, when the third reading of a Government bill comes on the floor of the Knesset, the Government bill is usually voted upon as it was originally introduced in the Knesset. For this reason, belief in the effectiveness of committees is quite low.

However, three committees are exceptions to this general rule. For various reasons, both the Finance and Labor committees have been given authority by both the Knesset and the Government to promulgate laws in their own small spheres of expertise, without needing the consent of either the Knesset or the Government. These committees, especially the Finance Committee, are thus considered quite powerful and influential, and consequently positions on these committees are highly sought.

The third exception to the general belief of committee ineffectiveness is the Foreign Affairs and Security Committee. It is interesting that this committee should be considered an exception to the general rule, because it has few powers. The committee is solely a debative body, devoting little time to drafting legislation and concentrating mostly upon policy discussion and evaluation. The reason that this committee is such an attractive one for MKs, quite clearly, is that so much of Israel's politics is related to this area; a member of this committee will be privy to more classified information than a member of, say, the Interior Committee. Whenever members of Knesset listed the two or three committees of which they most desired to be members, the two committees that were most often listed were Finance and Foreign Affairs, although in those interviews in which Members remembered to make distinctions with regard to effectiveness, Finance was always mentioned as "having teeth," and Foreign Affairs was described as "toothless, but interesting."

As indicated previously, seats on committees are given to parties, and are then reassigned by party leaders to party members. Consequently, when a member bolts the party line in a committee or speaks out of turn too often, he or she may be limited to participation in the plenary sessions, having been either reassigned from one committee to another, or, in more extreme cases, having been stripped of all committee memberships. The total dependence of the individual member of Knesset upon party leaders, a point that is further developed later, is something that is omnipresent in the Knesset.

An elaborate framework of customs and traditions has evolved in the Knesset's brief history. The Fundamental Law (the Knesset) indicated that the Knesset would be master of its own procedure; if procedures are not set down in law, the Knesset simply follows custom and precedent. The Rules of Procedure that are set down in law are said by members of Knesset to be extremely thorough, including discussions of the rights and powers of the Speaker and his or her deputies, committee behavior, the legislative process, individual behavior, etiquette, and forms of debate. There are over twenty "chapters" to the Rules of Procedure, units into which rules are organized.

As in other legislative bodies, legislators in Israel's parliament are expected to conduct themselves "properly" in the course of their activities. Propriety is a relative term and many an outsider is caught off guard at his or her introduction to the Knesset by the verbal barbs, interruptions, shouting, and heckling that are an accepted part of the day-to-day scene. Much of this behavior is undertaken in good humor, and appropriately disappears during formal occasions, but it is not uncommon for members to be evicted from the hall, sometimes for several days, as a response to deliberately obstructive behavior.

The Knesset sits for two terms a year, one in the summer and one in the winter. Under the Fundamental Law (the Knesset), the two terms must total at least eight months. After the Knesset has recessed, it may be reconvened in extraordinary circumstances at the request of either thirty MKs or the Government.

In order to provide the Knesset with a minimum of barriers to meeting, the Fundamental Law (the Knesset) specified no minimum number of MKs for a quorum. That is, any number of members present in the chamber at a time is a quorum, whether that number be 120 or 20. Partially because of this fact, attendance in plenary sessions varies widely, depending upon who is speaking, the legislation before the house, the importance of the vote to the Government, the expected closeness of the vote, and so on. Generally attendance ranges from 20 to 75 percent of the membership on the floor when the Knesset is in session.

One of the major characteristics of parliamentary governments around the world is the institution of question time, and this institution flourishes in the Knesset. Unlike the practice in some other parliaments, however, questions in Israel's Knesset can only be submitted in writing, although oral supplementary questions are permitted. Members submit their questions to the Speaker in triplicate, who forwards them to the appropriate minister. The Speaker may disqualify questions if they do not follow procedure; they must ask questions rather than make assertions, they may not deal in hypotheticals, and the like.

When the minister has prepared a response, he reads his formal response aloud in the Knesset at which time the member who submitted the question is permitted to orally submit a supplementary question. In fact, many members plan their supplementary questions at the same time they frame their original questions; the written question is simply a requirement to be met before they can ask an oral question of the minister in question in the plenum.

The institution of question time serves several functions. It permits the individual member to acquire information from the

Government that he or she might not be able to acquire any other way. ("Does the Government plan to build a road from town A to town B?") It enables members, especially members of the Opposition, to criticize the Government and its policy. ("Why has the Government insisted on following this weak economic policy in the face of rapid inflation?") And it is a way for individual members to bring to the attention of ministers problems in individual ministries. ("Does the minister of commerce know that it has taken sixteen months to process a work permit for individual B?") The important thing about parliamentary questions is that the public is watching. The press is in the Knesset gallery, and question time, especially the oral supplementary questions, makes good material for the evening news.

In addition to parliamentary questions, two other institutions of a similar nature in the Knesset merit further mention, the Motion to Add to the Agenda and the Urgent Motion to Add to the Agenda. When a member feels that there is a subject not on the Government's agenda that is of sufficient importance to warrant the Knesset's attention, he or she may make a Motion to add this question to the agenda. This motion must be submitted in writing to the Speaker, who passes a copy of it along to the appropriate Government minister, so that the minister can prepare the Government's position on whether this matter should be added to the agenda or not, which may take several days or several weeks. When the Government's response is ready, the sponsor of the motion is given ten minutes to explain to the Knesset why this motion should be passed, and the minister involved is given time to present the Government's position. The Government's position may be to support the motion, to oppose the motion, or to suggest that the motion be sent to committee for discussion. A vote is then taken on the original motion; if it passes, the matter is scheduled for the Knesset.

An Urgent Motion to Add to the Agenda allows matters to be added for immediate discussion. This motion must be submitted to the Speaker the morning before the day of proposed debate, and the Speaker and the Deputy Speakers decide whether the topic is sufficiently "urgent" to be handled in this manner, or whether the motion should be treated as a normal Motion to Add to the Agenda. If the Knesset Presidium (the Speaker and the Deputy Speakers) believe that the topic is sufficiently urgent, the motion is passed along to the appropriate minister who must be prepared the following day to indicate the Government's position on the matter. If the Urgent Motion is passed, debate takes place that day on the matter, rather than being put on the Knesset calendar for discussion some time in the future, depending upon the Knesset's work load as is the case with a regular Motion to Add to the Agenda.

In functional terms, there may not be much difference between the parliamentary question and the two kinds of motions for the agenda; each gets the attention of the media, and each can be used to call the Government's attention to policy alternatives and as a vehicle for criticizing Governmental policy. A member who is simply interested in acquiring information, such as the amount of a Government subsidy to the beet industry, will be more likely simply to submit a written question than to introduce a Motion to Add to the Agenda. There is no doubt, though, that in cases in which the Opposition would like to critize the Government, a motion to add is preferable to a question, because if the motion passes then a full-fledged debate takes place.

Although parliamentary questions legally cannot be controlled, the party leaders act as a screen between MKs and ministers. Members of the Government coalition parties must "clear" their questions with appropriate party leaders before they ask them; failure to do so may result in a strong disciplinary action. Members of Opposition parties ask considerably more questions than do Government coalition members and follow them with considerably more supplementary questions.

The system has a potential problem of having no real constraints upon the ministers to make sure that they always answer the questions that are asked of them.[8] By statute, a minister is given twenty-one days in which to respond to a written question, and may obtain a twenty-one day extension if necessary. However, ministers occasionally completely ignore questions that they perceive as being "difficult." Many Opposition MKs complain that they have submitted questions to the foreign minister, for example, and three months later have not yet received any response to their questions. With the volume of questions they receive, ministers can be selective as to which questions they will answer.

The question of the control of motions to add to the agenda is closely related to the previously mentioned items, as well as to the ability to introduce legislation and to control votes on the floor of the Knesset. The Government coalition whip on the floor of the Knesset controls the behavior of all members of coalition parties. The coalition party members cannot introduce legislation without receiving prior permission of the coalition leadership, nor can they speak on the floor without such permission, with the exception of heckling other members speaking.

Debate itself may be the central characteristic of parliamentary bodies throughout the world. Regardless of the true role of legislatures in the power structures of the governments in which they are found around the world, the one thing that legislatures always do is debate. The Knesset does not deviate from this rule, and debate is the vehicle by which it moves as it does. Debate may ensue from a bill, in which case debate occurs after the first, second, and third readings of the bill, which are discussed shortly, from a Motion to Add to the Agenda, or from a statement by the Government. Votes of confidence and nonconfidence would fall into the latter category. Knesset debates can be classified by one of two labels, personal debate and party debate.

Personal debate, which is the less significant of the debate in the Knesset, is usually employed either in "nonpolitical" matters, which the Knesset is discussing but which are not related to legislation pending before the house, or in matters of legislation on which opinions are not divided along party lines.

Party debate, by far the bulk of Knesset debate, takes place in relation to votes of confidence and nonconfidence, foreign policy, the budget, and any matter that the Government regards as significant (which means virtually any bill introduced by the Government). When this kind of debate takes place, the Knesset committee decides how much time to allow for the total debate, say four hours (240 minutes), then divides the total time by the total number of MKs yielding a time-per-member figure (240/120 or 2 minutes per member).[9] This amount of time is then given to the party leaders in the Knesset to do with as they please. The leaders may choose to permit everyone in their party to speak for the allotted time per member, or they may choose to pool all the time into one longer speech; it is entirely up to the party leader. In many cases the party leader himself will speak, or the entire party time will be given to a senior party member who is considered the party's spokesman on the given issue, for instance, a party expert on economic questions. Total debate times usually range from two to ten hours.

In addition to debate, the major function of legislatures is legislating, or passing laws. The legislative process in the Knesset follows the standard parliamentary model fairly closely; only a brief discussion of the process is needed here. An initial distinction must be made between Government bills and private bills. Private bills are any bills not introduced by the Government, whether by members of the Government coalition parties or by members of the Opposition parties. Numerically, private members' bills are a very small minority of the total number of bills processed by the Knesset annually. In the Sixth Knesset, for instance (1961-65), out of 166 laws passed by the Knesset, 156 (94.4 percent) were introduced by the Government, 6 (3.2 percent) were introduced by private members, and 4 (2.4 percent) were introduced by committees.[10]

Private bills in the Knesset are apportioned to the parties by a "key"; each party is allowed to introduce approximately three private bills per seat it holds in the Knesset per session. This being the case, the party leaders are very careful as to what they allow to be introduced as part of their party's quota of bills. Since MKs rarely are permitted to introduce their own bills—the party leadership usually has proposals for the party's entire quota of private bills—and since the mechanisms for making motions to add to the agenda are so cumbersome, most MKs are more likely to attempt to speak through the urgent motion to add to the agenda. These motions are neither controlled directly by party leadership nor by party quotas. The ordinary pressures of party discipline might, however, still be sufficient to dissuade an MK from taking advantage of this vehicle of communication if his or her topic is sufficiently controversial.

The bulk of the Knesset's work, as indicated previously, comes from Government-introduced legislation. This legislation usually is written by a Government ministry, which then passes the proposed legislation to the cabinet for revisions or policy refinement. The legislation is then "tabled" in the Knesset, and entered as an item for the agenda. The bill must "lie on the table" (be available for MKs' examination) for at least forty-eight hours before discussion on it begins. As with other limitations, this forty-eight hour rule may be waived by the Knesset committee if it so wishes.

The first stage in the legislative process is called the first reading. The minister in charge of the bill begins with an explanation of the contents of the bill, and a line-by-line reading of the proposed law. After the minister has finished presenting the bill, debate on the bill begins. This first-reading debate is usually a general one, and when the vote comes at the end of the debate Government bills invariably are passed and sent to committee; private members' bills rarely meet with the same results.

The bill is sent to whichever committee has jurisdiction over that area of legislation. The committee may deal with a bill for three months, or three hours, depending upon the importance of the bill, the committee's work load, and the willingness of the committee to cooperate with the Government manager of the legislation. Bills have been known to be reported out of committee on the same afternoon on which they were initially referred to committee; in the opposite manner, some bills have languished in committee for over a year before being reported out. The committee has the power to revise the bill, even to the extent of virtually rewriting the bill if it seems it necessary to do so. However, the Government retains the power to "recall" a bill to the Knesset floor in the exact form in which it was sent to committee if it believes that the committee has significantly altered the bill away from its intended direction.

At this stage the second reading takes place. This is the final major hurdle the bill must pass, because bills that pass the second reading invariably pass the third reading. Another debate takes place at this point, but in this debate only members of the committee may participate; all other members are in attendance only to vote on the bill, section by section.

If no amendments to the committee report are adopted, the third reading follows immediately after the conclusion of the second reading. If there are amendments, the third reading is postponed for one week to allow members time to consider the amendments. However, even if amendments have been proposed, if the Government requests an immediate third reading, the third reading takes place immediately after the second reading. Following the third reading of the bill, the bill is voted on as a whole.

As already indicated, discipline in the Knesset is strictly controlled. This is especially the case in the parliamentary vote, which is why roll-call analysis of MK behavior would not supply meaningful data. On virtually all legislation in the Knesset, both in committees as well as on the floor of the plenary session, the "whip is on," in that individual MKs *must* follow the party line. Failure of a member to vote with the party could certainly result in a change in that member's position on the party list in the next election, or removal from a prestigious committee in the Knesset. Although an MK cannot be expelled from the Knesset for going against his or her party, pressures brought upon an individual in that position both by the public as well as by Knesset colleagues have caused more than one MK to resign his or her legislative seat.

On a very small minority of issues, usually on either extremely controversial or extremely incidental issues, the party will take the "whip" off. In actuality, MKs almost never vote against their parties; this is almost a truism in parliamentary governmental systems. A member of Knesset who feels very strongly about an issue and against his or her party's policy, is most likely to go to the Knesset restaurant for a long cup of coffee in the middle of a roll call, so as to miss his or her name being called in the vote. This sometimes can be effective, and occasionally absence in itself can be a sufficient act of insubordination to warrant punishment by party leaders. From time to time, if the vote is sufficiently close, the party whip will pull in reticent members—sometimes literally—from the restaurant or elsewhere to make sure that these members vote on a given issue in the correct direction.

As indicated in chapter 1, the physical plant of the legislature itself might play a significant role in the legislature's performance of its role to a maximum degree in the political system in which it is found. Although the Knesset building itself is modern and new (it was opened in 1966), an examination of its structure suggests several interesting implications for legislative behavior in Israel.

The Knesset itself is a building of five floors. The first floor is composed entirely of committee meeting rooms and of offices of committee chairmen and their staffs. The Knesset printing office also occupies space on this floor. The second floor is called the "Government's floor," and has offices for cabinet members away from their ministry offices, rooms for cabinet conferences, and some extra rooms that are used as dormitory rooms (only) for coalition parties when the Knesset is in all-night session. The third floor is composed of a public cafeteria, the members' restaurant, the library, a small post office, the offices of the Speaker, and the Plenary Hall. The fourth floor includes the spectators' gallery and room for official banquets, plus offices for the public relations staff and press. The fifth floor is entirely made up of party offices, caucus rooms, and rooms for party members to use as dormitories in case of long sessions.

Missing in this description is an area of offices for members of Knesset, a secretarial/stenographic pool, or a legislative services bureau. These do not exist in the Knesset, which again indicates the relative role of the individual MK in the Knesset framework. When members receive mail—and they receive a good deal of mail—they must read, act upon, and answer their mail by themselves; they do not have legislative assistants or secretaries. Many banks of telephones are scattered around the building, which the members may use for official calls, and MKs are allowed free postage for official work, but all work must be done by the members themselves, with one important exception.

The exception lies in the party organization. Each party is given an annual allowance of 420,000 Israeli pounds for each seat that it controls in the Knesset. (This amount was raised in November, 1975, from an earlier allowance of 292,000 pounds.)[11] This money goes toward defraying party expenses at the party's discretion, either within or outside the Knesset. Most parties in the Knesset have two or three secretaries working on the fifth floor in the office of the party whip, and these secretaries are the only secretarial help available for MKs. For the small parties, with four or five members in the Knesset, this means that a nonparty leader might have access to secretarial help one-fifth or one-sixth of the time. In the fifty-one member Labor alignment, or the thirty-nine member Likud bloc, it is obvious that no staff help will be available for the backbencher, which further highlights the MKs' dependence upon the party organization for help. If the member is a good party worker, it is possible that the whip will give the MK some small access to secretarial help or to help by the party's staff workers. If the member doesn't follow party instructions to the letter, he or she must find other sources for secretarial help.

On June 26, 1975, a bill was passed that supposedly would alter this system drastically, for the better. This bill established individual legislative allowances for legislative assistance, either research assistants or secretaries, depending on what the individual MK wanted. By the time the bill was out of the Finance Committee, whose chairman opposed the idea, the allowance given to each MK had been cut to 2,700 pounds a year, approximately $200 at the time, although this allowance is adjusted annually to keep pace with inflation. The committee staff was also increased, and additional staff members were placed at the disposal of the committee chairmen; a similar increment applied to the staff of the Speaker. It is doubtful that this action will help the individual legislator increase his or her effectiveness, since it will be necessary for many MKs to pool their allowances in order to pay for one full-time assistant.

The members of Knesset do have a library, which is modern and of a respectable size, but only two librarians work in the library, and no legislative reference service is available to help with research and the drafting of legislation. Again, the entire burden of initiative falls on the individual MK, with only committee chairmen and party leaders having access to secretaries or legislative assistants.

This situation has obvious severe implications for the role of the individual MK. A member of a national parliament who is entirely dependent upon his or her party leaders for staff help, research assistance, permission to introduce legislation, committee membership, and even election to the legislature (through his or her position on the party electoral list) cannot be an autonomous segment of the legislative system, nor can he or she be very innovative. We now turn to an examination of the question of individual legislative behavior.

The Member of Knesset

Two different and distinct types of legislative behavior may be discerned in any type of legislative system, an intralegislative behavior and an extralegislative behavior. These types of behavior may be represented as shown in Figure 4.1. Once this important distinction in the types of legislative behavior is made in the

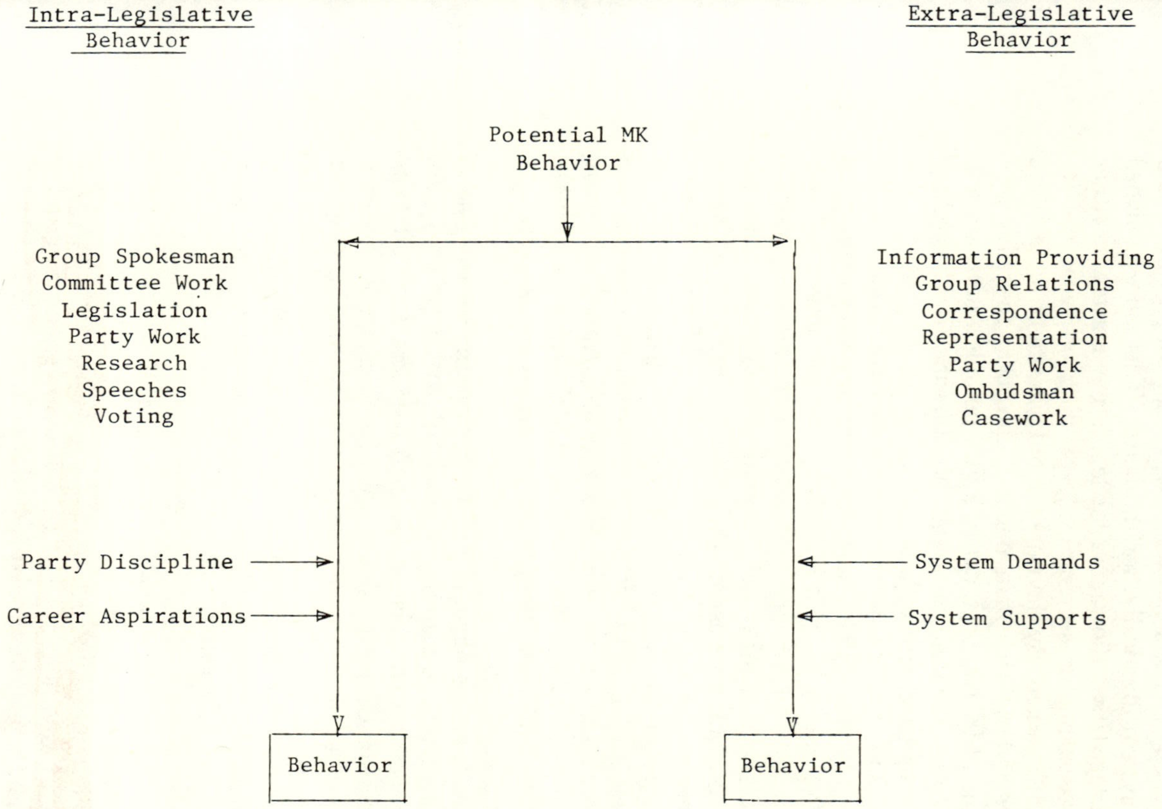

Intra-Legislative Behavior

Extra-Legislative Behavior

Information Providing
Group Relations
Correspondence
Representation
Party Work
Ombudsman
Casework

System Demands
System Supports

Potential MK Behavior

Behavior

Group Spokesman
Committee Work
Legislation
Party Work
Research
Speeches
Voting

Party Discipline
Career Aspirations

Behavior

Figure 4.1
A Schematic Representation of

Israeli case, it becomes possible to discuss behavior analytically in the Knesset; without the distinction, any discussion of legislative behavior would be ambiguous.

A noted and distinguished Knesset-watcher in Israel is Lea Ben-Dor, a former editor of the *Jerusalem Post*[12] who argues that there is no "individual behavior" to speak of within the Knesset. Outside the Knesset, MKs perform the traditional roles of representatives, helping their constituents with problems and providing information, community leadership, and the like. Inside the Knesset, however, the MK's behavior is a different story. In the Knesset MKs do not behave in an autonomous manner. The entire set of rules of behavior is highly formalized by the parties, and almost no possible action by the MKs with regard to their parties is left unregulated. The members of Knesset are elected as members of parties, pieces of the party list, and they therefore behave as pieces of the corporate party body in the Knesset. If they fail to conform, the members simply do not find themselves on the party's list at the next election. One noteworthy example of this threat being executed is Shulamit Aloni, who was a Labor party maverick in the Seventh Knesset. She disobeyed the formal party rules, debated against party positions, attempted to introduce bills against the wishes of her party, and spoke out against party policy too often to be tolerated by party leaders. She was left off the party list for the Eighth Knesset. (It is worth noting that Aloni formed her own party list for the Eighth Knesset elections and won reelection to the Knesset with two new party colleagues. Apparently, the public approves of mavericks!)

Lea Ben-Dor is perceptive in her evaluations of behavior in the Knesset, as well she should be, having been a political reporter in Jerusalem since 1935. Different aspects of legislative behavior within the Knesset, as portrayed in Figure 4.1, are all clearly influenced by the specter of party discipline, which forces all behavior within the legislature into a party mold. Although party considerations must be taken into account in extralegislative behavior, they are a much smaller factor, often to the point of having no influence at all, and consequently leave the individual member of Knesset virtually autonomous in his or her actions.

Figure 4.1 shows the relationship between intralegislative behavior and extralegislative behavior. As can be seen, virtually all aspects of behavior in the Israeli legislative system are influenced by party; they are either limited by party, apportioned by party, or directly controlled by party. If a member of Knesset has no career aspirations in the Knesset, he or she may opt to be more of a maverick, but since being in the Knesset is a "good job," most MKs are not anxious to openly antagonize their party leaders.

Being in the Knesset is a "good job" because the status of being an MK is high. In spite of the fact that it is generally recognized, both within and outside the Knesset, that individual members of Knesset "don't do anything" within the Knesset, the status of the job remains high because of the kinds of behavior that are left open in the extralegislative sphere of Knesset membership. The Knesset is the highest elective office possible in Israel, and because of this fact the MK is held in some esteem by the populace.

Members of the Knesset are in a position to perform a great number of services for the public, all of which bolster the esteem in which the MK is held. They respond to correspondence and provide information and policy positions to their constituents. The members make speeches and attend rallies, and actively represent groups in the Knesset, either occupational groups, ethnic groups, age groups, sex groups, or whatever groups they are elected to represent. The members perform ombudsman work, a great deal of which may be the area in which the average member of Knesset spends most of his or her time and receives most of his or her glory. Citizens write, telephone, or visit the MK and complain that one or another government ministry is giving them the "run around." The members contact the appropriate ministers, who are in the Knesset daily, who in turn contact the directors-general of the ministries involved, and sooner or later the problem is resolved. Actually, the MKs' success ratio in this type of activity is quite high, possibly because the political-bureaucratic system in Israel is gauged to this personalistic type of approach to problems.

In any case, once one distinguishes between intra- and extralegislative behavior, one can see the remarkable difference in effectiveness in individual legislative behavior that exists in Israel. In aspects of intralegislative behavior, the individual MK is highly limited and constrained, and is consequently highly frustrated and cynical. It is thus no surprise that of the members of Knesset interviewed for this study, over 83 percent indicated that they considered themselves accountable to their party or party leaders for what they did as a member of Knesset, and not to the public, and 74 percent indicated that individual MKs had "little," "very little," or "no influence" in the formation of government policy. (The figure rises to 93 percent when the response "generally little" is included in this category.)

In extralegislative behavior, however, members of the Knesset do not feel as cynical or helpless. They indicate that they receive a great deal of mail and that they spend a great deal of time, many say most of their time, responding to this mail. Several MKs responded, quite candidly, that since they knew there was nothing for them to do in the plenary sessions except to raise their hands when instructed to do so, they seldom went to the sessions, but instead spent their time in casework and helping their constituents.

Summary

The Israeli political system is a highly developed party system, with a great number of political parties playing very significant roles in terms of legislative behavior. The Knesset is organized and run along party lines. The Speaker and Deputy Speakers are all chosen on a partisan basis, although the Knesset puts the "nonpartisan" label upon these offices by traditionally having these officers elected unanimously after the party leaders agree who will hold them. Committee chairmanships are given to parties, which then in turn assign the chairs to loyal party members and good workers who will follow party directives. In one incident in the Eighth Knesset, a Likud (Opposition) chairman of a subcommittee bolted party ranks and passed a Government bill out of his subcommittee with his approval (which didn't matter in any case, since the Government controlled a majority of the full committee). The Likud subcommittee chairman was promptly stripped of all his committee assignments, and his entire life as a parliamentarian was limited to motions for the agenda in the plenum, since he wasn't even given an allowance of a single private member's bill.[13]

In addition to committee assignments, debate time is given to party leaders, who may parcel it out as they see fit among party members in the Knesset. As indicated, private members' bills are handled in a similar manner, with the parties receiving an "allowance" of approximately three bills per seat they control per session.

Voting in the Knesset is strictly along party lines, and in most cases a dissenting member of Knesset will choose an auspicious moment to visit the restaurant for a cup of tea. But if the vote is sufficiently close the party whip will "invite" the dissenting member to return to the party body in the plenum.

Physical facilities in the Knesset similarly are organized around the political parties, with the individual member being dependent upon his or her party leadership for any assistance in research or correspondence. This is yet another aspect of the members' total dependence upon their parties.

This dependence of members upon their parties has its toll in the feelings of inefficacy and cynicism felt by many members of Knesset. The members feel, in regard to those tasks that have been labeled intralegislative, that they are no more than robots—many MKs used this term in their statements—and they question their usefulness in the legislature. The suggestion has been made by some simply to give party leaders the appropriate number of proxy votes and let them do all the voting, since in any case all votes go in the direction dictated by party leaders.

In extralegislative tasks, however, the affective tone of MKs is entirely different. They are active and functioning, and most feel highly effective in their roles of ombudsman and representative. In this role, the members contribute a great deal to perceived governmental legitimacy by illustrating a responsiveness of the government to demands by citizens that might not be there but for their actions.

The Israeli Knesset obviously does not perform in the same manner as do some legislative bodies in other political systems, but it must be kept in mind that every political system has its own idiosyncrasies that affect political behavior. In the Israeli political system that idiosyncrasy is the highly (if not overly) developed state of political parties. Many of the "weaknesses" of the Knesset can be attributed to the fact that the Knesset is a parliamentary legislature, one in which the legislature by definition is led by the executive, and consequently one in which legislative control over the executive, and legislative innovation in legislation, will not be a maximum.

Notes

1. Joseph LaPalombara, *Politics within Nations* (Englewood Cliffs, N.J.: Prentice-Hall, 1974), p. 119.
2. Asher Zidon, *Knesset: The Parliament of Israel* (New York: Herzl Press, 1967), p. 40.
3. Ibid, pp. 53–54.
4. See the *Jerusalem Post*, January 16, 1974, p. 1.
5. Asher Zidon, *Knesset*, p. 55.
6. These committees were the following: Finance; Foreign Affairs and Security; Knesset; Constitution, Law, and Justice; Labor; Economics; Education and Culture; Interior; Public Services; and State Controller.
7. See the *Jerusalem Post*, January 21, 1974, p. 3.
8. Asher Zidon, *Knesset*, pp. 143–46.
9. In order to provide the small parties (one or two members) with some debate time, Knesset rules state that no party shall have less than 10 minutes' time in a four-hour debate, and fifteen minutes in a five-hour debate.
10. S. Weiss and A. Brichta, ''Private Members' Bills in Israel's Parliament,'' *Parliamentary Affairs* 23(1969):p. 25.
11. *Jerusalem Post: Overseas Edition*, November 4, 1975, p. 1.
12. Interview with Mrs. Lea Ben-Dor at the Jerusalem Post Building, Jerusalem, March 21, 1975.
13. Approximately one year after this event took place, the MK won recognition by the Speaker as a single-member party (independent), thus regaining some rights to introduce legislation and debate.

5

The Member of Knesset

Thus far we have examined the general structure of the Israeli political system, and the manner in which the legislature operates within the Israeli political system. We now turn our attention to the individual unit of the system, the member of Knesset. Who are the members of Knesset? What backgrounds do they bring with them to the Knesset? In this chapter we undertake to answer these questions, examining not only the general demographic background characteristics of the legislators but also the political socialization processes they experienced prior to reaching the national legislature.,

Demographic Characteristics

A general description of members of Knesset would begin much as a description of members of parliament in most other nations. It would indicate that the legislature is older than the general population, has a higher male population than the general population, and underrepresents minorities in the general population (see Table 5.1). Over 89 percent of the MKs interviewed in this study were men. (This proportion increases if the MKs not interviewed are included in the figures, since *all* of the women members of Knesset were interviewed.) This 10 percent representation for women MKs (which actually becomes 7.5 per-

---

*Portions of this chapter were previously published as parts of "Political Socialization and Political Interest in Israeli and Canadian Legislators: A Comparative Examination," *Political Science Review*, (August, 1980):1–27; and "Political Consciousness and Political Events: A Study of Israeli and Canadian Members of Parliament," *Political Science*, 31, no. 2 (December 1979):88–107.

cent when all MKs are included) is certainly not representative of the proportion of women in the Israeli population. It should be noted, however, that this proportion is not greatly different from that found in many European parliaments, and it is much higher than the comparable figure of the United States Congress of approximately 3.5 percent.

Members of the Eighth Knesset were born between 1899 and 1945, spanning an age range of from thirty to seventy-six years of age at the time of the interview, with the average age being 52.9 years. The difference between these ages and those of the general population is worth noting. In the entire Knesset membership, only two MKs (1.7 percent) were younger than thirty years of age, whereas 60 percent of the 1973 Israeli population was

Table 5.1

General Descriptive Characteristics of MKs

	Percent	(N)
Sex		
Male	89.5	77
Female	10.5	9
Age		
30–39	11.8	10
40–49	27.1	23
50–59	31.8	27
60–69	28.2	24
70 or older	1.1	1
	100.0	85
$\overline{X}$ = 52.9 years		
Median = 53.2 years		
Religion		
Jewish	96.5	83
Moslem	2.3	2
Christian	-	-
None	1.2	1
Frequency of Religious Activity		
More often than once a week	17.4	15
Approximately weekly	4.7	4
Occasionally, less than weekly	4.7	4
Holidays or special events only	50.0	43
Never	23.2	20

younger than thirty years of age.[1] The rapid increase in the native-born population of Israel did not start until after the creation of the State, and is, therefore, still too young to be found in the Knesset. Knesset membership thus still reflects an age composition and an immigration characteristic that are not representative of the current Israeli population. To a great extent many of Israel's "Founding Fathers" are still in the Knesset. The fact that the average age of MKs is just shy of fifty-three years, whereas 60 percent of the population is younger than thirty years of age, attests to the relatively old age of the Knesset members.

That Israel is a Jewish state is not questioned in the modern world. One of the major reasons for the creation of Israel was this specific purpose; the general population of Israel reflects this fact. In 1976, the non-Jewish population in Israel made up only 15.3 percent of Israel's population. Although 15 percent of the Israeli population is not Jewish, this segment of the population is politically a "silent minority," with only about 3 percent of the seats in the Knesset held by non-Jewish members.

Although 96.5 percent of the MKs indicated that they are Jewish, they are quick to make a distinction between being *ethnically* Jewish and *religiously* Jewish. Indeed, as Table 5.1 indicates, the vast majority of the MKs interviewed were *not* particularly active in religious matters. The table shows that only 22 percent of the members of Knesset stated that they attended religious services "more often than once a week" or "approximately weekly," whereas 23 percent indicated that they "never" attend religious services. In the 1890s, when Theodor Herzl was arguing for the ideas he had expressed in his written work *Der Judenstaat*, there was a great deal of debate over whether *Der Judenstaat* should be translated as "The Jewish State"—actively religiously Jewish—or "The State for Jews"—not necessarily actively religious at all. Over the last thirty years the tendency appears to have been decidedly in the latter direction.

Rearing

The Israeli population is largely composed of immigrants. Almost 44 percent of the total present Israeli population of slightly more than 3.3 million people—nearly 1.5 million people—was not born in Israel, but migrated there.[2] This figure is even greater in our sample of MKs, in which 63 percent of the MKs interviewed were not born in Israel.

This difference between the sample immigration ratio and the immigration ratio of the population at large should not be surprising, considering that the members of Knesset are older than the general population; the "old guard" still, to a very large degree, controls the political infrastructure of the political system.

Not only are members of Knesset to a very large degree immigrants, but they come from a variety of nations. The members of Knesset interviewed in this study were born in a total of seventeen nations, indicated in Table 5.2.

The fact that the members of Knesset come from such a variety of backgrounds makes the Israeli legislature among the most unique in the world. It also means that the MKs bring with them to the legislature a variety of norms, attitudes, and behaviors that are of significance in the overall process of legislative behavior. Although the members interviewed in this study come from seventeen different countries, it should not be assumed that their multicultural backgrounds stop in these seventeen settings. If we go back one generation farther, we see an increasing number of cultural influences in the backgrounds of MKs. Table 5.2, which provides information about the parents of members of Knesset, indicates the multifaceted nature of the background variable.

This assortment of ethnic identifications, which were subsequently passed along to the members of Knesset as children, is significant in the development of their political attitudes and political consciousness. It meant minimally for the individuals that their initial identifications and attitudes were oriented around foreign (to Israel) locations for the most part, a fact that did not in itself promote the development of an "Israeli" or "Palestinian" identity.

Although the thirty-one MKs (36 percent) who were born in Israel/Palestine (hereafter referred to as Israel) were reared in Israel, the other fifty-five MKs indicate a variety of backgrounds. Just less than 5 percent of the MKs were born outside of Israel, but moved to Israel when they were very young and thus considered themselves to have been reared in Israel. Forty-three percent of the members were reared in their place of birth, not in Israel, and moved to Israel after their childhoods. Several members (14 percent) indicated that they had been reared in both their

Table 5.2

Geographic Backgrounds of MKs

Country	MK Born	MK Father Born	MK Mother Born
Middle East			
Israel/Palestine	31	12	12
Syria	1	1	1
Iran	1	1	1
Iraq	3	4	4
Turkey	1	1	1
Eastern Europe			
Russia	9	21	21
Lithuania	3	4	6
Rumania	2	-	2
Hungary	1	1	1
Poland	20	31	26
Western Europe			
Germany	4	2	2
Austria	2	2	2
North America			
United States	2	-	1
Mexico	1	-	-
Africa			
Tunisia	1	1	1
Morocco	3	3	4
Yemen	1	2	1

place of birth and in Israel, and said that since they had moved during their childhoods, both locations were important to them. Just two members (2.3 percent) indicated that they had been reared in a country other than where they were born or Israel.

The actual migration of the members of Knesset occurred under a variety of different circumstances. The ages at which immigration took place ranged from one to forty-one, with a mean age of immigration of 18.4 years. Of the members of Knesset interviewed, more than one-quarter (27 percent) made the move to Israel alone and about half that figure (14 percent) migrated with a spouse. Just less than one MK in four (23 percent) moved to Israel with his or her parents.

The large majority of the members of Knesset interviewed who were not born in Israel were active in either Jewish or Zionist organizations before they migrated to Israel. Of those who were

Table 5.3

Jewish/Zionist Organization Membership prior to Migration

	N	Percent Immigrants	Percent Total MKs
Belonged to no groups	(15)	27	17
National Zionist organization	(6)	11	7
Beytar	(6)	11	7
Mizrahi	(6)	11	7
Agudat Israel	(3)	5	3
Mapam	(9)	16	10
Mapai	(2)	4	2
HaHalutz	(3)	5	3
Other	(5)	9	6
	55	N = 55	N = 86

Positions Held in Organizations	N	Percent
Belonged to no organizations	15	27
Belonged, but held no office	22	40
Held office on local level	2	4
Held office on national level	15	27
Held office on international level	1	2

active in such organizations, a sizable share held office and were active in the organizations (Table 5.3).

Most of the members of Knesset spent "most years" that they were growing up in a large city (70 percent). Although the Kibbutz population in Israel only comprises 3 percent of the general population, 31 percent of the MKs interviewed indicated that they had lived on a Kibbutz at some point in their lives.

EDUCATION

Members of legislatures of most Western democratic systems are highly educated, and members of Knesset are not exceptions to this rule. Only three of the MKs interviewed in this study had less than a high school education; one of those was a Bedouin who had never had *any* formal education, one MK had six years of schooling, and one had eight years of schooling. Over 20 percent of the MKs had finished either high school or Yeshiva and ter-

Table 5.4

Education of MKs

	Percent	(N)
Highest Level of Education		
No schooling	1	(1)
Six years	1	(1)
Eight years	1	(1)
Finished high school or Yeshiva	22	(19)
Some college, no degree	8	(7)
College degree (B.A. or B.S.)	26	(22)
Graduate work but no degree beyond B.A.	1	(1)
M.A. or equivalent (includes law)	29	(25)
Ph.D., LL.D., or equivalent	10	(9)
Attended some university or college	76	(65)
Location of college or university		
Israel	52	(45)
Iraq	1	(1)
England	2	(2)
Germany	5	(5)
Austria	2	(2)
Poland	3	(3)
Russia	1	(1)
United States	8	(7)
Not applicable, did not attend	24	(21)
Have college or university degree	66	(57)
Attended graduate school	26	(22)
Attended professional school	21	(18)
Have a degree from a graduate or professional school		
Graduate degree	19	(16)
Professional degree	15	(13)
Multiple degree	6	(5)
Type of professional degrees		
Law	19	(16)
Theology	2	(2)
Highest degree obtained		
None	34	(29)
B.A. or B.S.	27	(23)
M.A. or M.S.	12	(10)
Ph.D., Ed.D., or D.Sc.	10	(9)
Law	15	(13)
Other	2	(2)

Location of graduate education		
Israel	22	(19)
England	3	(3)
France	1	(1)
Germany	3	(3)
Austria	2	(2)
Switzerland	1	(1)
United States	8	(7)

minated their educations at that point. Seventy-four percent of the MKs interviewed attended at least some college; 66 percent graduated from college or had higher formal education, as indicated in Table 5.4. The MKs obtained their formal educations in a variety of settings. Colleges were attended in Israel, Iraq, England, Germany, Austria, Poland, Russia, and the United States; graduate or professional schools were attended in Israel, England, France, Germany, Austria, Switzerland, and the United States.

PROFESSIONAL BACKGROUNDS

In the same manner that their personal and family backgrounds are many and varied, so too are the professional backgrounds of the members of Knesset interviewed. Although *all* of the MKs interviewed indicated that they considered their positions as MKs to be their principal occupations, their occupations before entering the Knesset varied widely. Thirteen percent of the group were involved in agricultural settings prior to becoming legislators. Twenty-three percent were in business. Fully one-half of the sample was to be found in the professional world. Twelve percent of the respondents were skilled or unskilled workers. One MK, the Bedouin, was not able to relate to the question and indicated that he had no occupation before becoming a member of Knesset. These groups are broken down more fully in Table 5.5.

Political Socialization

Political socialization has been conceptualized as ''The process by which the individual acquires attitudes, beliefs, and values relating to the political system of which he is a member and to his

Table 5.5

Occupational Backgrounds of MKs

		Percent	N
Agriculture		13	(11)
Kibbutz (7)	Moshav (4)		
Business		23	(20)
Private business (1)	City government (3)		
Party executive (3)	Civil service executive (5)		
Union executive (4)	Banker (1)		
Industry (3)			
Professional		50	(43)
Lawyer (15)	Diplomat (1)		
Doctor (1)	Social worker (1)		
Party worker (2)	Jurist (1)		
Teacher/Educator (11)	Rabbi (5)		
Engineer (1)	Journalist (5)		
Sales worker/Merchant/Clerical		6	(5)
Merchant (1)			
Clerk (2)			
Secretary (2)			
Skilled/Unskilled worker		6	(5)
Weaver (1)			
Factory worker (2)			
Unemployed		2	(2)

own role as a citizen within that political system."[3] Socialization has been defined as "those developmental processes through which persons acquire political orientations and patterns of behavior."[4] The important point in these and other conceptualizations is that socialization is conceived as a process; it is an ongoing event that is not finished as long as the individual is still able to perceive his or her environment and respond to it.

Many different factors have been suggested by political scientists as having the greatest influence in the socialization process. Greenstein indicates that "among the most obvious sources" of political socialization in the United States are parents, teachers, neighbors, members of the extended family, peers, the media, and those whose views are transmitted through the media.[5] Langton suggests that the family, the school, and the peer group are the major influential factors in the socialization process, and he suggests that these factors interact to influence political attitudes or behavior.⁶ Others have suggested that socioeconomic status may be of significance in the socialization process.⁷

The central questions to be examined in this analysis include the following: How old was the individual when he or she first became aware of politics? What kind of event does he or she remember as his or her first political awareness? When did he or she first become interested in politics, as distinct from merely being aware of the existence of politics? At what age did he or she first identify with a political party? In answering these questions data are used that deal with the political environment in which the individual was reared, as well as personal background data that include information pertaining to the individual's family as well as to the respondent's emotional reaction to political events of his or her time.

Many socialization theories rest upon the assumption that the individual receives environmental stimuli and responds to these stimuli as may be appropriate. That is, there are agents (human, societal, political, or others) from which the individual learns, and receives norms and role cues, and in response to which the individual acts. Examples of this are (a) a child learning that he or she is a "Herutnik" from his or her parents (the parents are the agent, party identification is what is learned); (b) an individual witnessing a war and becoming a pacifist (the events in the war are the agent, pacifism is the acquired response); or (c) someone voting on election day (prior discussion and identifications and the election itself are the agents and the vote is the response). In all these cases we can see that the individual interacts with his or her environment.

Implicit in this assumption is the corollary assumption that the *types* of stimuli an individual perceives—or, put another way, the kinds of events the individual experiences—vary historically, culturally, ethnically, and geographically. These historical, cultural, ethnic, and geographic factors can, in some situations more than others, have a significant impact upon the socialization process. To give one example, the environmental stimuli perceived by a child growing up in 1932 varied tremendously depending upon whether the child was Jewish or not Jewish. Furthermore, there is variation among Jews reared in Germany, Palestine, the United States, and Russia. Similarly, being a Jew in Germany in

1912 was different than being a Jew in Germany in 1938 or 1940.

Political Awareness

The age at which the individual first becomes aware of politics marks the beginning of the early political socialization process; that is, the time at which the individual first becomes sensitive to political stimuli in his or her environment. Legislators were asked the question "What is the first aspect of politics or public affairs that you were aware of? How old were you at that time?"[8] The ages of the members interviewed, and the nature of the events they recalled, were noted in their responses to the questions. Additional questions were asked pertaining to the political environments in which they were reared, including questions dealing with their parents' political interests and activities, and the amount and nature of political discussion in their homes.

Culture, as well as the historical period in which one is reared, affects the type, duration, and extent of environmental stimuli perceived. To take one example, one of the women MKs was born and reared in Iran, and did not migrate to Israel until after she was married. She insisted during the interview, and maintained through a great deal of probing, that she was *never* aware of politics or public affairs until after she moved to Israel. In Iran, women simply were not expected to pay attention to such matters, and she could remember no event in her childhood that had the slightest connection with anything political. It was not until she and her husband were setting up household in Israel that she had any exposure, that she could recall, to even a discussion of politics.

Although this kind of cultural influence largely can determine whether or not an individual is exposed to political stimuli, history clearly also provides a control over the type, duration, and extent of stimuli. Table 5.6 presents the average ages of first political awareness of legislators, with the members of Knesset being divided into age cohorts. Members of Knesset who were born between 1910 and 1925 were initially aware of politics at a later age than either those born prior to 1910 or those born after 1925. This difference can be explained by what was happening in the world during those time periods.

Table 5.6

Average Ages of First Political Awareness of Four
Cohorts of Israeli Legislators

When Born	$\overline{X}$	S	N
I. Pre–1910	9.8	3.4	9
II. 1910–1925	11.6	3.2	43
III. 1926–1936	11.2	5.2	26
IV. 1937–1947	10.7	5.0	7

To begin, we must introduce a "time-lag" concept: a child will not, and indeed cannot, be aware of political stimuli as early as the day he or she is born. A certain level of development must be attained prior to any perception of politics. Our data show that most children first become aware of politics between the ages of nine and twelve years, although the reported ages range from three years to thirty years. By the time a child born in the first (i.e., prior to 1910) cohort was at an age at which he or she was beginning to be aware of contemporary politics, World War I was brewing or had already begun. The war provided these children with a stimuli-filled environment, and it is not surprising that they had lower ages of first political awareness than children "coming of age" (e.g., reaching the nine- to twelve-year-old range) in the period between the world wars.

The data also show that persons born in the third cohort, 1926–1936, were aware of politics at an earlier age than persons born between 1910 and 1925. If the nine-to-twelve-year "time-lag factor" is added to the years delimiting the third cohort (1926 and 1936), we have a period ranging from 1935 (1926 + 9) to 1948 (1936 + 12), years roughly approximating the duration of World War II.

Further supporting this hypothesis is the small group of Israelis who were born in the fourth cohort, after 1936. Their initial age of political awareness is even lower than that of the cohort "coming of age" during World War II. This can be explained by an examination of the increased importance of Zionism in post–World War II Europe and Palestine. The "Jewish Problem" was quite likely to have been talked about after World War II, both in Europe and in Palestine, and a Jewish child growing up either in the Middle East after the Balfour Doctrine had been handed down after World War I, or in Europe after World War II, was likely to hear a good deal of discussion about politics and public affairs. Further evidence of this is presented later in an examination of the object of the child's initial political awareness.

The argument can be made that the data indicate a fluctuation in age of first political awareness that varies with major world political events. For the MKs (who were for the most part either in Europe or the Middle East at the time) the "war situation" changed from being one of World War II and Hitler to being oriented toward the struggle for *Eretz Israel* and a homeland for the Jewish people, a struggle that has not yet been resolved. Thus, for the MKs a "war situation" continues to exist.

In a manner similar to the "when" of legislators' rearing, the "where" also appears to be associated with the age of first political awareness—for reasons similar to those previously expressed. Table 5.7 shows that those individuals who were born in certain areas of the world became aware of politics and public affairs at an earlier age than those who were born elsewhere. MKs who were born in Russia, and the Arab Middle East and Africa were the latest in developing a political awareness. Their relative slowness in becoming aware of politics may be a consequence of cultural factors such as those already mentioned; politics and public affairs were "adult" activities in these cultures, and children were not encouraged to take part or be interested in politics.

With the exception of the three MKs who come from North America, whose extremely low average age of first awareness of politics may simply be attributable to a small sample size, it appears that the more politicized or strife-ridden the area in which the individual was born, the earlier he or she became aware of politics. In the non-Palestinian Middle East and Northern Africa, individuals were late in developing any political awareness. In Russia, political awareness came earlier, three years on the average, than in the African group. Those individuals who were born in Palestine had an early age of first political awareness, nearly the same as that of MKs born in Europe as a whole. MKs born in Germany or Austria had the lowest average age of first political awareness of any group in our sample, excluding the three North Americans, less than nine years of age, which supports a "proximity-to-event" hypothesis.

Table 5.7

Average Ages of First Political Awareness of Israeli Legislators by Location of Birth

Where Born	$\bar{X}$	S	N
North America	7.7	1.5	3
Europe (all)	10.2	3.5	32
Europe (Germany and Austria only)	8.8	2.9	6
Palestine/Israel	11.0	4.4	31
Russia	12.0	3.6	9
Middle East/Africa	15.0	3.0	11

Note: Africa here includes Yemen, Morocco, and Tunisia. These nations are grouped with the "Arab" Middle East (Syria, Iran, Iraq, and Turkey) because of their predominantly Moslem natures.

Historical and cultural factors may be geographically confined, and geographical factors may be said to influence the age at which one begins to be aware of the political world. In addition to these influences upon the age of initial political awareness, the data show that the initial age of political awareness is also influenced by several factors suggested by "traditional" socialization theory. These factors include parents' political interests, the parents' activity in politics, and the home environment generally.

The home environment, and specifically the political cues received from parents, has an influence upon the age of first political awareness. Table 5.8 shows the difference in the age of first political awareness between children with active and interested parents and children without active or interested parents. This difference is not consistently statistically significant. Children with active fathers were aware of politics on the average of one and one-half years earlier than children with inactive fathers. *All* the MKs interviewed indicated that their mothers had been "inactive," politically. That is, interviewees indicated that although their mothers may have been interested in politics, none was actively involved in politics. This finding may be explained by the cultural values that prevailed in Eastern Europe and the Middle East at the time.

One explanation for the ambivalent behavior of the data may be that the extrafamilial environments of the MKs were richer in political stimuli than were the comparable nonfamilial en-

Table 5.8

Average Ages of First Political Awareness of Israeli Legislators and Parental Politics

	$\bar{X}$	S	N
Father active in politics	10.3	3.6	16
Father inactive in politics	11.8	4.1	67
Father's interest very strong	9.6	4.5	26
Father's interest quite strong	12.5	3.9	20
Father's interest not very strong	10.6	3.9	16
Father's interest weak	10.3	2.2	4
Father had no interest	12.3	3.2	12
Mother's interest very strong	10.1	3.8	12
Mother's interest quite strong	9.8	4.8	15
Mother's interest not very strong	11.4	4.1	31
Mother's interest weak	11.8	4.6	8
Mother had no interest	12.6	3.1	20

vironments of Americans, who have generated so much of the data on the importance of the family. For example, as a child, an MK may have been less dependent upon his or her father's political interest for an initial exposure to political stimuli because there were so many other political stimuli to be found in the child's environment outside the family.

The data support the general hypothesis that politically active parents are associated with politically stimulating home environments. Legislators who indicated that their fathers were politically active were more likely during this same period of time to have personally known officeholders[9] ($r = .57$), more likely to have indicated that there was political discussion in the home ($r = .26$), more likely to have known others who were "active in politics or public affairs" ($r = .59$), and more likely to have known others who were "inactive but very interested in politics and public affairs" ($r = .44$).

The data also show that interest alone on the part of the father or mother was sufficient to approximate the effect of activity on the dependent variable. Those legislators who indicated that their fathers were interested in politics also indicated that there was political discussion at home ($r = .35$), that they personally knew officeholders ($r = .24$), that they knew others who were politically active ($r = .22$), and that they knew others who were very interested in politics or public affairs, although not active ($r = .49$). This should come as no surprise since there is a strong relationship ($r = .34$) between interested fathers and active fathers. Table 5.9 illustrates these relationships.

Although some of the strong associations that exist among several variables and the age of first political awareness have been pointed out, it is equally important to examine the "what" of the process: the subjects of the legislators' first political awareness. Table 5.10 presents responses to the question "What was the first aspect of politics or public affairs that you were aware of?" The data show that several of the "traditional" factors were the objects recalled by some of the legislators. Some of the legislators remembered hearing political discussions in the home, going to political meetings, or joining political groups. Some indicated that their first political memory was associated with their schooling, in some cases a book they read, in others a lesson from a teacher. Fully 25.6 percent of the MKs cited such factors.

Other events or issues were also mentioned. Few of the MKs (only 4 percent) mentioned some kind of election as their first recollection of politics, considerably less than we would find in a study of Americans, for example. The major orientation of the MKs was clearly in a direction more or less unique to Israel, as indicated by the frequencies of responses such as "Zionism," and specific references to experiences and events of World War II.

Table 5.10 illustrates a general association between the events recalled and the average age of first awareness of the legislators. As may be seen, certain kinds of recollections were associated with earlier average ages of first awareness of politics than others. Those who referred to World War II had considerably earlier ages of first political awareness ($\bar{x} = 9.1$ years) than those who referred to factors related to the school ($\bar{x} = 12.3$ years).

The general rule suggested by the data in Table 5.10 is that as the age of first awareness of politics increases, the *nature* of the awareness changes from one requiring less cognitive difficulty to one requiring greater cognitive difficulty. For example, for many of the MKs, their knowledge of World War II was personal, requiring no research or effort. One merely had to live in Europe at the time to know of the existence of the war. The ages associated with the family and the youth group are also low, because they,

Table 5.9

Correlation Analysis of Family Environments of MKs:
Political Awareness

	Father's Interest	Mother's Interest	Discussion in Home	Father Active	Mother Active	Knew Officials	Others Active	Others Interested	S.E.S.
Age of first awareness	.18	.23	.05	.12	-	.21	.19	.27	.05
Father interested in politics	-	.81	.35	.34	-	.24	.22	.49	.02
Mother interested in politics	.81	-	.16	.24	-	.15	.20	.52	.01
Political discussion in the home	.35	.16	-	.26	-	.22	.19	.24	.22
Father politically active	.34	.24	.26	-	-	.57	.59	.44	.04
Knew officials	.24	.15	.22	.57	-	-	.46	.43	.09
Knew Others who were active	.22	.20	.19	.59	-	.46	-	.70	.03
Knew Others who were interested	.49	.52	.24	.44	-	.43	.70	-	.12

Correlations shown are absolute values of coefficients.

Table 5.10

Subjects of Initial Political Awareness of Israeli Legislators

	Percent	N	$\overline{X}$ Awareness Age
Elections (National, local, unspecified)	3.5	3	10.3
Zionism (e.g., Discussions in home, local activities, plans to emigrate)	14.0	12	11.7
Family (e.g., Discussions in home, family member or friend active)	10.5	9	9.9
School (e.g., Books read, teachers)	8.1	7	12.3
Factors Related to Palestine/Israel (e.g., pre-Independence riots, Balfour Doctrine, War of Independence)	33.7	29	11.6
Anti-Semitism in community	7.0	6	14.2
War, generally (e.g., Russian Revolution, Algiers; *not* World War II or Israeli War of Independence)	5.8	5	10.8
War, Specifically World War II (Includes references to Hitler, concentration camps, purges, and the like)	10.5	9	9.1
Membership in or joining political youth group	7.0	6	9.8

too, were events that required a low level of cognitive development to be perceived in the child's (home) environment.

Learning about politics or public affairs through the school, which is found to be associated with a later age of first awareness in Table 5.10, is a different *type* of process, requiring more individual effort and capability—a different level of cognitive difficulty. It is interesting to note the pattern in which the factors cluster. The age at which MKs were aware of "Zionism" issues closely approximates the age at which they were aware of "Israel/Palestine" issues, but is considerably different from the age at which they were aware of "anti-Semitism." Similarly, the "family" and "youth group" factors apparently were cognitively related, but separate from "Zionism" or "school."

For many reasons, anti-Semitism, as an issue, was not perceived until later in life, on the average. First, as a concept, anti-Semitism may be more difficult to understand than others and may be associated with a later age of first awareness either because of lack of cognitive capacity or because of perceptual difficulty. Second, in many areas in the Middle East and Eastern Europe, Jewish families lived in Jewish communities, and children raised in these communities would have had only Jewish children for playmates and friends. The child would not have been exposed to anti-Semitic comments until he or she was old enough to work or move farther away from the home (i.e., the early to mid-teens).

To recapitulate, it has been observed that one of the three "facets" of political socialization, the age of initial awareness of politics and public affairs, varies with different factors. The general environment in which the child is reared can have an impact upon the age at which the child first becomes aware of politics and public affairs. Here, "general environment" includes both geographic and historic factors. Where a child is born, and when he or she was born, may prove to be of significance in the individual's later political life. "Traditional" factors also have an impact upon the age of first political awareness. In this regard, parental propensities are of foremost importance because they, in turn, influence so many other variables in the home political environment. Finally, the nature of the event actually recalled appears to have had in impact upon the age of first political awareness. It was suggested that different levels of cognitive development may be required to perceive certain types of stimuli in the environment.[10] Some events associated with a first awareness of politics may require a more mature level of cognitive development than others before they can be perceived.

Political Interest

As was noted in the previous section, the world into which the individual was born made a difference in the age at which the individual became aware of politics. The same thing, it turns out, may be said for the development of political interest. The "war children," who "came of age" during war years, had earlier ages of initial political interest than did children reared in intervening years.

Although the age of first interest in politics increased for the interwar cohort, the age of first political interest declined in both the third and fourth cohorts, much as did the age of first political awareness, as indicated in Table 5.11. The relationship between

Table 5.11

Average Ages of First Political Interest and Awareness of Four Cohorts of Israeli Legislators

When Born	$\bar{X}$ Age Interest	S	N	$\bar{X}$ Age Aware
I. Pre–1910	13.3	6.5	9	9.8
II. 1910–1925	15.4	5.3	41	11.6
III. 1926–1936	14.8	4.6	25	11.2
IV. 1937–1947	14.4	8.8	7	10.2

these measures is illustrated in Figure 5.1, in which the "interest curve" almost parallels the "awareness curve." The age of initial political interest follows the age of initial political awareness by 3.5, 3.8, 3.6 and 3.7 years, respectively, through the four time periods. If the theories of Piaget[11] concerning cognitive development are valid, we may infer that children's interest in politics should follow by a fixed time period their awareness of politics, with the fixed time period depending upon the time required for the individual to reach a subsequent stage of cognitive development.

The data show us that the best predictor variable for the age of first political interest is the age of first political awareness. Not only do the data cluster very well around a single line ($r = .58$) but the relationship is direct, as the almost constant age differential indicates.

The age of first interest in politics for MKs was also strongly related to fathers' and mothers' political interest ($r = .27$ and $r = .23$, respectively), to the amount of discussion in the home ($r = .19$), and to the fathers' political activity ($r = .19$). In addition, knowing people who were active in politics seems to have affected the age of first interest in politics ($r = .25$), as well as did knowing people who were not active, but still very interested in politics ($r = .31$). Having known officeholders personally does not appear ($r = .13$) to have been of significant importance for the development of political interest, although it was of more importance for the development of initial political awareness ($r = .21$). These data are given in Table 5.12, a summary table from a correlation analysis done on these data.

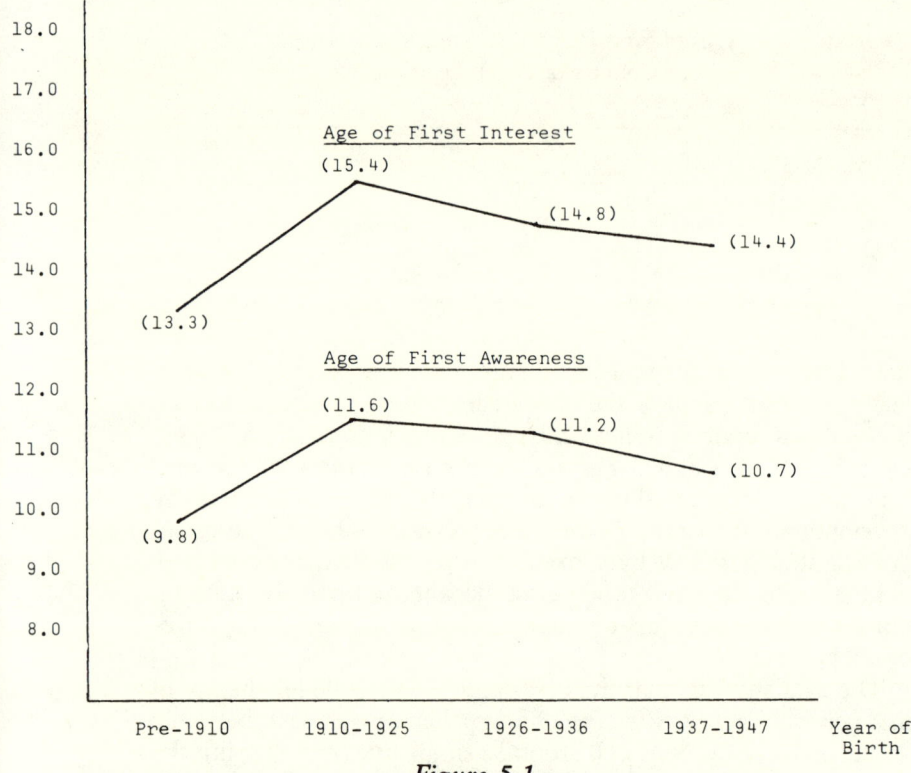

Figure 5.1

Average Ages of First Political Awareness and First Political Interest of Four Cohorts of Israeli Legislators

Table 5.12

Correlation Analysis of Family Environments of MKs: Political Interest[a]

	Age Aware	Father's Interest	Mother's Interest	Discussion in Home	Father Active	Knew Officials	Others Active	Others Interested	S.E.S.
Age of first interest	.28	.26	.23	.08	.19	.13	.14	.31	.04
Age of first awareness		.18	.23	.05	.12	.21	.19	.27	.05
Father interested in politics	.18	.81	.81	.35	.34	.24	.22	.49	.02
Mother interested in politics	.21	.35	.16	.16	.24	.15	.20	.52	.01
Political discussion in the home	.05	.34	.24		.26	.22	.19	.24	.22
Father politically active	.12	.34	.15	.26		.57	.59	.44	.04
Knew officials	.21	.24	.20	.22	.57		.46	.43	.09
Knew Others who were active	.19	.22	.20	.19	.59	.46		.70	.03
Knew Others who were interested	.27	.49	.52	.24	.44	.43	.70		.12

[a] Correlations shown are absolute values of coefficients.

Caution must be exercised when it comes to suggesting *causal* relationships, however. For example, the data show that the age of first political interest was related ($r = .43$) to closely following politics, but can it be said with confidence that people who were interested in politics earlier followed politics more closely? The latter may be a more plausible explanation, and therefore care should be exercised in suggesting causal relationships.

In a similar manner, where the individual was born appears to matter in terms of the individual's age of first political interest. Table 5.13 indicates that the ages of first interest parallel the ages of first awareness in terms of a geographic breakdown: the three MKs from North America were most precocious; the MKs from the Middle East and Africa were the slowest to develop; and the Russians, Europeans, and Israeli/Palestinians are in the middle in terms of their development of political interest. Again, MKs from the Western European countries (Germany and Austria) had an earlier age of initial interest than did the Eastern Europeans.

Table 5.13

Average Ages of First Political Interest of Israeli Legislators by Location of Birth

Where Born	$\bar{X}$ Age Interest	S	N	$\bar{X}$ Age Aware
North America	9.3	3.5	3	(7.7)
Russia	13.8	3.1	8	(12.0)
Europe (all)	14.5	5.6	30	(10.2)
Europe (Germany and Austria only)	11.6	4.9	6	(8.8)
Israel/Palestine	15.5	5.3	30	(11.0)
Middle East/Africa	16.9	3.7	11	(15.0)

In an examination of the "what" of the interest-developing process, some interesting differences from comparable answers that are related to the development of political awareness may be observed. Several of the factors that were suggested as the object of initial awareness failed to be cited as frequently in connection with political interest. Family, school, wars, elections, and Zionism were all recalled less often as the events associated with political interest than in connection with political awareness. In fact, only two categories of responses were cited more frequently for the interest question than had been cited for the awareness question, and both of these categories are significant for discussion here.

First, anti-Semitism was named slightly more frequently in these responses than it had been in the earlier responses, and since most categories of responses decreased in frequency, an increase of even a small degree is worth noting. It was suggested earlier that anti-Semitism may have been a concept that was cognitively too difficult for young children to grasp, and that consequently children didn't become aware of anti-Semitism until (a) they were sufficiently mature to grasp its implications, and (b) they had more exposure to non-Jewish individuals, something that children in a Jewish ghetto did not experience until they were older. The fact that anti-Semitism was cited more often by children at an older age ($\bar{x}$ = 16.2 years in association with political interest) than at a younger age ($\bar{x}$ = 14.3 years in

Table 5.14

Subjects of Initial Political Interest of Israeli Legislators

	Percent	N	$\bar{X}$ Age Interest	Percent Aware[a]
Elections (National, local, unspecified)	1.2	1	18.0	3.5
Zionism (e.g., Discussions in home, local activities, plans to emigrate)	12.2	10	16.9	14.0
Family (e.g., Discussions in home, family member or friend active)	7.3	5	12.9	10.5
School (e.g., Books read, teachers)	2.4	2	15.0	8.1
Factors related to Palestine/Israel (e.g., pre-Independence Riots, the Balfour Doctrine, War of Independence)	30.5	25	16.6	33.7
Anti-Semitism in community	9.8	8	16.2	7.0
War, generally (e.g., Russian Revolution War in Algiers; *not* World War II or War of Independence)	2.4	2	12.0	5.8
War, Specifically World War II (Includes references to Hitler, concentration camps, purges, and the like)	9.8	8	11.5	10.5
Membership in or joining political youth group	24.4	20	12.8	7.0

[a]This percentage indicates those individuals who mentioned an answer in this category as a response to the question pertaining to the subject of their first political awareness.

association with political awareness) lends credence to the earlier hypothesis.

Second, whereas "youth group membership or activities" was cited only 7 percent of the time as being associated with initial political awareness, it was named over 24 percent of the time as being associated with initial political interest. The number of individuals who associated the political youth group with their first political interest is proof of the effectiveness of the youth group in its primary task, to recruit and orient youngsters to a specific political position sponsored by a specific political organization. As was suggested in an earlier chapter, youth groups, both in Palestine/Israel and in other nations, sponsor activities and events to teach children about politics, and to attempt to win them to the folds of a specific party. Clearly the youth groups have succeeded in their goals.

The general trend in the Israeli responses was to move from a more passive type of event that was remembered in association with political awareness to a more active type of event that was remembered in association with political interest. The impressive increase in responses of "youth group activities" illustrates this trend, since nothing probably stimulates interest as well as activity or involvement.

This active-passive relationship does not contradict or weaken the cognitive development theory suggested earlier. Rather, it suggests that not only is cognitive development important in terms of what types of events are remembered in association with the ages of first awareness of politics and first interest in politics but so too is *general* development. That is, an eleven-year-old child might not be called upon to pass out pamphlets in a campaign, but a fourteen- or fifteen-year-old child might be asked to do just that. Consequently, the eleven-year-old child, in the more passive role, might only be aware of a political event, such as an election, whereas the fourteen-year-old, by virtue of his or her *participation* in the event, might reply that his or her *interest* was thereby aroused.

Party Identification

Political parties are, in themselves, of relevance for the larger political systems in which they are found, in terms of the structures they provide within the political system as well as in terms of the functions they perform for the political system generally. This section examines the age of initial identification with a political party on the assumption that in a system which is as party oriented as the Israeli system has been demonstrated to be, the age at which an individual begins to identify with a political party is an important milestone in the individual's process of developing political activity. A subsequent aspect of this process, recruitment to political office, is examined and discussed in the next chapter.

The development of party identification, which may be defined as a feeling of proximity to, and oneness with, a political party organization, appears to be a phenomenon that differs markedly from the development of an initial awareness of, or interest in, politics or public affairs. Although awareness may be considered as merely knowing of the existence of a given phenomenon (e.g., politics), and interest may connote a "caring about," identification indicates a ". . . sense of personal attachment which the individual feels toward the group of his choice."[12] As such, identification may be found to be *less* dependent upon many of the environment variables discussed earlier and *more* dependent upon the existence and structure of parties, issues, events, cognitive developments, and "internal" feelings and predispositions.

By way of illustration, as has been previously noted, *where* a child was born and reared affected his or her age of initial awareness of, and interest in, politics because of (a) proximity to cataclysmic events such as wars, and (b) the stage of development of the state in which the child was reared. Knowing of the existence of a given phenomenon and caring about its outcome may influence awareness and interest, but need not influence feelings of closeness with a political organization. Such feelings are more likely to be the result of the availability of parties and "identification factors" including shared or adopted beliefs, attitudes, and values of the party, as well as knowing someone who belongs to the party, being attracted by party leaders, and so on.

Similarly, the (temporal) world into which the child was born made a difference in the child's age of initial awareness of, and interest in, politics because of the type of events taking place at the time. These events may be more important for awareness and interest than for identification, since identification with a party may take place for reasons that are unrelated to specific political events of the day.

An examination of the relevant data supports these arguments. Neither the "when" nor the "where" aspects of the external environment significantly affect identification formation. Although historical and geographical factors did not significantly affect variations in the process of party identification, the familial political environment did influence the ages of initial identification with a political party. Table 5.15 indicates the variations in the age of initial party identification with several of those home political environment variables that have been discussed. Many of these breakdowns are statistically significant, and whereas some are not, several of the categories that fail to achieve statistical significance are nonetheless theoretically interesting.

Table 5.15

Average Ages of Initial Party Identification of Israeli Legislators and Parental Politics

	$\bar{X}$	S	N
Father active in politics	14.7	5.8	16
Father not active in politics	16.8	5.2	66
Father's interest very strong	15.6	5.5	26
Father's interest quite strong	18.4	6.3	20
Father's interest not very strong	14.4	3.7	16
Father's interest weak	16.8	8.3	4
Father had no interest	17.1	3.9	16
Mother's interest very strong	16.8	4.2	12
Mother's interest quite strong	16.2	8.5	15
Mother's interest not very strong	15.8	4.1	31
Mother's interest weak	17.3	6.7	8
Mother had no interest	17.6	4.2	19
Discussion of politics in home	16.3	5.5	69
No political discussion in home	17.8	4.4	16
Great deal of discussion	16.3	5.7	38
Some discussion	16.4	6.1	20
Not much discussion	15.6	4.1	11
Knew officials	15.5	6.5	8
Did not know officials	16.6	5.2	77

For example, children with politically active fathers initially identified with a political party approximately two years earlier than did children with politically inactive fathers. In the same manner, having known public officeholders is associated with an earlier political identification, as is having had political discussion in the home. For all these factors, the differences in ages of initial party identification are in the same direction: having active fathers, knowing public officials, and having had political discussion in the home are all associated with earlier ages of initial identification. These differences, though, are not as great as they could be.

Part of this finding may be explained by the Israeli party system. The impact upon MKs of membership in political youth groups has been mentioned. As children a number of the MKs were introduced to politics through a youth group, whether in Poland, Russia, Argentina, or Palestine. This introduction was not accomplished through a rational, intellectual decision on the part of the child to join, for example, Hashomer HaZaire rather than HaNoar HaDatit, but rather the decision was usually made by a parent, who took the child to the group of the parent's choice and registered the child for membership. Thus, the parents of the MKs, by putting their children in this type of nonfamilial political environment, were to some extent providing their own replacement as political role models. This action may explain why the family and home envirionment generally are not as significant for the MKs as they have been shown to be in the United States, for example.

Accordingly, it may be noted that whereas both the ages of initial political awareness and initial political interest correlate fairly strongly with childhood environment among the MKs, the relationship of the age of initial identification with childhood environment is considerably weaker for them ($r = .13$ as compared with .25 and .31, respectively) as illustrated in Table 5.16.

From the list of reasons for initial identification with a political party provided in Table 5.17, it is clear that the lower segment of the list is composed of more passive types of factors. The importance of the political youth group has already been mentioned, and the manner in which the child is passively enrolled in such groups has been discussed. In the same manner, a religious home background, especially for an orthodox child, made a feeling of af-

Table 5.16

Correlation Analysis of Family Environments of MKs:
Party Identification[a]

	Age Aware	Age Interest	S.E.S.	Childhood Environment[b]	Father's I.D. Same[c]	Mother's I.D. Same[c]
Age of identification	.27	.27	.01	.13	.09	.11
Age of awareness		.58	.06	.25	.05	.03
Age of interest	.58		.04	.31	.20	.23
S.E.S.	.06	.04		.08	.08	.08
Childhood environment[b]	.25	.31	.08		.15	.09
Father's Identification Same as Respondent's First I.D.[c]	.05	.20	.08	.15		.95

[a]Correlations shown are absolute values of coefficients.
[b]The variable "childhood environment" is a composite variable describing the child's home political environment, including parents' activity, interest, discussion in the home, knowing officials, and knowing others who were active or interested.
[c]The variables dealing with parents' identification being the same as the respondents' initial identification are "dummy" variables with shared party identification coded as "1" and unshared identification coded as "0."

finity with a religious party more likely to come earlier than it otherwise would. Israel's "religious" parties are not wholly political by any means; in fact, they are more oriented to the religious than to the political world. Consequently, a child who lived in a very religious home and who would be more likely to be aware of his or her religious organization also would be likely to be aware of the political activities of that organization. Since the child already would belong to the organization for religious reasons, his or her political identification was, in a manner of speaking, "preformed." Of the MKs who indicated that "religious home background" was a factor in their initial party identification, 92.3 percent identified with a "religious" party.

Other factors and events are associated with initial identification for the MKs as we move along the temporal ladder. "Underground experiences" in the War of Independence and Zionism are temporally proximate, and they are logically related. Seventy-five percent of those who indicated "underground ac-

Table 5.17

Average Ages of Initial Party Identification of MKs and Why They Identified with the Party

Years	
22.0	
21.0	21.2 Kibbutz (12%)
20.0	
19.0	20.0 School (5%) 20.0 Charismatic Individual (6%)
18.0	
17.0	17.4 Platform (81%)
16.0	16.2 Zionism (16%)
15.0	15.5 Underground Experiences (5%)
14.0	14.4 Youth group (33%) 14.2 Family (33%)
13.0	13.4 Religious home (15%)

tivities" as the reason for their initial identification identified with the Herut party, the political organization that grew out of the Irgun/paramilitary organization of the War of Independence. Identification with a party because of its platform or because of a charismatic individual, schoolwork, or Kibbutz or Moshav membership, were also listed by MKs as reasons for their initial party loyalty.

Summary

This chapter has tried to learn who the members of Knesset *are* and to learn more about their individual backgrounds in terms of demographic characteristics and the development of their attitudes and values. MKs are as diverse a lot as one would find in any national legislature in any national setting.

Demographically, MKs are older than the bulk of the Israeli population and trace their roots to a variety of national and cultural settings. They are generally a highly educated group of individuals, coming from a variety of occupational backgrounds but primarily the professional world.

The political socialization process is a complex phenomenon that is dependent not only upon variables in the immediate environment, such as parents' interests and activities, discussions in the home, and the like, but is also dependent on factors considerably beyond the sphere of the family. Specifically, the world in which the MKs lived, both when they were born and where they were reared, made a difference not only in when they developed their initial awareness of politics and interest in politics but also in the content of that event. Political party identification was more dependent upon political structures outside of the family, although familial factors are also important.

Learning who the members of Knesset are is important, but it does not really help us to understand how these individuals were selected to belong to the political elite while so many of their countrymen were not. The next task is to examine the process of political recruitment in Israel, the "pathway to parliament," to appreciate how the Israeli political system affects *who* ultimately becomes a member of the Knesset.

Notes

1. *Israel Government Yearbook* (Jerusalem, 1974), Table II/5, p. 42.
2. Ibid., Table II/19, p. 45.
3. Edward Greenberg, *Political Socialization* (New York: Atherton, 1970), p. 3.
4. David Easton and Jack Dennis, "The Child's Image of Government," *The Annals of the American Academy of Political and Social Science* 261 (1965):7.
5. Fred Greenstein, *Children and Politics* (New Haven: Yale University Press, 1965), p. 12.
6. Kenneth Langton, *Political Socialization* (New York: Oxford University Press, 1969), p. 20. See also Richard Dawson and Kenneth Prewitt, *Political Socialization* (Boston: Little, Brown, and Co., 1969), p. 6.
7. See, for instance, the following: Michael Parenti, "Ethnic Politics and the Persistence of Ethnic Identification," *American Political Science Review* 61 (1967):717–26; or Lewis Froman and James Skipper, "An Approach to the Learning of Party Identification," *Public Opinion Quarterly* 27 (1963):473–80.
8. The exact wording of all the questions used in this study may be found in the Appendix.
9. Pearson product-moment correlations have been used in all correlation analysis performed in this study. Although traditionally Pearson correlation coefficients are used solely for interval level data, Norman Nie and others suggest in their book *Statistical Package for the Social Sciences* (New York: McGraw-Hill, 1975, p. 267n) that "several social science methodologists argue that the Pearson correlation coefficient. . . may be used even if the data satisfy only the assumptions of ordinal-level measurement." See also Edward Tufte, "Improving Data Analysis in Political Science," *World Politics* 21 (1969):641–54; or Sanford Labovitz, "Statistical Usage in Sociology: Sacred Cows and Ritual," *Sociological Methods and Research* 1 (1972):13–38.
10. See Jean Piaget and Anne-Marie Weil, "The Development in Children of the Idea of the Homeland," *International Social Science Bulletin* 3 (1951):561–78.
11. Ibid.
12. See Angus Campbell et al., *The Voter Decides* (Evanston, Ill.: Peterson, and Co., 1954), p. 88.

6

The Recruitment of Members of Knesset

One of the major assumptions underlying the study of individual legislative behavior is that "who the legislators are affects the product generated by the systems of which they are a part."[1] That is, there is some belief that legislatures can be seen as more than simply conglomerates; it *does* make a difference who becomes a member of a legislature, because the behavior of the whole can be seen as a sum of the behavior of a number of individuals.

Thus, if legislative output can be regarded as being affected by individual legislators' behavior (this does not, of course, suggest that *every* individual legislator will be of significance, simply that *some* individuals *may* be of significance), there is a justification for studying those factors that can be seen to affect individual legislators' behavior. That which affects individual legislative behavior can similarly affect, to varying degrees, the output of the legislature.

It is clear from an examination of the literature that there is no agreement on a single definition of the term "recruitment."[2] Although theorists agree that political recruitment can be conceived as a process, definitions suggested in the literature differ and these differences are not always of an insignificant nature. Recruitment has been broadly conceived as the function of the political system which "recruits members of the society and of particular subcultures . . . and inducts them into the specialized roles of the political system, trains them in the appropriate skills, provides them with political cognitive maps, values, expectations, and affects."[3] Almond suggests that the recruitment function

The Recruitment of Members of Knesset

"takes up where the general political socialization function leaves off."[4]

Part of the definitional problem is that the term "recruitment" is used to cover two actual processes, *initial recruitment to* politics, and *promotion within* the political infrastructure. Jacob has attempted to develop this useful distinction in his work[5] by breaking the overall process down into components. Similarly, Patterson and Boynton are careful to distinguish between *political* recruitment and *legislative* recruitment. Political recruitment is the "process by which people enter the politically active subculture," becoming aware of, and responsive to, political stimuli. Legislative recruitment, on the other hand, "largely takes place in the politicized stratum. There it is a matter of opportunity, availability, and recruitment contact."[6]

The term "recruitment" is used in a broad sense in this chapter, although not as broadly as that suggested by Almond. The term includes a variety of political activities of the individual prior to his or her membership in the national legislature. Thus, included in this conceptualization of the term "recruitment" are not only the individual's recruitment to the Knesset, including the process of party selection and endorsement, but also some of the individual's earlier political activities and experiences.

There is theoretical justification for this broad interpretation of the term. If attention were to be focused only upon the individual's recruitment to (selection for) candidacy for the legislative position, it would be hard to determine some continuity between early individual socialization described in the last chapter and subsequent candidacy. By ascribing a broader interpretation to recruitment, it is possible to encompass a larger segment of the process of political maturation, and to trace the growth of the individual's involvement in politics through initial political activity, candidacies, and offices held prior to becoming a candidate for national legislative office.

As was shown in the last chapter, the socialization of children to politics could be affected by variations in many different factors. Among these factors are the home environment; the parent's political predispositions and activities; the ethnic, cultural, and geographic area in which the individual resides; and the precise time period during which these socializing events occur.

In addition to dealing with many of these factors, this chapter focuses upon other facets of the respondents' political lives prior to their incumbency in legislative offices. Attention is directed to the growth of their political interest subsequent to their initial political interest by examining their friends' levels of political interest, how closely the respondents followed politics, how well informed they were, and how important politics and public affairs were to them while they were growing up. Additionally, the respondents' histories of larger-scale political activity, including any candidacies, offices held, and the manners in which they came to be placed in nomination for seats in the legislature are discussed.

In parliamentary democracies there are many different pathways to parliament, and Israel is no exception to this rule. Figure 6.1 illustrates several (although not necessarily all) of the different possible routes that might be taken between the points of complete political inactivity on one hand, and membership in the national legislature on the other. Activity in political groups may be seen as a link—although not a mandatory one—between the socialization process and later recruitment to political activity. Political group membership may include nothing more than attending a party meeting once a month, or simply paying organizational dues, and not really participating at all, and thus may be seen simply as an extension of party identification. On the other hand, political group membership may entail considerably more activity than simply meeting and talking. It may entail full-scale party work, such as attending or organizing rallies, electoral work, work in the party infrastructure, and so on.

Although several different types of activity are listed hierarchically in Figure 6.1, they are not necessarily experienced in the order indicated in the figure. Indeed, some of the stages may be skipped entirely. As indicated, political group membership may include party work, and these two conditions may thus be experienced simultaneously. Similarly, one might be elected to a party office immediately after joining a political group, and thereby reach those stages simultaneously.

Figure 6.1 suggests six alternative routes that can be taken to membership in a national legislature. An MK who successfully ran for a public office prior to entering the national legislature would be included in the sixth group in Figure 6.1. If the MK ran

I.	No Political Experience	— —			In National Legislature
II.	No Political Experience	Political Group Member	— —		In National Legislature
III.	No Political Experience	Political Group Member	Party Work	— — — — — — — — — — — — — — — —		In National Legislature
IV.	No Political Experience	Political Group Member	Party Work	Party Officer	— — — — — — — —	In National Legislature
V.	No Political Experience	Political Group Member	Party Work	Party Officer	Ran for Office	In National Legislature
VI.	No Political Experience	Political Group Member	Party Work	Party Officer	Ran for Office — Held Public Office	In National Legislature

Figure 6.1

Prelegislative Political Experience of Israeli Legislators: Pathways to Parliamentary Office for such an office, but never won, he or she would fall in the fifth category. If he or she held party office, but never ran for a public preparliamentary office, the member would be included in the fourth category. The third category includes individuals who were sufficiently active to work for the party prior to entering the legislature, but who never held party or public office. The second category is comprised of individuals who joined political groups, but who indicated that they never worked for a party prior to being elected to the legislature. The first category includes those rare individuals who "parachuted" into the national legislature, without having been overtly involved in politics prior to their election.

Figure 6.1 depicts six possible and plausible routes to membership in a national legislative body. It does not, however, exhaust all the possibilities. Indeed, to comprehensively include every possible combination of preparliamentary political activity would lead to an unwieldy set of factors that would be quite difficult to analyze.[7] This chapter does not attempt to empirically validate or invalidate the theoretical model suggested in Figure 6.1., but examines several stages of political activity of the MKs prior to their membership in the Knesset with a goal of understanding how individual MKs reach their positions. These data will explain patterns of individual legislative behavior that are encountered in the next chapter.

Early Patterns of Recruitment

The discussion in the last chapter regarding the ages of initial political identification of MKs is an appropriate point from which to begin an examination of the recruitment process, for in many cases identification may be seen as the initial step along the road to party activity. It was previously observed that the availability of political youth groups for the future MKs was significant in their political socialization. The fact that a formal, organized structure existed specifically to recruit children to politics and to "teach" them about politics—and subsequently to channel them to political activity with a specific political party—also had an effect upon the political recruitment process. Once the individual is aware of, and interested in, politics and public affairs, he or she begins what may be called the "early" stage of the recruitment process: developing political beliefs, attitudes, and values. At the same time, the individual is establishing orientations toward the political world for anchoring these beliefs, among which are included developing an identification with a political party, joining political organizations, and becoming politically active in general. In this "early" stage of the recruitment process the effects of both the political system and political structures can be clearly seen.

Table 6.1 illustrates patterns of "early" political recruitment, and the patterns observed are quite striking. Over 80 percent of the MKs belonged to political groups while they were in high

Table 6.1

"Early" Recruitment Patterns of Israeli Legislators

	Percent	N
Group Membership		
Member of political group in high school	83.3[a]	(70)
Member of political group in university	75.7[b]	(50)
Member of political group outside school	82.6[c]	(71)
Friends' Interest in Politics:		
Most friends interested	31.4	(27)
Some friends interested	59.3	(51)
Few friends interested	9.3	(8)
Follow Politics:		
Very closely	66.3	(57)
Somewhat closely	29.1	(25)
Little	4.6	(4)
Informed:		
Better than average	62.8	(54)
About average	36.0	(31)
Less than average	1.2	(1)
Importance of Politics:		
Important and mattered	72.9	(67)
Not important/didn't matter	20.9	(18)

[a] Based upon an N of 84, two MKs were never in high school.
[b] Based upon an N of 66, twenty MKs were never in university.
[c] This and other MK figures based upon an N of 86.

school; over 75 percent of the MKs who went to university belonged to youth groups; and over 80 percent of the MKs belonged to political groups outside of school at about this same time. The magnitude of these figures may be attributed, at least partially, to systemic factors. That is, political youth groups did exist in abundance in the future MKs' political worlds, wherever they happened to be. Therefore, future MKs were not "superjoiners" who would overcome any obstacle in order to join a political youth group, although this might have been the case for some, but rather such political structures were both plentiful and accessible in their political environments and were taken advantage of by the future MKs.

Similarly, other measures of "early" recruitment show high levels of politicization of the MKs. Only 9 percent of the MKs had "few" friends who were interested in politics; less than 5 percent of the MKs followed politics "little"; only 1 percent of the MKs considered themselves informed "less than average." In short, Table 6.1 presents a picture of a highly politicized group of individuals whom we would not be surprised to find in parliament.

These data suggest several things. First, it seems clear that at least a part of the early recruitment process is completely system-dependent. That is, many of the MKs joined political groups in school because the groups already existed and because many of their friends were members and not out of a basic ideological commitment to the movement. In political systems in which such groups did not exist, such as the American system, it would not be reasonable to expect to find such a high proportion of "joiners" as the MKs evince.

Second, the data illustrate a "two-step" pattern. Not only does the system influence which structures exist but in turn the existence of those structures promotes other phenomena, such as greater interest in politics, greater awareness of politics, and higher levels of information. If most MKs belonged to political groups as children and were interested in politics, it is reasonable to assume that their friends also would be interested in politics, since their friends would most likely also be members of political groups. Similarly, responses to the question dealing with how closely the respondents followed politics suggest that an individual will, by virtue of his or her membership in such a group, follow politics more closely than someone who does not belong to such a group.

The data suggest that two different processes are at work in the general recruitment process. One process deals with "internal" or "emotional" recruitment—the level of awareness, interest, information, importance of politics, and so on. The second process deals with "external" or "structural" recruitment, which is most clearly measured by group-related activity. The bifurcated nature of the recruitment process is also illustrated in the relationship of recruitment to some of the environmental variables utilized in the last chapter.

Table 6.2 indicates that among future MKs, CHILDENV—a composite variable combining parents' political interest and activity, discussion of politics in the home, and whether the respondent personally knew officeholders—is consistently more strongly associated with what we have called the "internal" recruitment factors than with the "external" or "structural" factors. Thus, the degree of politicization of the child's home environment, as measured by CHILDENV, appears to be better associated with the importance of politics to the individual ($r = .25$), as well as with the individual's being well informed ($r = .25$), and following politics closely ($r = .21$), than with belonging to political groups outside the school ($r = .12$), in university ($r = .10$), or in high school ($r = .16$). The differences between some of these zero-order correlations are not sufficiently large to enable us to make grand statements about these relationships, but the theoretical pattern is supported by the data. This pattern supports the assumption that group membership was to a large degree influenced more strongly by systemic factors than by socialization factors in the individual's home background.

There is considerable variation among the many factors that can be said to make up the "early" phase of the recruitment process, although it is difficult to say exactly where childhood socialization ends and "early" recruitment begins. The data illustrated in Table 6.1 show two paths along which one might move toward political activity. An individual could belong to a political group, whether or not he or she was well informed or cared a great deal about politics, and could thereby become active in politics. Alternatively, the individual could care about politics, follow politics closely, and be well informed about politics, even if

Table 6.2

Correlation Analysis of Variables in the Early Recruitment of Israeli Legislators

	Age of Interest	Age of I.D.	Age of Activity	CHILDENV	H.S. Groups	University Groups	Nonschool Groups	Friends Interested	Follow Politics	Well Informed	Politics Important
Age of first awareness	.58	.28	.05	.27	.16	.20	.12	.22	.22	.11	.29
Age of first interest	*	.27	.03	.32	.11	.15	.20	.31	.43	.30	.31
Age of first ID	.27	*	.42	.12	.22	.02	.12	.13	.15	.18	.12
Age first party activity	.03	.42	*	.00	.21	.20	.11	.14	.08	.18	.09
CHILDENV	.32	.12	.00	*	.16	.10	.12	.16	.21	.25	.25
H. S. group member	.11	.22	.21	.16	*	.55	.69	.37	.20	.10	.23
University group member	.15	.02	.20	.10	.55	*	.66	.13	.17	.11	.10
Nonschool group member	.20	.12	.11	.12	.69	.66	*	.26	.31	.16	.16
Friends interested	.31	.13	.14	.16	.37	.13	.26	*	.35	.20	.34
Follow politics closely	.43	.15	.08	.21	.20	.17	.31	.35	*	.65	.61
Well informed	.30	.18	.18	.25	.10	.11	.16	.20	.65	*	.52

Correlations shown are absolute values of coefficients.

he or she did not belong to organized political groups. These two routes are not mutually exclusive, since many legislators were both members of political groups and were also interested, well informed, and followed politics closely. The interesting question these data lead us to ask is: which of these two roads, if either, had a greater effect in promoting an early age of political activity? We now turn our attention to an examination of this question.

Patterns of Later Recruitment to Party Activity

The Knesset is a "party" legislature; that is, in the Israeli political system candidates run for political office primarily on the basis of a party label; the party's support of the individual's candidacy does not come merely for the asking. On only a very few occasions have individuals been placed on a party's Knesset list in a "realistic" position without having first spent a number of years in the party hierarchy prior to election time.

Thus, in the Israeli political system a crucial point in the recruitment process is the point at which the individual first becomes an active party worker, the "birth" of his or her politically active self. Here we investigate the time in the respondent's life when he or she first became active in politics. Subsequently, we examine the respondents' pre-Knesset careers to see what offices, if any, they held, if they were ever unsuccessful candidates for any office, and whether they volunteered for candidacies or were recruited for office. Additionally, we study patterns of party officeholding prior to their becoming a candidate for national legislative office.

Table 6.2 shows that the age of initial party activity for the MKs is not related to the age of their initial political awareness or to the age of their initial political interest, but *is* strongly related to the age of their initial party identification. (Correlation coefficients are .05, .03, and .42, respectively.) Although party activity develops independently of awareness and interest, it is strongly related to the age of initial party identification. This may be explained by the existence of political groups in Israel: when MKs first identified with a political party, they joined a political group (sometimes these occurred simultaneously) that engaged them in political activity. Thus, identification led to a group membership that led to party activity.

The age of initial party activity is not related ($r = .00$) to the child's home political environment, CHILDENV, which supports the argument that this stage of the recruitment process is relatively independent of early life stimuli, and depends instead upon formal structures that may or may not be present in the political environment. There were no noteworthy differences in the average age of initial party activity between individuals with politically interested fathers (or mothers) and individuals with parents who were not interested in politics. Similarly, parental activity, discussion of politics in the home, where the respondent was born, when the respondent was born, and whether the respondent personally knew officeholders had no impact whatsoever upon the respondent's age of initial party activity on the aggregate level.

A strong association *may* be seen to exist between party activity and political group membership, as shown in Table 6.3. For the MKs, belonging to a political group in high school was associated with an earlier age of activity of approximately three years. Belonging to a political group outside of school was associated with approximately two years' difference in the age of activity.

From the data presented in Table 6.3 we can conclude that in different systems different structures play significant roles in the encouragement and development of party activity, and political youth groups are significant in Israel. In Table 6.2 the correlation coefficient between the age of first party activity and group membership for the MKs is noteworthy in regard to high school groups ($r = .22$), university groups ($r = .20$), and nonschool groups ($r = .11$). This suggests that these groups are quite important in the Israeli context for the encouragement of party activity.

The data presented in this section indicate that political structures influence socialization and recruitment patterns. For the MKs, the existence of highly organized and active political groups encouraged their early recruitment and party activity.

Patterns of Officeholding and Candidacies

The discussion of differences in patterns of candidacies and officeholding in Israel reveals apparent structural idiosyncrasies. In many instances the legislators' responses to one of the interview questions has a meaning that would be totally out of place in

Table 6.3

Average Ages of First Party Activity and Group Membership of Israeli Legislators

	X	S	N	Significance
In high school group	18.5	6.6	67	
Not in high school group	22.7	8.2	11	.05
In university group	17.9	4.9	47	
Not in university group	21.1	10.9	15	n.s.
In nonschool group	18.8	7.1	68	
Not in nonschool group	21.0	5.3	11	n.s.
Overall	18.7	6.7	77	

another political setting. This situation limits the types and extent of conclusions that may be drawn from the data, but a proper analysis of the data should enable us to posit limited conclusions and hypotheses.

If party activity is indeed a major factor in the process of political recruitment, then an examination of party officeholding may be useful. It has been suggested in this study that the Israeli party system is a multiparty system and that the intensity of party activity is much stronger in the Israeli system than in many other parliamentary settings. If party work and experience is very important in the recruitment process in Israel, we would expect to find that a high proportion of MKs had held party office prior to their election to national legislative office. The data presented in Table 6.4 show this to be the case.

Table 6.4 shows clearly that MKs were virtually all party officeholders prior to their legislative membership. To a large degree this statistic relating to party officeholding may be attributed to idiosyncrasies involved in the study. In most cases, public office in Israel comes when (or after) one has attained sufficient party rank; one must have served the party prior to being placed in a "safe" electoral position. This is true whether one is running for a position on a city council or in the Knesset. In asking MKs a question relating to party work, we are for the most part asking only individuals who held "safe" ballot positions (since few "marginal" positions are elected) if they were active in

Table 6.4

Patterns of Officeholding of MKs prior to
Legislative Candidacy

	Percent	N
Held party office	96.5%	(83)
Held public office	51.2	(44)
Number of preparliamentary offices		
None	48.8	(42)
One	18.6	(16)
Two	14.0	(12)
Three	12.8	(11)
Four or more	5.8	(5)
Two or more	32.6	(28)

their party, which is not dissimilar to asking rabbis and priests if they are actively religious.

Additionally, patterns of party activity and patterns of officeholding may be attributed to party structure as well as to electoral structure, although the two clearly are related. As was suggested in chapter 2, parties in Israel are constantly active, and party offices in Israel are therefore more easily perceived and more attractive to politically active individuals. Party *officeholding* is a virtual prerequisite for election to public office in a system (i.e., Israel) in which party leaders construct all electoral lists.

There is a wide range of officeholding experience available to politicians *outside* of the party hierarchy, as well. These offices in many cases are more visible than party offices because they are public offices. To some degree these possibilities are limited by systemic factors: Israel has a unitary system of government, in which one may hold public office at either the local or national level—there is no intermediate level of office. This means, minimally, that there are fewer ''public'' offices for which to compete in Israel than in other nations. To complicate the analysis further, the term ''public office'' has different meanings in different contexts. The MKs took a broad view of the term ''public office'' and included in their responses to the question offices they had held in any public-related organization, thus including in the analysis offices in labor unions, for example, in addition to local and national governmental office.

The Recruitment of Members of Knesset

The decision to allow nongovernmental offices to be included as responses by the MKs to the interview questions was consciously determined. The Histadrut (national labor union) is a prime recruiting structure in Israeli politics, and it was determined that exclusion of Histadrut offices from this analysis might result in the exclusion of valuable information about the recruitment process in Israel, which is generally an undesired result.

It can generally be stated that most MKs held prior public office. The data in Table 6.4 are certainly influenced by the group of MKs that was studied. In interviewing MKs we interviewed individuals with generally long and successful histories of party work; if these characteristics were not present in the individuals being interviewed, the individuals would very likely not have been placed in "realistic" positions on their respective electoral lists and would not be in the Knesset today. Thus, we are in the same position as when we asked individuals if they had held party office: by virtue of the fact that we asked the question of members of Knesset rather than unsuccessful also-rans, we limited our interviewing to those who, for the most part, held offices and had successful campaign experiences, or who had some other kind of outstanding party work backgrounds.

The pathway to the Knesset for many MKs was a long one. This path might have begun with work for the local party, followed by being placed in an "unrealistic" position on the party electoral list, being elected to local party office, having one's name slowly rise on the ballot, being elected to local municipal office, and finally being given a "realistic" place on the party list for the Knesset. For many MKs this pattern could take ten or twenty years. Indeed, one MK interviewed reached the Knesset at age seventy-three after working in his party organization since the age of twenty-five and having been on his party's Knesset list—in "unrealistic" positions—since the elections for the First Knesset.

The number of offices held prior to election to the national legislature, illustrated in Table 6.4, generally repeats the pattern already established. Not only did most of the MKs hold office but they held many offices, as well.

Interesting patterns may be found in the *types* of offices held by legislators prior to their entering the national legislature. Table 6.5 shows variations in the types of offices held by MKs prior to

Table 6.5

Types of Preparliamentary Offices Held by
Israeli Legislators

	Percent Held No Office	Percent Executive Administrative	Percent Legislative	Percent Judicial
Most recent	48.8	41.9	8.1	1.2
First	67.4	20.9	10.5	1.2
Second	81.4	16.3	2.3	0
Third	93.0	4.7	2.3	0

their entrance into their legislature. In *every* case presented in Table 6.5, the Israelis held a substantially higher proportion of "executive-administrative" offices than they held "legislative" offices.

This pattern is undoubtedly the result of the structural differences that were alluded to earlier, and of the types of office available to candidates in Israel. The fact that Israel does not have a federal system of government may be a partial explanation for the lower proportion of legislative offices held by MKs: where states or provinces do not exist, one obviously cannot hold a seat in a provincial legislature. Similarly, the existence of elected Histadrut offices and other bureaucratic (administrative) offices in Israel affords a partial explanation for the higher proportion of MKs who held executive-administration positions.

Table 6.6 shows data relating to the *level* of offices held by MKs, and these data support the pattern of the data in Table 6.5. In the interests of economy we describe only those offices that were held most recently prior to the MKs' entering the national legislature.

The type of office that was most often held by MKs was an executive-administrative office, as indicated in Table 6.5. Table 6.6 shows that the bulk of MKs held their offices in party organizations, where more executive and administrative positions were available.

It can thus be seen that officeholding is dependent upon more than socialization variables and the political background from which the individual emerges. Holding a political office is

The Recruitment of Members of Knesset

Table 6.6
Levels of Preparliamentary Offices Held by Israeli Legislators

	Percent	N
Local office	12.8%	(11)
National office	3.5	(3)
Party office	24.4	(21)
Union office	9.3	(8)
No office held	48.8	(42)

especially dependent upon system-related factors such as *available offices* (if no government exists between the local and national levels, one obviously cannot hold a position in such a government), *electoral considerations* (whether individuals are elected by party lists or by single member districts, for example), and the *type of party system* within which one must operate. A party system such as one finds in Israel, based upon an electoral list system, has certain implications for prospective candidates and officeholders, such as much party work and seniority being expected prior to receiving a "safe" or "realistic" position on the party's electoral list. These implications may well affect *who* reaches for a position of power.

Not all individuals who are candidates for office, however, are *successful* candidates for office. Theoretically, we could expect many individuals in our sample to have run unsuccessfully for office one, two, or several times before they finally won an election. We might expect some of the legislators to have had no successful electoral experience prior to becoming candidates for a national legislative position. In some instances it might be reasonable to assume a loss as a candidate would be considered by party leaders as a necessary political experience.

When MKs who were officeholders before their entry into the Knesset were asked if they had ever been unsuccessful candidates for an office before they were elected to their preparliamentary office, an interesting pattern of responses was offered. Those MKs who were elected to preparliamentary office had never lost an election prior to winning that office. *None* of the MKs who held office prior to their seat in the Knesset remembered ever having lost an election, which is remarkable in itself. Although it would be expected that our sample would not include many individuals who had lost past elections, the fact that *no* MKs in the sample had ever lost an election is remarkable.

At least part of this pattern in the data is the result of the nature of the Israeli electoral system combined with the manner in which one can define the term "lost" in an electoral sense. Many MKs' responses suggested that if one's name was placed on a party electoral list in a marginal position by the party leaders, one's failure to be elected could be perceived not as having "lost" an election but rather as having been in an "unrealistic" position on the ballot in any case, and therefore not *really* having been a candidate. When such statements were made by MKs in the interview, and when the interviewer asked whether this meant that the individual "ran unsuccessfully" or "lost," the respondent replied in the negative. Party *lists* can lose: individuals whose names are in unrealistic positions on party lists do not lose; they simply do not win office.

Much the same pattern may be observed for those MKs who did *not* hold a preparliamentary office. None of the MKs in this group indicated that they had been an unsuccessful candidate. Again, any loss was attributed to party lists. The MKs insisted that they could not be called unsuccessful candidates, because being on the party list in a moderate position was not *really* being a candidate, it was merely an indication of an association with the party. A candidate is someone who campaigns and attracts voters to the party list. People at the very top of the party list do this, and therefore people at the very top of the party list are the only *real* candidates. Furthermore, people at the very top of the party list invariably win office; therefore, all real candidates are victorious.

Since party activity is a virtual *sine qua non* for receiving a party's endorsement, then the individuals who were never preparliamentary officeholders must have been active in some other capacity before receiving their party's nomination. The great majority (94.2 percent) of legislators had been active in their party organizations in one capacity or another prior to becoming candidates for a parliamentary seat. Thus, although many MKs may never have held preparliamentary office, or even been a candidate for such an office, they certainly were politically active prior to their candidacies for parliament.

The Recruitment of Members of Knesset

Before an individual may be either a successful or an unsuccessful candidate for office, whether the office involved is in the party or in a local or national level government, he or she must *become* a candidate for the office. This being the case, it may be useful for us to examine the pathways leading to the candidacies of the legislators in our sample to see if any systematic variations in patterns of candidacy occur. We focus our attention both upon those individuals who had previously been candidates (successful or unsuccessful) for another office and upon those individuals for whom candidacy for the Knesset was their first attempt at elected office.

Table 6.7 reflects the manner in which party systems can influence recruitment patterns to preparliamentary office. Assuming that legislators' recollections of how they came to be candidates for preparliamentary office are accurate, it is clear that most MKs were recruited by their parties to be candidates for preparliamentary office. The data in Table 6.7 also reflect the great saliency of party and party leadership in the recruitment process in Israel.

A great deal of this pattern can be attributed to the political and electoral systems involved. Whenever a group of five or six party leaders are entirely responsible for the construction of a party's electoral list (as is the case in Israel), candidates are very likely to be recruited, and only rarely will an individual have the opportunity to ''volunteer'' for office and be assigned a ''safe'' or ''realistic'' position on the party list.

A much larger percentage of MKs volunteered for candidacy for the Knesset than volunteered for pre-Knesset candidacy, as shown in Table 6.7. Undoubtedly part of this increase may be ex-

Table 6.7

Recruitment to Candidacy of MKs

	Preparliamentary Candidacy		Knesset Candidacy	
Volunteered	2.3%	(2)	15.1%	(13)
Recruited	37.2	(32)	58.1	(50)
[No preparliamentary effort]	48.8	(42)	-----	
Don't know/no answer	11.6	(10)	26.7	(23)

plained by the greater attractiveness of Knesset office as compared to lower offices in Israel. Indeed, membership in the Knesset is the highest elected office in the land. Another part of this pattern of variation, however, may be explained by the fact that many individuals who were not "self-starters" earlier—in the sense that they were recruited to candidacy for lower office rather than seeking it themselves and volunteering—were "started" by the party's recruitment of them to candidacy for lower elected office. These individuals thus became "self-starters" when the opportunity existed for them to become candidates for the Knesset.

The differential impact of party organizations and electoral systems on the recruitment process is reflected in the respondents' answers to the question: "What, in your opinion, were the reasons that you received the party's nomination at that time [when the respondent was nominated]?" Many of the responses offered by MKs to this question openly discuss system-level structures; other responses merely imply the existence and importance of such structures.

Many reasons suggested by MKs for their receiving nominations (positions on party lists) would not fit into other political contexts, as has already been suggested. Almost 11 percent of the MKs indicated that they received their nominations because of their membership in a party sponsored Kibbutz or Moshav. Over 12 percent of the MKs suggested that they were nominated because of the support of a specific public group, in one instance the Tel Aviv Women's Association. These two instances reflect the different recruitment style that exists in Israel. When party list makers construct their electoral lists, they often place people on their lists solely to win the support of specific groups in the public, such as women in Tel Aviv, or farmers. References by MKs to party work, experience, and activity far exceeded what might have been expected, as seen in Table 6.8. Over 80 percent of the MKs suggested that party activity, in part at least, was responsible for their receiving their nominations. Others suggested that holding party office, party seniority, party leadership in general, or support of a specific party faction were responsible for their being placed on the party list. This is indicative of the role played by parties in the Israeli political system, and the method of parliamentary recruitment resulting from the combination of party roles and electoral systems.

Table 6.8

Reasons Offered by MKs for Their Receiving Legislative Nominations

	Percent	N
History of party activity	80.5	(66)
Success in previous office	25.6	(21)
Support of specific party faction	17.1	(14)
General party seniority	14.6	(12)
Helped organize party	12.2	(10)
Union activity	12.2	(10)
Support of specific public group	12.2	(10)
Kibbutz or Moshav membership	10.9	(9)

The political system itself is perhaps the most crucial variable in an explanation of why recruitment in Israel is the way that it is. The number of offices available, the number (and structures) of parties competing for these offices, and the (electoral) manner in which the parties compete are all significant in the recruitment process.

Summary

In the course of this chapter we have seen some remarkable characteristics of the recruitment processes that affect legislators in Israel. Through an examination of some of these characteristics we have learned a good deal about several of the stages through which MKs pass on their paths to parliament.

What we call "early" recruitment may, in fact, be perceived as two processes rather than one, an "internal" recruitment and an "external" recruitment. "External" recruitment was not associated with the socialization/home environment variables we examined in chapter 5, but instead was dependent upon such factors as those structures that exist in the political system.

The fact that the political systems in which the MKs were reared offered more structured opportunities for children to become involved in politics accounts for a great deal of the high politicization of the MKs as children. Most MKs belonged to political groups in high school and university simply because more of these groups existed, having been already formed by political parties, and the time and energy required to form such organizations was not required in their particular situations.

In an examination of correlation coefficients it was shown that the age of initial party activity, a later phase of the recruitment process, was generally not related to the socialization process. The age of initial activity was only very weakly related to both the ages of first political awareness and first political interest (which were themselves strongly associated) but was strongly related to the age of initial party identification. We can see the existence of a triangular relationship among first awareness, first interest, and first identification, with initial party activity connected *through* first party identification, a demonstration of the importance of party in the recruitment process.

The childhood environment variables examined in the last chapter (e.g., parents' interest and activity in politics, discussion in the home, etc.) had no significant association with the age of initial party activity. Political group membership, however, did have a significant association with initial party activity, and individuals who belonged to political groups were politically active earlier than individuals who did not belong to such groups.

We also saw that patterns of officeholding and candidacy vary, as do patterns of recruitment to candidacy. Party systems, existing party structures, and party powers, as well as electoral regulations, are highly influential in how one becomes a *candidate* for a public office, as well as in how one is *elected* to such an office. Levels and types of offices are also variables in the recruitment process.

Patterns of party officeholding may be attributed simply to the characteristics of Israeli politics. Israeli parties are very centralized, highly regimented, and structured, and holding party office is therefore of great significance for one with political aspirations. As theorists have suggested, much of the explanation of why party systems are the way they are may be attributed to electoral systems. That Israel is a single national electoral district with proportional representation and a list ballot is of great significance in explaining not only why the party system is the way it is but also why the party system exhibits such great influence in the general recruitment process in Israel.

Notes

1. Allan Kornberg, *Canadian Legislative Behavior* (New York: Holt, Rinehart and Winston, 1967), p. 42.
2. For a discussion of the debate over the nature of the term "recruitment," see Harold Clarke and Richard Price, eds., *Recruitment and Leadership Selection in Canada* (Toronto: Holt, Rinehart and Winston, 1977), p. 7.
3. Gabriel Almond, "Introduction: A Functional Approach to Comparative Politics," in *The Politics of the Developing Areas*, ed. Gabriel Almond and James Coleman (Princeton, N.J.: Princeton University Press, 1960), p. 3.
4. Ibid.
5. Herbert Jacob, "Initial Recruitment of Elected Officials in the United States," *Journal of Politics* 24 (1962):705–18.
6. Samuel Patterson and G. Robert Boynton, "Legislative Recruitment in a Civic Culture," *Social Science Quarterly* 50 (1969):264.
7. For example, based upon the seven stages of political activity indicated in Figure 6.1, some of the routes by which one could reach office would be: 1-5-7, 1-2-4-7, 1-2-3-4-7, and so on. The number of possibilities is enormous.

Part III
Legislative Attitudes and Behavior

7

Legislators' Perceptions of the Israeli Political System

Once the members of Knesset have reached the legislature, they find themselves in a new environment. This environment, which comes with being a member of Knesset, might be very similar to a previous position the MK has held, or it may be an entirely new experience, with new role expectations, new role behaviors, and new flexibilities required.

This chapter deals with the attitudes and perceptions of the individual members of Knesset toward the role of being a member of Knesset. The discussion includes an examination of the ideas the MKs held concerning what the job of being a member of Knesset required, and what differences they found once they were in office. We examine some of the informal rules of behavior that are of importance in the Knesset, seeing who follows the rules, what the sanctions are for not following informal norms, attitudes toward these norms, and the manner in which these rules or norms affect one's ability to function as a legislator. We also examine legislators' views of Knesset procedures, and see which procedures MKs feel should be changed, and why. We learn who the perceived "influentials" are in the Knesset, and why individuals are perceived by their peers as being influential. Finally, we discover which ministries and which committees of the Knesset are perceived as being the most important in the Israeli political system. This information is used in the next chapter, which is concerned with actual legislative behavior in the Knesset.

Perceptions of the Job

Surprisingly, three out of every four members of Knesset interviewed (sixty-five of eighty-six) indicated that when they *first* were elected they did *not* "have any ideas about what the job of being an MK required." This is especially surprising in light of the data discussed in the last chapter, which demonstrated the "professional" or at least "paraprofessional" nature of the Israeli politician. When so few "outsiders" receive nominations from the party, it is not at all unreasonable to assume that those who are nominated will have a very good idea about what to expect when and if they are elected.

The MKs interviewed did not, however, support this assumption. Most members responded that they wanted to be members of Knesset to "help" people or to "enact policy," but when they were pressed to be a bit more specific, to indicate what the job of being an MK required, most indicated that they really did *not* know what to expect. Of the twenty-one MKs who did have some ideas about what to expect in the Knesset, four found things "somewhat different" from what they had expected, indicating specifically that (a) more time was required for the job than they had expected, and (b) they could actually accomplish less than they had thought they would be able to. Of those for whom things worked out "pretty much as expected," the major expectations of the job were: working in committees (10), representing people and constituency work (2), drafting legislation (2), doing legal work and making public statements (2), and doing "lots of general jobs" (5).

The experience of being an MK obviously had different effects upon different individuals. Members were asked, "Of all the things you did during that first year, which did you find were the most gratifying?"; virtually all of the responses of substance focused upon one of two factors, either general Knesset activity or casework. The responses to this question are summarized in Table 7.1. Over a third of the MKs indicated that it was committee work, specifically, that they found most gratifying, with the next largest group of respondents indicating that "being in a position to help specific groups" was the most gratifying characteristic of the job.

Table 7.1
Gratifying Characteristics of the MK's Job

General Knesset Activity	(37)	43%
Committee work (29)		
Speechmaking (3)		
Being in the public eye (2)		
Public speaking (3)		
The Legislative Role	(34)	39%
Passing laws, generally (7)		
Housing legislation (1)		
New settlements legislation (1)		
Arab-Jewish relations legislation (2)		
Helping create the state (5)		
Helping constituencies (12)		
Women's rights legislation (3)		
Ecology legislation (1)		
Religious legislation (2)		
Holding formal position of Deputy Speaker (4)		
Having influence (3)		
Nothing—everything was frustrating (4)		
Other (4)		

There was not quite the same degree of consensus among MKs when they were asked the companion question, "And what did you find the most burdensome and onerous?", although noteworthy pluralities did occur in a couple of areas, as can be seen in Table 7.2. Clearly the largest "burdensome" area had to do with the plenary sessions of the Knesset. More than one MK in three responded that having to listen to others' speeches was generally an unpleasant task; this finding certainly parallels the suggestions of many MKs that the plenary session as an institution needs to be reevaluated.

Paperwork was another burdensome area indicated by a number of members of Knesset. This statistic is especially meaningful when it is recalled that most of the MKs do not have secretaries and must do all of their own correspondence, research, and the like. This point emphasizes the vulnerability of the individual MK to the system within which he or she must operate.

Table 7.2

Burdensome Characteristics of the MK's Job

General Knesset work	(5)	6%

Plenary sessions, generally
  Listening to others' speeches (20)
  Other (11)
	(31)	36%

Amount of time required, generally	(11)	13%

Politics, generally
  Party discipline (4)
  Other (5)
	(9)	10%

Specific Issues
  Paperwork (13)
  Policy decisions (4)
  Others (13)		

Legislative Roles

The concept of legislative "roles" is not a new one, and has long received a good deal of attention in the literature.[1] A role, whether in or out of a legislature, may be defined as "a set of expectations about behavior in a position held by the incumbent of that position and by incumbents of related positions."[2] In the legislative sense, a role is more than simply expectations of what the job will require; it includes rules of behavior, expectations held by an individual of how he or she should interact in his or her role with incumbents of related roles. Formal rules in the legislature cover part of this process. Knesset procedure and Knesset norms of etiquette and behavior, which were discussed in chapter 4, certainly apply to individuals' perceptions of the legislative role.

Role behavior, however, goes beyond simply the formal rules of the legislature. Studies have found that informal "rules of the game" are very significant in legislative behavior. Matthews, in his study of the U.S. Senate, and Kornberg, in his study of the Canadian House of Commons,[3] have both pointed out the importance of being an "insider," of following the "unofficial rules of the game." The assumption here is that if one wants to be an effective legislator, if one wants to "get along," one must "go along." Further, and related, the assumption implies that if one does *not* follow the informal rules of behavior, the norms, or the folkways, one will not be an effective member of the legislature. There may, in fact, even be certain penalties imposed upon individuals who do not go along with these "informal" rules.

Members of Knesset interviewed in this study were asked a series of questions dealing with these types of "informal" rules. MKs were asked if they agreed or disagreed with the statement that "Every legislature has its unofficial rules of the game, certain things that members must do and certain things they must not do if they want the respect and cooperation of their legislative colleagues." Almost half of the respondents (forty-one MKs) said that there were no rules of an informal nature, and these respondents maintained through the series of questions that these kinds of informal norms simply do not exist in the Israeli legislature.

Although a majority of the MKs (52 percent, or forty-five of eighty-six MKs) indicated that there were informal norms in the Knesset, there was not a strong consensus as to the character of these rules. Of the forty-five MKs who responded positively to this question, over a quarter said that the only rule in the Knesset, official or unofficial, was to obey the directions of the party leader. The bulk of the other responses followed this same line, with respondents indicating that "informal rules exist, but they are all made formal either by the party or by the Knesset Committee," that "all unofficial Knesset rules are official party rules," and so on.

When members were asked if they could "name several of your fellow members, regardless of party or position, who are most respected for following these 'rules of the game'...," their responses were quite interesting. Although the respondents were almost evenly divided between the two major parties (thirty from the Labor alignment and thirty-one from the Likud alignment), members of the Likud party were named considerably more often as individuals who are respected for following the rules of the game. The leader of the Opposition at the time, Menachem Begin, was named more frequently than anyone else (twenty-three times).

When we list the top sixteen names in terms of the frequency with which they were mentioned as being respected for following the rules of the game, we find an impressive group of individuals. Three party leaders were named, Rabin of the Labor alignment, Begin of the Likud, and Aloni of the CRM, although Rabin was named only twice and Aloni only once to Begin's twenty-three times. Six committee chairmen were named, including Tamir of Interior (five times), Kargman of Finance (four times), Navon of Foreign Affairs (now president, seven times), Warhaftig of Laws and Constitution (once), Bader of State Controller (seven times), and Arbelli of Labor (once). In addition to these noteworthy individuals mentioned as being respected were six present (at the time) or former cabinet members, including Abba Eban, Moshe Dayan, Zevulon Hammer, Pinhas Sapir, Shimon Peres, and Haim Zadok.

These responses give the reader the clear impression that positions of formal influence and power correspond highly with informal influence and with the perceived behavior of following whatever "informal" rules there happen to be. This should come as no surprise, since we have already seen that the major informal rules involve following the directives of party leaders, and that the individuals who are credited with following these rules the best *are* the party leaders.

Members were further asked about sanctions that were utilized if one did not follow these "informal rules": "How do other members make it difficult for these people when they don't follow the 'rules of the game'?" Of the sixty-three legislators who responded to this question, 13 percent indicated that even though there were rules of an informal nature to be followed, people "don't do anything if you don't follow them." A larger number of respondents (21 percent) said that people "can't do anything" to the "mavericks" of the Knesset. Five MKs indicated that ostracism or exclusion might be the result of not following informal rules. By far the largest number of respondents indicated that the primary result of too much "outsider" behavior would be party discipline. The MKs indicated that party discipline would either result in a reduction of a member's speaking time or opportunity to introduce legislation (16), or in the member's position on the party election list being placed in jeopardy.

Earlier we saw that parties *do*, in fact, exercise this latter option when, in the opinions of the party leaders, individual members are not sufficiently following the party directives. These responses indicate that the message has been received, and members are aware that if they go too far, they may put themselves in potentially difficult situations.

How members learned of these informal rules is an interesting study in socialization in its own right, whether they were quietly taken aside by their party leaders after they received their nominations (positions on the party list) and told "look, we expect certain behavior out of you in exchange for your safe position on our electoral list," or whether these informal rules simply are learned from observation once one is elected to the Knesset.

Members were asked "How did you learn of these rules?", and their responses indicate a variety of socialization techniques, for socialization is the correct term to describe the learning of new patterns of behavior that are appropriate to a new situation. Of the members who would talk about this ($n = 47$), over half (thirty-one) indicated that they learned of these rules on their own after taking office, simply through observation. A number of respondents indicated that they learned about these informal norms from others after taking office, either from other MKs, from party colleagues who were not in the Knesset, or from advisors or friends.

Reaction to the existence of these rules was slightly tilted in a negative direction, although the majority of MKs who would discuss this aspect of their jobs were neutral. Only one MK indicated "strongly liking" these informal rules, whereas seven indicated they "liked" the system in which one knew what to expect and what was expected of oneself. Fifteen MKs said they were "neutral" about the system, eight MKs said they "disliked" the system, and another seven "strongly disliked" the framework of informal rules.

In spite of their mixed reaction to the existence of these rules, the vast majority of the respondents (twenty-three of thirty-eight) indicated that they felt their ability to accomplish their goals was unaffected by the existence of these party norms. Only two MKs indicated that their ability to accomplish their goals was increased or greatly increased, whereas thirteen indicated that their ability to accomplish their goals was decreased or greatly decreased.

Similarly, most of the respondents indicated that their "likelihood to act" was unaffected by these rules. The same two respondents indicated that they were more likely to act or much more likely to act, and again thirteen indicated that they were less likely to act or much less likely to act because of these rules.

The Legislators and Knesset Procedure

The importance of the party in the Knesset is something that has already been discussed at length, and could be considered as one of the major themes of this study. Party is the central organizing, electing, and orienting force in the legislature, and accordingly we should not be surprised to see that whatever informal rules exist in the Knesset are classified as being predominately party rules and regulations. Further, it is entirely consistent with the broader political context that perceived sanctions for violating these rules are primarily party sanctions: lower electoral list positions, decreased opportunity to participate in the Knesset, and so on.

The theme of the vulnerability of the individual legislator that was discussed earlier was broadly indicated by the members of Knesset in their responses to questions dealing with changes in procedure in the Knesset. Members were asked: "Are there any changes in procedure or in the way the Knesset operates that you think would make it easier for you to accomplish your goals?" Eighty of the eighty-six respondents (93 percent) indicated that there *were* changes they would recommend. Up to three responses, or recommended changes, were recorded per respondent; the responses could generally be placed in one of five categories: facilities and staff, legislative power, Knesset procedures, party discipline, and electoral procedure.

By far the largest numbers of suggestions for change made by these respondents were in the general area of facilities and staff help. Staff help and secretarial assistance were suggested by sixty (75 percent) of the MKs; an additional thirty-six responses indicated "research assistance," "greater information resources," and "better working facilities (offices)." This characteristic of the operation of the Knesset, the generally nonsupported role of the individual MK, is clearly keenly felt by the MK and is a situation that individual MKs would be quick to change, if they could.

The second largest number of suggested changes came in the area of the relative lack of power of the Knesset in relation to the Government. Several MKs specifically indicated giving "more power to the Knesset to use against the Government." Sixteen responses were concerned with the power of the committees in the Knesset, with nine respondents suggesting that committees be given more power to modify Government legislation, five suggesting committee reorganization, and two suggesting more committee staff.

Knesset procedures were the object of a number of responses of MKs. These comments focused on structures discussed in chapter 4 and specifically recommended a variety of changes in Knesset procedure that the respondents believed would make the operation of the legislature not only more efficient but also more "truthful" and "realistic." Other recommended changes were that speeches be shorter, and that less time be spent in the plenum generally, since "nobody's mind is changed" by speeches in most cases, and formal speeches were simply a matter of "show, not substance" because MKs vote in the direction indicated by their party leaders, rather than in the directions they would individually prefer to vote.

Another recommended change that would directly affect a structure discussed in chapter 4 would be a change in the format of question time. Several MKs suggested that questions in the Knesset should be modified to follow more closely question time in Commonwealth nations and should include oral, as well as written, questions. These MKs believe that this change would make question time more spontaneous and lively, rather than giving the ministers advance warning of all questions they will be asked.

Finally, many members suggested that attendance in the plenary sessions, when the entire Knesset was in session, should be made mandatory. They argued that "Knesset business" is a farce when only 20 or 30 percent of the membership is in attendance. The argument was made that if every member were there, people would start taking the Knesset's business more seriously, so that required attendance would in effect upgrade the quality of business of the Knesset itself.

Another category of suggested changes in Knesset procedure was very specific: decrease the influence that parties have over individual MKs and provide more freedom for the MKs from party discipline. The interesting point about these responses is that there were so few of them. Only eleven out of 258 possible responses (up to 3 responses for each of 86 MKs) indicated that party discipline should be reduced. This could either be explained by (a) a belief that party discipline is *not* too strong, and therefore the respondents do not feel that it should be reduced, or (b) a belief that party discipline is *so* strong that it *cannot* be reduced, and therefore the respondents do not bother to even discuss the matter.

The final broad category of suggested changes dealt with elections, with a number of MKs indicating a belief that the Israeli electoral system should be changed from the proportional representation single national list system it currently employs to a system of single-member districts, similar to that used in the United States. This is a theme to which we will return in the last chapter.

Legislative Expertise

Virtually all legislators felt that there was a "particular area of work in the Knesset" in which they had become expert, over 90 percent, in fact ($N = 78$). Table 7.3 is a list of their responses, showing the wide variety of perceptions of expertise indicated by the MKs. Of the general responses, the one most frequently given dealt with the broad area of legislation; of the specific responses, the most frequent responses dealt with finance/economics, and security and defense.

Members of Knesset were subsequently asked how they acquired their expertise and whether their expertise was in one, two, or several areas. Their responses fell into several broad categories.

First, a number of the respondents (15 percent) indicated that pre-Knesset work or experience was the primary source of their expertise. This type of response was offered by a very high proportion of those who indicated that they were experts in finance; many had been bankers prior to becoming members of Knesset. Similarly, a number of those who indicated expertise in "security and defense" relied upon their former military backgrounds for a large share of their expertise.

The largest group of MKs, however, indicated that their expertise came from committee work in the Knesset (45 percent). These respondents indicated that it was the hearings, witnesses,

Table 7.3
Areas of Indicated Expertise of Members of Knesset

	N
General	
Legislation	6
Fundamental Laws	4
Knesset rules	4
Electoral reform	1
Committee work	1
Specific	
Aliyah/Immigration	4
Agriculture	5
Arab relations	4
Education	7
Environment	3
Finance/economics	15
Foreign affairs	8
Housing	3
Interior	1
Labor	8
Religion	2
Security and defense/military	14
Social welfare/health	5
State controller	4
Budget	1
Public service	1
Women's issues	1
Consumer protection	1
Tourism	1
Poverty	1

and debates that went on behind the closed doors of the committee meeting rooms that served as the basis for their expertise. Several individuals indicated that "just being in the Knesset" made them the experts that they were in their respective areas ($n = 5$). One hearty individual indicated that he had done a great deal of research in order to acquire his expertise. The third largest group of individuals (23 percent) indicated that it was a combination of pre-Knesset experience coupled with committee work in the Knesset that made them the experts they were.

The notion of committee expertise is characteristic of most legislative bodies around the world that have committee structures. The original reason for the development of the committee as a legislative institution may have been to promote specialization and expertise, based upon the awareness that nobody can be an expert in every field of inquiry. This norm is present in the Knesset in which the members belong to committees. Most MKs ascribe the source of their expertise to committee work (fifty-seven, or 66 percent), regardless of the ultimate role of the committee in the overall legislative process.

Expertise and Cabinet Membership

Interestingly, expertise was *not* mentioned by even one member of Knesset as a criterion for becoming a member of the cabinet. This supports the suggestions offered in chapter 3 about how and why cabinet members are selected. When members were asked ''From your own experience and based on the experience of others, what do you think are the principal criteria applied to select cabinet members?'', there was no doubt that party leadership was the major factor. Table 7.4 shows the responses to this question; clearly the two most significant characteristics of the responses are the frequency with which party is mentioned, and the absence of the mention of expertise.

Table 7.4

Criteria Applied for the Selection of Cabinet Members

Seniority. Members of ''eligible'' factions with the greatest seniority are chosen	51%
Leaders of party factions are chosen	35
Parties have internal elections for ''their'' cabinet positions	5
Popularity within the party	6
Decisions by party caucus	2

The norms of party loyalties and traditional coalition partnerships that were discussed in chapter 3 were very much indicated by members of Knesset in their responses to these questions. Members of parties traditionally in the opposition (the Likud, Moked, Rakah, and so on) saw no possibilities at all of their reaching the cabinet, assuming that the Mapai-dominated coalition continued to hold power.

When members were asked what their chances of being a member of the cabinet would be "if, in the next election, you were reelected and your party were a part of the Government," the themes of seniority and party hierarchy continued to be echoed. Most of the members interviewed were not very optimistic about their chances for joining the cabinet. As Table 7.5 indicates, over 60 percent of the respondents indicated that their chances were either "not so good," "poor," or that they had "no chance" at all.

Almost invariably, those MKs who responded in the first four categories of responses to the question "what are your chances for becoming a member of cabinet..."(ranging from "I am a member of cabinet now" to "good"), were *also* the individuals who responded in the first four categories to the question "why do you think this is so?". In other words, individuals who thought that they had at least a good chance to belong to the cabinet felt this way primarily because of their party seniority. Equally invariably, individuals who responded that their chances for becoming a member of the cabinet were "not so good," "poor," or that they had "no chance," responded that the reasons for these bleak outlooks had to do with low seniority, being too independent of party discipline, or that their party's "quota" of cabinet positions was filled and there was no chance for another cabinet position going to his or her party unless someone died. Members were very much resigned to these statuses, with over 80 percent indicating that there was nothing they could do that they felt could improve their chance to belong to the cabinet.

The association between these two sets of responses is quite high. In fact, in a cross-tabulation analysis of the two sets of responses indicated in Table 7.5, an almost linear response was visible, yielding a Tau B of .767, significant at better than the .0001 level. *Every* individual who responded in the first three categories in 7.5A responded in either the first or second category in 7.5B. Similarly, *no* individual who responded in the last three categories of 7.5A responded in the first three categories of 7.5B. These data are illustrated in a presentation of the data in Table 7.6.

Table 7.5

Cabinet Opportunities for MKs

A.	"What would you say are your chances of becoming a member of the cabinet if in the next election you were elected and your party were a part of the Government?"		
	1. Is minister now/could be any time	10%	(9)
	2. Excellent	1	(1)
	3. Very good	6	(5)
	4. Good	16	(14)
	5. Not so good	41	(35)
	6. Poor	13	(11)
	7. No chance	7	(6)
	8. DK	6	(5)
B.	Reasons offered by MKs for their likelihood of their becoming cabinet members		
	1. Responds that he or she is/was a minister	10%	
	2. Could be if he wanted to, but declined in order to hold another office that excluded a cabinet portfolio	3	
	3. Party seniority is high	16	
	4. Seniority is increasing	5	
	5. Seniority is low/new MK	46	
	6. Too independent of party discipline	6	
	7. Party wouldn't be invited/other	8	
	8. DK	5	

This association indicating that party seniority is the primary variable in the consideration of cabinet material ties in with the theme developed throughout the book of the dependence of the individual MK upon his or her party and his or her party organization. One clear result of this relationship is that the member of Knesset, if he or she wants to remain a member of Knesset, must be "sensitive" to the wants and needs of his or her party. In other political systems if one has the firm backing of a specific geographic constituency one can afford to be somewhat of a maverick, because one's base of power, fundamentally, rests with the electorate. In Israel this clearly isn't the case, and one's political life lies in the hands of the party leaders who construct the electoral list.

A clear indication of this, and an indication that members of

Legislators' Perceptions of the Israeli Political System

Table 7.6

Likelihood of Cabinet Membership for MKs

Reason	Already in Cabinet or Excellent	Very Good	Good	Not So Good	Poor No Chance	Don't Know
Am/have been a cabinet member	9	1	0	0	0	0
High seniority	1	4	9	0	0	0
Seniority increasing	0	0	4	0	0	0
Low seniority	0	0	0	29	8	3
Too independent of party leaders	0	0	0	1	2	2
Party quota already filled	0	0	0	5	1	1
Totals	10	5	13	35	11	6

$r = .83$ sig. $= .00001$ $B = .932$
$Tau_B = .767$ sig.0001

Knesset, as well as Knesset-watchers, perceive this to be the case are the responses of members of Knesset to the question: "To whom do you consider yourself accountable for what you do as an MK?" Eighty-one percent of the members of Knesset responding to the question indicated that they felt responsible to their party. Almost 13 percent (12.7 percent) took what might be considered a "Burkean" approach and responded that they felt responsible for what they did to themselves only. Only two MKs (2.3 percent) indicated a feeling of responsibility to the public.

This feeling of dependence upon the party, which is translated into responsibility or accountability to the party, is further translated into a feeling of collegiality. That is, there is a clear perception on the part of the members of Knesset that everyone on the "team"—in the party in the Knesset—shares the same goals. In fact, when members were asked "Do you feel that there are differences between what you want to accomplish and what your party colleagues in the Knesset want?" over 95 percent of the respondents (82 of 86) answered "no."

"Influentials" in the Knesset

Even though there may be a sense of camaraderie in the Knesset, there is still an apparent division between the "insiders" and the "outsiders," those with power and those who as yet do not share power. Individuals in a specific political party may feel themselves on the same team, but that does not necessarily mean that everyone thinks that he or she is the captain of that team, or even (to continue the analogy) an officer, for that matter. It thus becomes possible to speak of an elite within an elite.

Gaetano Mosca once wrote that

> In all societies . . . two classes of people appear—a class that rules and a class that is ruled. The first class, always the less numerous, performs all political functions, monopolizes power and enjoys the advantages that power brings, whereas the second, more numerous class, is directed and controlled by the first.[4]

What we can see in operation in the Knesset, as we would in any legislature we examined, is a pattern of elitism in which a minority of the members of a population (admittedly a small and elite one in its own right) dominates the majority. Even the small body that makes the rules for the greater society exhibits characteristics of elitism, for here, too, there are the rulers and the ruled.

Members of Knesset were asked the question "Who, in your mind, are the ten most influential members of this Knesset, regardless of party?" and were subsequently asked "Why are these people influential?" Their responses support the "elite within an elite" hypothesis that there is a distinct minority that is recognized by members as composing the "inner circle" of Knesset decision making.

Fifty-four different members of Knesset, 45 percent of the total, were named at least once as being among the most influential members of Knesset. Of these, however, only twenty-four were named by three or more different individuals. In addition to examining which individuals were "nominated" as being influential, it is useful to include a discussion of *why* these individuals were perceived as being influential. An analysis of who these twenty-four individuals are and why they are considered influential reveals a great deal about the nature of influence in the Knesset.

Five categories of responses for "why" the influentials had influence were offered by our respondents, including "formal position in the Knesset," "formal position in a party," being a "member of the Government or having influence with a minister," and "having a large following." Code sheets also included other options, such as "general knowledge," "having a flexible opinion," being an "up-and-coming MK," and "being active," but these responses were not offered once for the influentials.

Table 7.7 indicates a remarkable consensus on *why* most influentials have influence. In fact, the more often someone was nominated as being influential, the greater was the likelihood that consensus would develop. A couple of examples will substantiate this. Menachem Begin, who subsequently became the prime minister, was "nominated" as an influential thirty-two times, more than anyone else, even the then prime minister. Thirty-one of the thirty-two nominations of Begin were made because of his "formal position in the party," that is, as head of Likud. Itzhak Rabin, who was prime minister at the time of the survey, was nominated twenty-five times, and twenty-two of these nominations were because he was a "member of the Government." Out of the twenty-four influentials indicated in Table 7.7, there was a consensus on why the individual had influence (at least 75 percent of the responses in one category) nineteen times. All of the members of Knesset listed primarily in the third category ("being a member of the Government or having influence with a minister") were, in fact, members of the cabinet. All of the members listed primarily in the first category ("formal position in the Knesset") were committee chairmen. And virtually all of the members primarily listed in the second category ("formal position in party") were either party leaders or party whips.

There is, then, a clear indication of a consensus on why individuals have influence in the Knesset. Influence comes with formal position, either in the Knesset, in the party, or in the Govern-

Table 7.7

"Influentials" in the Knesset

M.K.	Times Nominated	Formal Knesset Position	Formal Party Position	Formal Government Position	Other	Percent of Nominations in one category	Formal Position Held
Y. Allon	6			5		83%	Foreign minister/Deputy prime minister
S. Aloni	3	1	1		2	33	Formed new party
S. Arbelli-Almozlino	6	6				100	Labor Committee chairperson
S. Erlich	4		4			100	Likud party officer
M. Begin	32		31		1	97	Likud leader
Y. Bader	11	2	9			82	Likud whip/State Controller Committee chairperson
Y. Ben-Ahron	4		3		1	75	Labor party whip
I. Galilee	4			4		100	Minister without Portfolio
M. Dayan	7		2		5	71	Former defense minister
Y. Horwitz	3		2		1	66	Economics Committee chairperson
Z. Hammer	4		3		1	75	N.R.P. party whip
Z. Warhaftig	3	1	1	1		33	Laws, Constitution Committee chairperson
M. Wertman	10	1	9			90	Labor party floor leader
Y. Navon	8	8				100	Foreign Affairs and Security Committee chairperson

M. Nissim	5		5		100	Likud party whip
P. Sapir	4	1	1	2	50	Minister of finance
S. Peres	20		1	17	85	Minister of defense
H. Zadok	13		1	12	92	Minister of justice
I. Kargman	15	14	1		1	93	Finance Committee chairperson
Y. Rabin	25	1	1	22	88	Prime minister
E. Rimalt	11		10	1	91	Likud faction leader
Y. Raphael	3			3	100	Minister of religious affairs
Y. Tamir	9		8		1	89	Interior Committee chairperson
Y. Rabinowitz	10	1		8	1	80	Minister of housing

ment. What these data do *not* tell us, and what they will not tell us, is the causal relationship between influence and position. That is, do the "influentials" have influence because of their formal positions, whether in the Knesset, in the party, or in the Government, or do these individuals have their formal positions because they already had influence, and the position was simply a reward for, or a vestige of, possessing this influence.

We can speculate that the relationship may work in both directions. That is, an individual who previously had little influence, who is appointed to a specific political position, perhaps as a result of a coalition agreement, may acquire a great deal of influence solely as a result of his or her being an incumbent of a position of power. On the other hand, an individual who acquires a great deal of influence through more informal relationships will, in the Israeli political system, find his or her influence formalized in relatively short order at least with a formal position in the party hierarchy.

There is a high degree of consensus among the members of Knesset as to which are the most important formal positions to hold in the Knesset. Table 7.8 indicates that over 50 percent of the MKs indicated only three ministries as being among the "five most important ministries in the Government today," Foreign Affairs, Defense, and Finance. Five other ministries were named ten times or more, including the Prime Minister's Office and the ministries of Justice, Labor, Education and Culture, and Interior. It should come as no surprise that the ministers of Foreign Affairs, Defense, Finance, Justice, and Labor, as well as the prime minister, were all named to the "influentials" list, as well as the minister of Religious Affairs and one minister without portfolio.

To a large degree there is a similar consensus as to the "five most important Knesset committees." Only the Foreign Affairs and Security Committee and the Finance Committee were named by over 50 percent of the respondents as being important, whereas the Knesset, Constitution, Labor, and Education and Culture Committees were named ten times or more. The chairmen of the Finance, Foreign Affairs and Security, Constitution, and Labor committees were on the "influentials" list, as well as the chairmen of the Interior, State Controller, and Economics committees.

Table 7.8
Influential Government Ministries and Knesset Committees

A.	Influential Government Ministries	
	Ministry	*Nominated By*
	Prime Minister's Office	(38)
	Foreign Affairs	(61)
	Defense	(76)
	Justice	(22)
	Police	(2)
	Labor	(17)
	Housing	(9)
	Education and Culture	(40)
	Transportation	(0)
	Finance	(71)
	Health	(4)
	Commerce and Industry	(5)
	Immigrant Absorption	(4)
	Agriculture	(4)
	Communications	(1)
	Tourism	(0)
	Interior	(18)
	Religious Affairs	(5)
	Social Welfare	(3)
B.	Influential Knesset Committees	
	Constitution, Laws, and Justice	(26)
	Knesset	(15)
	Finance	(78)
	Foreign Affairs and Security	(63)
	Labor	(25)
	Economics	(7)
	Education and Culture	(10)
	Interior and Environment	(6)
	Public Services	(3)
	State Controller	(3)

In sum, then, it is evident that there is a clearly identifiable "elite" within the Knesset, and that this "elite" is strongly associated with positions of formal power, either in the party, in the Knesset, or in the government. It is speculative whether influence precedes power or positions of power build influence, but cases may be suggested to substantiate both causal pathways.

Summary and Conclusions

This chapter focused upon many of the perceptions of the Israeli members of Knesset. We saw that the members had a wide range of perceptions of the role of being an MK prior to their assuming that position, and the data illustrated the fact that the MKs perceive a variety of gratifying as well as burdensome aspects of their job.

An investigation of the concept of a legislative role, including role expectations, yielded mixed results. There apparently are certain informal "rules of behavior" that exist in the Knesset, but the distinctions between these informal rules and other, similar, formal party and formal Knesset rules is apparently fuzzy to many of the MKs. The broadest consensus that could be discovered was that informal rules for the most part simply echo the formalized party rules, and that the legislator's "role" in the Knesset is to a high degree defined by his or her party leader.

Legislators had a number of perceived improvements they would suggest to modify Knesset procedures. The bulk of these suggested modifications were directed at the relative impotence of the member of Knesset. Most suggestions were directed either to (a) needing more staff/research help, or (b) giving more power to the Knesset. Members felt, as well, that internal Knesset procedures could be modified to make the Knesset a more efficient body.

The cabinet is perceived as a political body. That is, one does not attain cabinet rank primarily on the basis of skill or expertise, but rather on the basis of political power. This power may be derived either through seniority or through coalition negotiations. The data presented in Table 7.6 indicated the overwhelming importance placed on party seniority in the attainment of cabinet rank.

Finally, we saw that there is a clearly perceived "elite within an elite" in the Knesset, and that the membership in this elite was closely associated with positions of formal power. It was suggested that the causal relationship between influence and position could not be strictly determined, since examples of each causal relationship could be easily imagined.

This discussion of legislative perceptions has been designed to provide the final bit of groundwork for a discussion of legislative behavior in chapter 8. Now that the reader has been introduced to the general political system within which the Knesset operates, the procedures in the Knesset itself, the socialization and recruitment of the legislators, and the perceptions the legislators hold, he or she is in a position to understand not only the causes but also the explanations of the legislative behavior of Israeli MKs. It is to such an examination that we now turn our attention.

Notes

1. See, for example, Raymond Hopkins, "The Role of the MP in Tanzania," *American Political Science Review* 64 (1970):754–71; or Allan Kornberg, *Canadian Legislative Behavior* (New York: Holt, Rinebhart and Winston), especially chapter 6.
2. Kornberg, *Canadian Legislative Behavior* p. 8.
3. See Donald Matthews, *U.S. Senators and Their World* (New York: Vintage, 1960); or Kornberg, *Canadian Legislative Behavior*.
4. Gaetano Mosca, *The Ruling Class*, ed. and rev. by Arthur Livingston, trans. Hannah Kahn (New York: McGraw-Hill, 1939), p. 50.

8

Legislative Behavior in the Knesset: Intralegislative Frustration and Extralegislative Effectiveness

The Israeli Knesset presents the observer with a study in the intricacies of political power. The Knesset is legally and constitutionally supreme in the Israeli political system, "giving birth" to the Government, with the power to remove the Government any time it feels the Government no longer deserves its support. As has already been pointed out, the Knesset also does the hiring and firing of the president of the state. Similarly, the Knesset is supreme in terms of legislative policy; since the Fundamental Laws are simply majority acts of the Knesset, the Constitution may be amended, modified, or withdrawn completely, all at the pleasure of the Knesset.

Yet, this book has been a study of the ineffectiveness of the individual legislator, and of the entire legislature for that matter, in "flexing" its legislative muscles. Because of the extremely tight party discipline that results at least in part from the Israeli electoral system and the "list" ballots that are so critical both for the political party organizations and for the individuals involved, the successful candidate, the one who is elected, is in an extremely vulnerable position. On the one hand, he or she is protected "constitutionally" by parliamentary immunity so that he or she may perform his or her "mandate" with as few external pressures to worry about as possible. On the other hand, the successful candidate knows how he or she was elected, and realizes that the party leaders are watching his or her every move. The member knows that in the Knesset "in order to get along you have to go along," and that a failure to show oneself as a team player may easily result in one's not being included on the team the next time around.

The picture presented of the member of Knesset, then, is one of an emasculated legislator, one who although he or she has the constitutional power to speak out without fear of governmental reaction must be concerned with his or her *party's* reactions. If this were the entire picture, we would be correct in asking why anyone bothers to hold these positions, why individuals spend a great deal of time, effort, and money, to become MKs. The fact of the matter is that members of Knesset do considerably more than sit in plenary sessions waiting to be told how to vote.

In this chapter we undertake a thorough and comprehensive examination of Israeli legislative behavior. We look at a variety of behaviors that fall within the realm of party discipline and those that fall outside of the realm of party discipline. Figure 4.1, which is reprinted here as Figure 8.1, represents potential MK behavior in the Israeli legislative system. In this chapter we investigate a number of behaviors that may be conceived as being part of this framework for analysis, with the ultimate goal being a more complete understanding of how and why the Israeli political system operates in the manner that it does.

Legislators and the Government

The formal relationship between the legislators and the Government is a contradictory one, especially for legislators of the Governmental parties. On one hand they are (theoretically) expected to exercise some degree of control over the Government, and to be prepared to vote against the Government in the event they feel it is doing something improper. On the other hand, party discipline guides them to follow the directions of their party leaders, who happen to be the leaders of the Government as well. The members of Opposition parties feel no such cross-pressures, because their role is to continually oppose the Government.

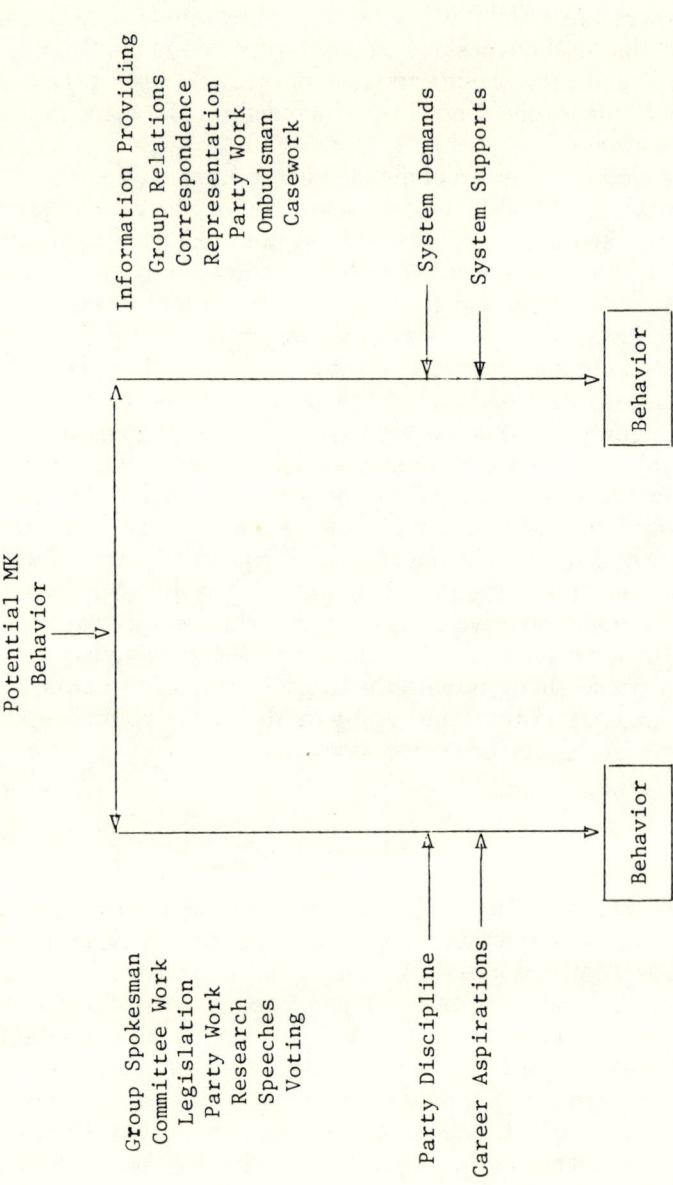

Figure 8.1

This portrait of controversy is one that perhaps implies more antagonism and hostility than really exists. In day-to-day life, when *major* policy debates are not being undertaken in the legislature, there is a remarkably low level of hostility between and among members of the Knesset, regardless of their party loyalties. After all, MKs are professional politicians, who must continue to work together, and one of the informal norms of behavior in the legislative world is one of impersonalization: don't make personal attacks, and don't take attacks on policy and positions personally. MKs have roles as members of committees, and as members of ethnic, geographical, and occupational groups, and many of these ties and identifications serve to weaken the pull of party conflict in the Knesset.

There is a great deal of contact between members of Knesset and the Government. For members of the Government parties, this contact takes place both within the Knesset and also within party caucus meetings. For members of the Opposition parties, the contact primarily takes place in the Knesset, as is pointed out shortly. Members of Knesset were asked how often they contact cabinet members—any cabinet members—in an average month, and their responses were indicative of an open Government, with a great deal of communication between legislators of both parties and members of the governing parties.

There is a great deal of contact between legislators and cabinet ministers. More than one MK in three (34.9 percent) indicated that he meets with a cabinet member "quite often (at least daily)." Just over half of the MKs (51.2 percent) indicated meeting with cabinet members "often." Only a few MKs indicated that they meet with ministers "not very often" (3.5 percent) or "rarely or never" (5.8 percent). These data serve as a model of the way a parliamentary government is supposed to operate, with a great deal of interaction between the legislative and executive branches of government, and with the executive separate from, yet still a part of, the legislature.

This contact between legislators and members of the Government takes place in a variety of settings. Over four of five members of Knesset (82.5 percent) indicated that their contact with ministers took place "in the Knesset, generally." The second most frequent response was that contact took place over the telephone, usually with the MK calling the minister at his office in his Ministry building (30.2 percent). Another response offered by a number of legislators was that their primary place of contact with ministers was in committee meetings, when the minister was invited to testify before the committee (24.4 percent). In short, we see a system in which there is a great deal of contact in a variety of settings.

There is a clearly perceived hierarchy of ministries in the eyes of the legislators in terms of which ministries are contacted more often than others. Table 7.8 indicated that several ministries were perceived as being "more important" than others. Only eight ministries out of nineteen, Defense (88 percent), Finance (82 percent), Foreign Affairs (71 percent), Education and Culture (46 percent), the Prime Minister's Office (44 percent), Justice (26 percent), Interior (21 percent), and Labor (20 percent) were named by at least one-fifth of the respondents. The interesting point here is that the ministries that were indicated by most MKs as being "most important" were *not* in every case the same as the ministries that were indicated by the MKs as being the offices of the ministers they contacted most often.

Table 8.1 shows responses to the question "Which ministers do you contact most often?" As the data indicate, there is a considerably wider dispersion of responses than was indicated in response to "important" ministries. The ministries that cannot really be included in the "glamorous" category, such as the ministries of Police, Housing, Health, Commerce and Industry, Immigration and Absorption, Agriculture, and Social Welfare, all showed marked increases in the frequencies with which they are indicated by MKs as being contact targets.

This should come as no surprise, though. In their "nonpolitical" roles, in which the MKs serve as ombudsmen, information gatherers, and troubleshooters, they are much more likely to have to go to the "nuts and bolts" agencies of the governmental organization than to the more philosophical or policymaking branches. Thus, the Ministry of Foreign Affairs, which is mentioned by 71 percent of the MKs as being an important ministry, is mentioned by only 26 percent of the MKs as being contacted often. Conversely, the Ministry of Police is mentioned as being contacted considerably more often than it is mentioned as being "important" (19 percent as contrasted with 2 percent).

Table 8.1

Which Ministers Are Contacted Most Often

	Mentioned as Contacted		Mentioned as Important		Difference Percent
Prime Minister or his Office	23%	(20)	44%	(38)	− 21%
Foreign Affairs	26	(22)	71	(61)	− 45
Defense	29	(25)	88	(76)	− 59
Justice	24	(21)	26	(22)	− 2
Police	19	(16)	2	(2)	+ 17
Labor	26	(22)	20	(17)	+ 6
Housing	30	(26)	10	(9)	+ 20
Education and Culture	27	(23)	47	(40)	− 20
Transportation	8	(7)	0	(0)	+ 8
Finance	37	(32)	83	(71)	− 46
Health	20	(17)	5	(4)	+ 15
Commerce and Industry	15	(13)	6	(5)	+ 9
Immigration and Absorption	15	(13)	5	(4)	+ 10
Agriculture	15	(13)	5	(4)	+ 10
Communications	5	(4)	1	(1)	+ 4
Tourism	9	(8)	0	(0)	+ 9
Interior	24	(21)	21	(18)	+ 3
Religious Affairs	10	(9)	6	(5)	+ 4
Social Welfare	17	(15)	3	(3)	+ 14

Members indicate that the reasons for their contacts with ministries vary, but virtually all of the reasons indicated fall into one of two categories, either constituency matters or policy matters, or both. Policy matters may come to the attention of the MK through a constituent request, and as such a very large percentage of MK contacts may be constituent-initiated. Twenty-three percent (twenty) of the MKs indicated that the reasons for most of their contacts with ministers were policy questions. Fifteen percent of the respondents indicated that they contacted ministers for both reasons.

Members of Knesset are realistic enough to know that simply because they have spoken with a cabinet minister does not mean that their problem is resolved. One MK in four (twenty-two) indicated that they felt they were "very, or quite successful" in "getting what you have asked for or getting your points across." Twenty-one percent (eighteen) indicated that they felt that they were "generally successful." The same number felt that it "depends on the subject and the minister involved," sometimes their efforts met with a successful outcome, sometimes not. Only seven MKs felt that they were generally "not very successful" with ministers.

The usual pattern of communications in the ombudsman or information-seeking role of the legislator is predictable. An MK will receive a question or complaint from a member of the public, for example, a request for help from a new immigrant who is having trouble finding housing and a job. The new immigrant, we will call him Simon Tov, has gone to the respective ministries of Housing, Immigration and Absorption, and Labor, and has not received the assistance he needs. He is now at a point of desperation and is it possible that Haver HaKnesset (member of Knesset) Nayim (a fictitious name) can help him? Tov has selected Nayim because of some shared characteristic they have; perhaps Nayim immigrated from the same country that Tov has recently come from. Nayim may have had the same occupation prior to entering the Knesset as that in which Tov is trying to find a job. Or, Nayim may have lived on a Kibbutz, and Tov hopes that as a kibbutznik Nayim will be understanding.

In any case, Nayim is contacted by Tov. This contact may be by telephone, or perhaps Tov will come to the Knesset for a meeting, or maybe they will meet elsewhere. (This point is discussed later.) After Nayim hears Tov's problem, and decides that it is a reasonable problem and that there is a possible solution, Nayim will probably go directly to the ministers in charge of the respective ministries rather than to the ministries themselves and directing his questions and requests for help to civil servants. Many members of Knesset will take their problems to the head civil servants of the government agencies, but just as many will avoid the bureaucracy completely and start their search for a remedy to a given problem at the top.

The interview data show that almost half of the members of Knesset interviewed indicated that they "very rarely or never" ($N = 41$, 48 percent) contacted a high-ranking civil servant, but instead took their constituents' problems directly to the minister involved. The Israeli bureaucracy is geared to this clientele style of problem solving, and therefore to take a problem to a lower level is usually neither as effective nor as efficient as starting one's inquiry at the top.

At this stage Nayim will either call one of the ministers involved on the telephone or search him out in the Knesset, and recount Simon Tov's problem. If the minister is sympathetic, if there is no policy question involved that prevents him from coming to Tov's assistance, the minister will usually ask MK Nayim for a written note on the matter, which the minister will then pass along to the director-general of the ministry (e.g., the director-general of Housing, Labor), who will pass the note along to a lower-level bureaucrat, who will then help Simon Tov, much as this bureaucrat could have done in the first place, were he or she not too busy addressing an earlier problem that had been passed down along a similar route.

Although about half of the MKs will take the "high road" and start their search for help with the minister, a number will start with a telephone call to a high-ranking civil servant. Fully half of the respondents ($N = 43$) indicated that they call civil servants on the telephone to discuss constituency problems. The ministries in which members of Knesset feel most likely to contact civil servants are not, again, the ministries that are regarded as being "most important" in a policy sense, but are the ministries that are most oriented to the day-to-day problems of the public. The ministries of Housing (26 percent), Labor (17 percent), Education and Culture (15 percent), Health (14 percent), Interior (14 percent), Agriculture (13 percent), Commerce and Industry (10 percent), and Social Welfare (10 percent), were all named by 10 percent or more of the MKs as being targets of communications with civil servants. Of all of these ministries, only Education and Culture was included among the "top five" in terms of "importance." Generally, however, the frequency of communication between members of Knesset and civil servants is not of the same quantity as is the communication between MKs and ministers.

The parliamentary system that operates in Israel, then, is one that functions in the classical model. Although the legislature is the base of power of the Government, in that the Government derives its power from the consent and confidence of the legislature, in reality the situation is one of "cabinet supremacy," not "legislative supremacy." The legislature is, in fact, led by the Government, rather than vice versa. There is, however, still a great deal of communication between the MKs and cabinet members, especially in terms of constituency problems. The pattern of operation of the Israeli bureaucracy is such that in many cases a "constituent to MK to Minister to civil servant" communication link is much more efficient than simply a "constituent to civil servant" link. In this role, as an ombudsman and information seeker, the MK probably feels the least pull of party discipline of any of the roles he or she plays. This leads to members of Knesset spending greater amounts of their time outside of committees and the Knesset assembly hall, and more time in the service of their constituency. It is these components of legislative behavior to which we now turn our attention.

Legislators and Committees

We saw in chapter 4 that many members of Knesset consider their roles as members of legislative committees to be among the most satisfying and effective aspects of their jobs. That is, there is a general belief among members that debate in the plenum is simply "going through the motions," since speeches virtually never cause MKs to change their votes. Similarly, since the direction of one's vote is something that is "guided" by party discipline, the act of voting itself loses its importance as significant individual legislative behavior for many of the MKs. Committee meetings, then, are left as virtually the only forum in which an individual can behave in a more or less self-guided manner, although, as has been noted, action in committee that blatantly goes against the party is not immune from discipline or sanction.

Committee assignments are important to members of Knesset, for there is a hierarchy among legislative committees, and there are a limited number of places on each of the committees. The decision was made at the start of the Fourth Knesset (November 1959) to limit membership on the standing committees to nineteen members,[1] and this decision has served as a precedent since that time.

Members of Knesset belong to a varying number of committees, ranging from none to four. MKs who are part of the Knesset leadership—either the Speaker or one of the Deputy Speakers—may choose not to hold seats on committees. Members of the Government do not hold committee positions. MKs who chair important committees may choose to limit their activity to that one committee, if they wish. Of the respondents, 13 percent (eleven) held seats on three committees, 58 percent (fifty) held seats on two committees, 24 percent (twenty-one) held seats on only one committee, and four individuals held leadership positions and therefore did not participate in committee behavior.

Our sample of MKs included almost an even number of members of each committee, ranging from a high of twenty members on the Finance Committee to a low of twelve members of the State Controller Committee. Although membership on the committees was fairly evenly distributed, the committees to which the members indicated an interest in belonging was not evenly distributed, as Table 8.2 indicates.

Table 8.2

Committee Membership and Committee Interest

Committee	Respondents on Committee	Respondents Interested in Committee
Knesset Committee	16	4
Constitution, Law, Justice	14	8
Finance	20	19
Economics	13	3
Labor	14	12
Foreign Affairs and Security	16	21
Education and Culture	16	11
Interior	14	13
Public Services	15	10
State Controller	12	1

The range of interest is impressive. Some of the committees, notably the Foreign Affairs and Security Committee, and the Finance Committee, have a much greater attraction to members of Knesset than do most other committees, and some committees, most notably the State Controller, Economics, and Knesset committees, clearly have less drawing power. The three committees with the biggest appeal to members of Knesset are the three committees indicated in the fourth chapter as being the exceptions to the rule of committee impotence, Finance, Labor, and Foreign Affairs and Security.

Committee work in the Israeli Knesset, which is similar to

committee work in the U.S. Congress and many other national legislatures, consumes a very large share of the members' time. Thirty-seven percent (thirty-one) of the respondents indicated that they attended committee meetings "very often," more than six meetings a week. Another 46 percent (thirty-eight) of the MKs indicated that their committees met "often," at least four times a week. Twelve MKs indicated attending meetings "sometimes," and only two indicated attending meetings less than twice a week.

These data illustrate the relative importance of committees in the legislative behavior of MKs. Attendance in the plenum is low because the outcomes of votes and debates are known by all in advance on most issues. Committee behavior is another matter, however, because although the concept of party discipline exists in the committee, it is considerably more flexible in that forum in most instances (with the exception of major pieces of legislation), and committee norms encourage participation by all committee members, giving the individual MK the chance to take part in proceedings. When members were asked if they "generally stay for the whole or most of the meeting of a committee or do you generally leave early?" 94 percent (seventy-eight) indicated that they stayed for all of the meeting, and another 5 percent (four) indicated that they generally stayed for most of the meetings; only one MK indicated that he "rarely attended" committee meetings.

Committee preparation takes a good deal of time, as shown in Table 8.3. Although some MKs admit that they do little or no work in preparation for committee meetings, the great bulk of the members interviewed went out of their way to emphasize the amount of work they did to prepare for their meetings. As also indicated in the table, the members engage in a variety of activities in the name of preparing for committee meetings.

The overall impression that MKs have about the proper role of committees in the Israeli legislative system varies considerably, depending upon which member one talks to. Members were asked what the "principal function of committees" was, whether it was one of "shaping the substance of legislation, of providing an opportunity to present party positions on substantive issues, or of giving the individual MK an opportunity to participate in the policy process, or what?" As indicated in Table 8.4, there really

Table 8.3

Committee Work and Committee Preparation

A. Time spent in preparing for committee work.

None	13%	(11)
Little	6	(5)
Some	2	(2)
Moderate amount	8	(7)
Good deal	48	(41)
Great deal, a lot	10	(9)
Don't know/No answer	13	(11)

B. Types of preparation for committee meetings.

	Mentioned by	
	(N = 73)	
Reading documents, press	84%	(61)
Reading prepared by committee staff	30	(22)
Talking with public groups	23	(17)
Talking with experts	22	(16)
Unspecified research	15	(11)
Library work	11	(8)
Field trips	7	(5)
Letters, phone calls	3	(2)
Party caucus	1	(1)
Other	1	(1)

is no consensus on this question. One finding that may be gleaned from the data is that most MKs do not consider the committees to be totally ineffectual—only two MKs indicated that committees had "no functions" and were "useless." The general perception is that committees have a role in providing a forum for discussion and debate that may have variable influence on the substance of the legislation under examination, depending upon the specific legislation and the Government's attitude toward that legislation.

Virtually all of the members responding indicated that their work on committees had led them "to suggest policy changes or additions in areas of the legislation." Almost half of the MKs (41, or 48 percent) said that this happened "quite often," and almost as many (40, or 47 percent) said that this happened "frequently." These responses do not indicate how often these

Table 8.4

Perceived Functions of Legislative Committees

Mostly debate	23%	(20)
Specifically writing legislation	20	(17)
Depends on bill or committee	17	(15)
Generally shaping legislation	16	(14)
Party-line debate	10	(9)
Both shaping and discussion	9	(8)
No functions, useless	2	(2)
No answer	1	(1)

suggested policy changes or additions to legislation were either accepted by the committee in question or accepted by the Knesset from a committee report. These data are not available, but the MKs' responses certainly indicate a sense of efficacy, a perceived ability to have *some* degree of influence over both the substance and the direction of legislation coming before their committees.

This theme of relative efficacy and perceived impact is echoed by the data presented in Table 8.5, which indicates members' responses to the question "How could the influence of the individual member of Knesset on a committee be increased?" Only four MKs (5 percent) indicated that influence could not be increased under the present parliamentary and party systems; the rest of the MKs interviewed clearly felt, as reflected in the table, that there was (and is) some potential for influence in committees. The responses themselves are worth some examination. For example, *only one* MK indicated that he felt that his influence could be increased by having "less party discipline in committee"; apparently other MKs felt that this was not a factor affecting their influence in committees.

The most common response to this question touches upon a problem that has already been mentioned several times in this study, staff help. Just over two-thirds of all the respondents mentioned more staff help as a way of increasing the influence of the individual MK on a committee. The members again consistently mentioned the fact that any preparation for committee work had to be done by themselves, including reading, research, drafting legislative proposals, and the like, and they lamented the fact that time simply did not permit them to do as much preparation as they would like. Another large group of respondents (fourteen, or 16 percent) indicated a related aspect of this same situation. They indicated that the influence of members could be increased if more MKs would "do their homework and come prepared" to committee hearings. Again, many of the MKs admitted that they did *not* do their "homework" and came unprepared to committee precisely because they did not have time to do so; if they had staff help this situation would improve.

The other major response by members to this question focused upon the role of committees in the Knesset, generally. These members indicated that in order to increase the influence of individual MKs on committees the role of the committees vis-à-vis the Knesset (and the Government) would have to be improved. They indicated that committees would have to be given "teeth" so that their decisions would have some real meaning, and so that the Government could not simply disregard committee findings by insisting that bills be voted upon as they were originally introduced in the Knesset.

Many members of Knesset indicated that the committee chairman was very important in determining both the role of the individual committee as well as the effectiveness of the committee. An effective chairman is able to establish a good relationship in terms of communications and cooperation with the related Government ministry and civil servants, and this relationship, in turn, can give the individual MKs more influence in *their* rela-

Table 8.5

Factors That Could Affect MK Committee Influence

	Mentioned By (N= 82)	
Staff help	70%	(57)
Having committee decisions mean something; giving committees "teeth"	21	(17)
By MKs "doing homework" and coming prepared	17	(14)
Giving more power to committees	4	(3)
Requiring attendance	3	(1)
Having better chairmen	1	(1)
Less party discipline	1	(1)
Influence can't be increased	5	(4)

tions with the bureaucracy. The largest share of the respondents indicated that the most important role of the committee chairman was to select good topics for the committee agenda that were both timely and important. This factor alone, the members indicated, would make the difference between a committee being perceived as "important" or "influential" in the Knesset, and a committee being perceived as "insignificant." In all, 63 percent of the MKs responding to a question about the role of the committee chairman indicated that "selecting good topics for the agenda" was very important.

Several other roles that a committee chairman should play in order to be most effective in his or her job were also mentioned. Thirty-seven MKs responding indicated that they felt that a good chairman kept debate "under control" in committee hearings. It was felt if the chairman were able to keep debate under control—and this does not mean restricting debate, simply keeping it under control—then the committee would be able to accomplish more in the course of a meeting. Additionally, 37 percent of the members felt that a good chairman "invited good witnesses" to committee hearings. Again, the argument was made that good witnesses made for more productive sessions.

In short, many of the members see the committee structure as a major redeeming aspect of legislative behavior, one opportunity in which they can actively participate. In fact, when members were asked how much they participated in committee hearings, 65 percent indicated that they participated a "great deal," and another 12 percent (10) indicated that they participated a "fair amount." Only 16 percent of the MKs indicated that they participated "little" or "rarely."

Committees in the Knesset, then, are a significant structure in an examination of legislative behavior. The committees provide members with an opportunity to debate, discuss, and argue in an atmosphere that is not usually dominated by the pattern of party discipline that is characteristic of other types of intra-Knesset legislative behavior. In this sense, the committees are valuable both for what they do in a legislative sense, in terms of screening, amending, and modifying legislation, and for what they do in a psychological sense, in providing members with some perceived efficacy, opportunities for action, and perceived individual importance.

Legislators and the Knesset

In spite of the limited opportunities for individual and autonomous legislative behavior in the Knesset, members of Knesset do not completely withdraw from the Knesset plenum because of frustration or inactivity. When members were asked whether there were other ways, other than committees, in which they could influence the work of the Knesset, a number of alternative routes were suggested. Many of these routes we have already seen as being primarily symbolic, that is, not very effective or realistic in creating policy. Yet, members continue to suggest several possibilities, indicated in Table 8.6, as routes for individual MKs to influence the work of the Knesset.

Table 8.6

Areas Other Than Committees through Which MKs Could Influence the Work of the Knesset

	Mentioned by ($N = 85$)	
Through private member bills	44%	(37)
Through Motions for the Agenda or Urgent Motions for the Agenda	39	(33)
Through questions to ministers in question period	18	(15)
Through discussion in party caucus	15	(13)
Through public relations and press	11	(9)
Through speeches, generally	6	(5)
Through informal contacts with ministers	6	(5)

These data indicate that many of the legislative behaviors that were indicated in chapter 4 as being relatively ineffective in producing either legislation or change in the Knesset because of party discipline and other informal or formal Knesset rules are still regarded by many MKs as possible sources of influence in the Knesset. Members were quick to emphasize with these responses that influence and effectiveness had to be perceived as varying depending upon the legislation at hand and the Government's reaction to the legislation at hand. Governmental ambivalence or apathy provided the best environment for individual action and influence, because it meant that party discipline would be at a minimum.

As indicated earlier, attendance in the Knesset was not usually very high, with the exception of major votes during which virtually all MKs are present in the chamber to vote. Just one-quarter of the respondents, twenty-two, indicated that they spent a "great deal" of time on the floor of the Knesset. Another block of MKs, 31 percent (twenty-seven) indicated that they spent a "moderate amount of time, about average," in the plenum. Fully 38 percent said they spent "very little" time in the plenum, or attended "only rarely or not at all" (five MKs were unwilling to respond).

The MKs' responses show that most were skeptical at best, and cynical and rejectionist at worst, about opportunities for individual behavior in the Knesset. That is, they indicated that they continued to undertake activities such as introducing private members' bills, making motions for the agenda, and the like, but they really were not convinced that there was an overwhelmingly high probability of success for their endeavors. Many MKs stopped short of being cynical by taking a system-oriented perspective, indicating that the system simply was not designed for much autonomous individual legislative behavior in the Knesset, but rather was designed for the kind of party-dominated teamwork that exists in the legislature today.

Members inevitably commented that legislative ineffectiveness, party discipline, and possible frustration were fundamentally limited to the Knesset itself, to plenary activity, committee activity to a much less extent), speeches, private bills, and the like. Virtually all MKs pointed out that their behavior *outside* of the Knesset, their relationships with constituent groups, were basically uncontrolled and unregulated by the Knesset and their party organization, and as such they looked forward to spending time in these endeavors.

Legislators and Constituencies

The extralegislative sphere of activity is very important to members of Knesset in supporting their feelings of efficacy and usefulness, and a great deal of communication goes on between the MKs and their public. Because of the proportional representation electoral system within which they must operate, members of Knesset do not have strict geographical districts as do members of many other national legislatures. That is, since all of Israel is one national electoral district, no official districts are assigned to representatives.

This does not mean, however, that there are not "constituencies" in the political system and the legislative system. Constituencies exist, and they are as clearly defined and as consistently interpreted as if they were legal and official. As was mentioned in chapter 6 dealing with legislative recruitment, many legislators are recruited to the party lists primarily as an attraction to specific groups in the electorate, and it is clearly understood by all that if a given individual is elected to the Knesset, he or she will be the spokesman for the interest he or she was chosen to represent. This does not mean that an MK will turn away a member of the public with a problem if the individual does not fit into the MK's "constituency"; it simply means that in very many instances members of the public are aware that "their" MK is a specific individual, because he or she represents their representative interest group.

Members of Knesset communicate with all types of constituencies. When MKs were asked "Generally, what type of people communicate with you," virtually all the respondents indicated "all types" or "everyone" ($N = 81$). Most MKs maintain that although they might have been put on their party's electoral list to "represent" a specific group, their respective constituencies were considerably broader than simply the group they supposedly represented. Out of eighty-six respondents, only eleven indicated in their initial responses anything other than "everyone."

Subsequently, fifty of the respondents were able to identify more specific groups that were primarily oriented to them as contacts in the Knesset. Ten MKs (12 percent) indicated that they were primarily contacted by party members. This figure is at the same time high and low, because it indicates that many MKs are contacted by individuals who supported other political parties, but who see the MK as "theirs" in any case because of group identifications.

The bulk of the specific groups of constituents that were indicated by MKs were special interest groups or specific constituencies. A number of MKs—all the MKs from kibbutzim and moshavin—indicated that they were contacted by other kibbutzniks or moshavniks, not necessarily individuals from the same kibbutz or moshav, but individuals from *any* kibbutz or moshav. The feeling was that there are certain experiences or attitudes that all kibbutzniks and moshavniks have in common, regardless of party. Other groups mentioned were ethnic, occupational, or geographic. Responses such as "Bedouin," "Arabs," "laborers," "Sephardic Jews," and "residents of Dimona" were typical of these constituencies.

The interesting point illustrated by these responses is that although the party system in Israel is very highly developed, and party discipline and party behavior in the Knesset are second to none in strength in being able to regulate legislators' actions, when legislators are outside of the Knesset, their party labels somehow become less important. The members are still identified as belonging to a party organization, and they still communicate with party members, but a constituent who has a problem will still go to "his" MK, regardless of party.

Members of Knesset indicate that they receive a great deal of mail as a part of their link with the public. This causes the MKs some problem, as we suggested earlier, since MKs do not have secretarial assistance in handling all the correspondence that goes along with the job. Nevertheless, the MKs spend a great deal of time every day in correspondence, providing constituents with information, responding to questions and comments, and providing help whenever they can.

In all, 48 percent of the respondents (forty-one) indicated that they received a "great deal" of mail as part of their workload. Another 47 percent (forty) responded that they received "some" mail. Only 5 percent (five) indicated that they generally did not receive mail from the public. Mail received by MKs may be broken down analytically into two broad categories, public reaction to official matters and general constituency requests.

MKs indicated that mail communications from the public in reaction to official business was primarily directed at their Knesset speeches. MKs perceived that after they made a speech in the Knesset that was picked up by the media, mail regularly became oriented to that speech, either positively or negatively. Eleven MKs indicated that a good deal of their mail focused on the speeches they made in the Knesset. Other MKs indicated that they received a good deal of mail focusing on official business that either offered criticism of what the Knesset was doing (three MKs mentioned this), or offered suggestions for what the Knesset and/or the individual MK should be doing (ten MKs mentioned this).

By far the bulk of MKs' mail communications with the public falls in the area of general constituency requests. Ten MKs indicated that they received a great deal of mail requesting information about a variety of matters, from government spending on certain projects to how to get a variety of government permits. The majority of constituency requests were requests for help. In fact, fifty-nine of the respondents (69 percent) indicated that they had a good deal of mail focusing upon what could be called the "ombudsman" role, general requests for help. Another thirty-six respondents indicted that they also received mail asking for help with "personal" problems.

Mail is not the only link between MKs and the public; 91 percent (seventy-eight) of the respondents indicated that they received communications from the public in forms other than the mail. These other communications came by telephone ($N = 77$), outside of the Knesset in meetings with constituents ($N = 34$), from constituents who came to the Knesset with problems ($N = 45$), and occasionally even by telegram ($N = 2$). These various types of communications covered virtually the same concerns as did mail communications.

The extralegislative role of the MK is an important one to the MKs in providing them with a kind of behavior they can feel is beneficial and helpful to the public. This role is also important to the political system in helping to maintain support for the regime on the part of the public by showing the public that those who govern, those who enact the laws and policies of the regime, are paying attention to what the public thinks. The subtitle of this chapter, "intralegislative frustration and extralegislative effectiveness" is borne out by the MKs' responses to interview questions. With the possible exception of participation in committee activities, many MKs indicated that the major aspect of legislative life that they most enjoyed about being a member of Knesset was their ability to help the public.

Members were asked "Let's suppose that next week for some reason you had to give up being an MK. What would you miss most about not continuing in office?", and their responses clearly illustrate this point, as shown in Table 8.7. The two largest single categories of responses to the question "What would you miss most?" are committee work in the Knesset, and helping the public.

Table 8.7

Things MKs Would Miss Not Being in Knesset

Committee work	24
Helping people, being in the position to do so	17
Influencing legislation and policy	8
Activity	8
Being in the public eye	7
Holding formal Knesset position	4
Being in the center of things	3
Work in writing laws	3
Access to information	1
Other	11

These same two activities were again emphasized by MKs in their responses to the question "All in all, what aspects of an MK's job deserve more of his time and attention?" The single largest category of response was "helping the public" ($N=30$), followed by "committee work" ($N=23$). Many MKs also felt that the legislative aspect of their jobs, actually drafting laws, was something else that deserved more of the time and attention of individual legislators.

The activities that members felt deserved less of their time and attention are, as has already been mentioned, attendance in the plenum (having to listen to debates), and party work and party speeches in the Knesset.

Table 8.8

How MKs Feel Their Time Should Be Spent

	N
A. Activities deserving *more* time and attention	
Helping the public	30
Committee work	23
Legislation; drafting laws	18
Meeting people	8
Constituency work, generally	7
Specific Knesset issues	5
Becoming better informed	4
Keeping an eye on the government	1
B. Activities deserving *less* time and attention	
Attendance in plenum	16
Party work	15
Party speeches	11
Speeches in plenum	11
Social events	6
Committee work	3

Summary and Conclusions

The picture of legislative behavior that is painted by the interview data presented in this chapter is very likely typical of many parliamentary nations. That is, in a political system in which a legislator is primarily elected as a member of a political team and who is not really expected to exercise either innovativeness or autonomy, there is bound to be a great deal of frustration or cynicism on the part of the legislator, even if he or she knows what to expect prior to becoming a member of the legislature. Indeed, Mezey's essay on legislators in Thailand[2] clearly documents this. The Israeli instance, then, is not unique.

Analytically, legislative behavior may be separated into two spheres, intralegislative behavior and extralegislative behavior. This separation is necessary precisely because of the regimentation that occurs within the legislature: there is no point in undertaking roll-call analysis in a system of tight party discipline, and there is little point in examining individual legislative behavior that is neither expected nor encouraged. However, since individual behavior (in terms of autonomous behavior) is both countenanced and encouraged *outside* of the legislative body, as is the case in Israel, then an analytic separation of the two types of behavior not only is wise, it is necessary.

Within the legislature, Israeli members of Knesset generally feel constrained, as well they should. Most of their avenues of formal participation are "under the gun" of the party whip. Private bills, speeches, motions for the agenda, and, of course, voting, are all directed by party discipline. The only area within the Knesset in which the members are permitted to speak and participate semifreely, but an area that is still not entirely free of the influence of party discipline, is the legislative committee, and the data clearly show that members regard the committee as the point of their greatest efficacy and feel that more time and attention should be spent in that activity.

Outside of the Knesset members are relatively on their own and they find that their relations with their constituencies are extremely rewarding, even if they are quite time-consuming. Members believe that more of their time and attention should be spent in this kind of endeavor, and many indicated that the only aspect of their jobs that prevented them from being "robots" was their constituency work.

Legislative behavior in the Knesset, then, is a concept that must be understood in a specific context, the Israeli political system. Legislative behavior is at the same time quite insignificant and quite important. It is insignificant in that because of party discipline, who the legislators are really makes *very little difference* in the final product generated by the Knesset. Only a handful of individuals make a difference in the Knesset, and they are the party leaders who tell their party followers in the Knesset how to vote, what to say, and when to act. At the same time, it must be added that legislative behavior—and here we mean extralegislative behavior—is quite important in helping the system to survive, in educating the public, in political socialization, in political recruitment, and generally in maintaining and developing public support for the regime. Intralegislative frustration *can* be combined with extralegislative effectiveness to produce and support a democratic regime.

Notes

1. Ashner Zidon writes that "Beginning with the Fourth Knesset, the membership of the ... committees was fixed at nineteen." Ashner Zidon, *Knesset* (New York: Herzl Press, 1967), p. 207.
2. See Michael Mezey, "The Functions of a Minimal Legislature: Role Perceptions of Thai Legislators," *Western Political Quarterly* 25 (1972):686–701.

9

The Knesset in the Eighties

Introduction

This study was undertaken to gain a better understanding of those actors, structures, and behaviors that affect legislative behavior in Israel and thereby affect public policy, although policy questions were not directly addressed. The assumption was made that the legislature is important to study because policy decisions are made in that setting, regardless of the degree of individual legislative freedom or autonomy that might be exercised by members of Knesset.

The Israeli political system was surveyed in a broad way. We examined the constitutional and legal structures that are significant in the system and which influence the behavior of those actors who are significant in the operation of the Israeli political world. We saw the manner in which political parties and elections are structured, and the manner in which they, in turn, have profound consequences for political behavior in Israel.

The nature of coalition government as it exists in Israel was discussed in chapter 3, and a detailed historical analysis of cabinet formation and coalition behavior was presented. We saw that the very existence of coalition government has had significance for Israeli politics on several occasions, both in terms of policies that have been enacted by the Government, and in situations in which no policy was enacted, because the very fragile nature of the government coalition required inaction.

Although most of this study was directed to the individual legislator in the legislative system, the legislative system itself was also discussed. The Knesset was portrayed as a parliamentary system, and the role of the individual member of Knesset within that system was discussed. The thorough discussions of who the legislators are, demographically, politically, and attitudinally, included a description of the political socialization and political recruitment of MKs and the significance of several of their early-life political experiences.

Finally, we turned our attention to the legislator's perceptions and behavior in the contemporary political system. We examined the manner in which the legislator perceived his or her job, his or her colleagues, and the legislative system within which the legislator must operate. Data were presented describing what the legislator does within the legislative system.

The discussion of legislative behavior in the Knesset would not be complete without considering three additional points of interest. First, what *comparative* observations can we make about the structure of the Knesset and behavior in the Knesset as we have observed it? What significances or similarities or differences can be observed between the Israeli legislative system and other legislative systems? Second, does the 1977 ascendancy of Menachem Begin and the Likud and the termination of the thirty-year political domination of the Mapai-led Labor Alignment—temporary or not—affect any of the conclusions that have thus far been drawn? How can Mr. Begin's rise to power in 1977 be explained in light of the earlier discussions? Finally, we consider some of the proposed reforms before the Knesset and the future of the domestic Israeli politics, generally.

Some Comparative Observations

The Israeli political system is essentially a British-model parliamentary political system, but there are some significant deviations from the British model. Constitutionally, Israel does follow the Westminster model to a large degree, choosing to rely upon unwritten constitutional doctrines: the specific Fundamental Laws of Israel that deviate from the

Westminster model are attempts to clarify "fuzzy" aspects of the unwritten constitution.

The proportional representation electoral framework found in Israel is a major deviation from the Westminster model of single-member-district representation that is found in virtually all the Commonwealth nations. Not only is this deviation significant in its own right—as a structural deviation from the Westminster structure—but it is significant because of the *consequences* that flow from its existence: multiple political parties and increased ideological diversity. In other proportional representation systems, of which Italy is a good example, we find characteristics similar to the Israeli pattern: there are many political parties of a more ideological nature. Since there are many parties, no one party receives a majority of legislative seats, which necessitates the creation of coalition governments.

The history of political coalitions in Israel has been in some respects similar to, and in other respects different from, the experiences of other regimes. Israeli coalitions have been more stable than those found in Italy, for example, because once initial coalition agreements are made in Israel they are generally honored, resulting in general regime stability. The *number* of parties in the Israeli case, as well as other factors discussed in chapter 3 including ideology, loyalty to former coalition partners, uncertainty, and the national security issue, all serve to make the Israeli coalition-formation process unique.

Demographically, members of Knesset are typical of legislators in other systems. They are older than the general population, and minority groups and women are underrepresented in the legislative population. The members of Knesset differ markedly from legislators in other systems, though, in terms of the kinds of experiences they report as part of their early political socialization and recruitment. In this respect one of the factors that makes Israel a unique nation—its Jewish character—is of serious consequence in terms of the socialization processes reported earlier, with their focus on Zionism and Anti-Semitism.[1]

One term is paramount in a discussion of political recruitment, attitudes, perception, legislative roles, and legislative behavior of the individual member of Knesset: party. The

Knesset is typical of other parliamentary systems in that party discipline is of significance in voting in the legislature. The Knesset varies from other legislative systems, however, in the degree to which the party permeates the political environment. One of the major themes of this book is the importance of party in the Knesset, the *extreme* dependence of the individual member of Knesset on his or her party and party organization, and the results of this dependence. The main result of the power of the party is the impotence of MKs as evidenced by their intralegislative behavior. However, in extralegislative behavior, MKs tend to be active and efficacious.

The Ascendancy of Menachem Begin

Since the data utilized in this analysis come from interviews conducted with members of the Eighth Knesset (1973-77), a word about the effect of the passage of time on the findings reported here is in order. Because the focus of our analysis has been the legislative *system* and those factors that are influential in the legislative system, rather than specific individual legislative leaders, a change in the national leadership has very little consequence in terms of the applicability of those ideas that have been suggested.

Fundamentally, the Israeli political system did not change with the election of Menachem Begin in 1977. Israel is still a single national electoral district with proportional representation and an electoral list, and Begin's ascendancy had no effect on these structures. Party discipline, a concept that has been frequently mentioned in this analysis, is a tool that Begin has used during his thirty years in the legislative opposition. He did not indicate any intention of changing traditional patterns of behavior once he became head of the Government rather than leader of the Opposition.

It is obvious that a Likud government had certain implications for Israeli government, such as a Likud speaker of the Knesset, more Likud committee chairmen, and the like. There is no reason to believe, however, that Begin's rise to power in any way detracts from any concept that has been considered in our analysis; most of the MKs in the Ninth Knesset were also in the Eighth Knesset, and patterns of political socialization, political recruitment, legislative perceptions, and legislative behavior have not changed because of a change of the individuals who are in power.

It is safe to say that although many political observers in Israel were predicting another net Labor loss of votes in the 1977 Knesset elections, it came as a surprise even to the most ardent Likud supporters that the Likud coalition won a plurality of seats in the Knesset. We discussed in chapter 2 the historic gradual decline of the size of the Labor alignment in the Knesset and the correspondingly gradual increase of the Herut/Gahal/Likud opposition. Table 9.1 presents the results of the 1977 elections compared to the results of the 1973 elections, indicating a continuation of the historical pattern.

A comparison of the two elections reveals not a "mandate" for Mr. Begin and the Likud coalition but rather an extreme rejection of the Labor party. Labor has been gradually losing public support for the last several elections, winning sixty-three seats in 1965, fifty-six seats in 1969, fifty-one seats in 1973, and thirty-two seats in 1977,[2] but the drop in its support in 1977 was not simply an extension of past patterns—it went far beyond that. Credit for the Labor disaster may be attributed, at least in part, to two factors: Labor party leadership and the creation of a new political party, the Democratic Movement for Change.

The new Labor leader, Shimon Peres, indicated after the election that corruption in his party was the major cause of the Labor defeat in the election. During the Seventh and Eighth Knessot there were scandals in the Finance Ministry, the Bank of Israel, and personal financial illegalities committed by the Labor Prime Minister (Rabin) and his wife, among other events. These events simply led to the public perception of the Labor party as a whole becoming corrupt, and a good share of the public was looking for new leadership.

This led to the second factor, a new political party. The Democratic Movement for Change was created on the eve of the 1977 elections, and although this party drew suupporters from all across the Israeli ideological spectrum, including former Herut and Free Center supporters, members of the Citizens' Rights Movement, and others, its membership was *primarily* drawn from former Labor supporters. Individuals

Final Results of Elections to the Ninth Knesset May 17, 1977

	1977 Votes	1977 Percent	1973 Votes	1973 Percent	Gain/Loss %	Seats '77	Seats '73	Gain/Loss
Eligible Voters	2,236,293		2,037,478					
Votes Cast (%)	1,771,726	(79.2)	1,601,098	(78.6)				
Invalid Ballots (%)	23,906	(1.3)	34,243	(2.1)				
Key for Knesset Seat	14,173		12,451					
Likud	583,075	(33.4)	473,309	(30.2)	+ 3.2	43	39	+ 4
Alignment (Labor)	430,023	(24.6)	621,183	(39.6)	−15.0	32	51	−19
Democratic Movement for Change	202,265	(11.6)	-	-		15	-	+15
National Religious Party	160,787	(9.2)	130,349	(8.3)	+ 0.9	12	10	+ 2
Agudat Yisrael	58,652	(3.4)	60,012	(3.8)	+ 1.0	4	5	0
Poalei Agudat Yisrael	23,956	(1.4)				1		
Democratic Front for Peace and Equality (Rakah + Black Panthers)	79,733	(4.6)	53,353	(3.4)	+ 1.2	5	4	+ 1
Shelli (Moked, 1973)	27,281	(1.6)	22,147	(1.4)	+ 0.2	2	1	+ 1
Shlomozion (Ariel Sharon)	33,947	(1.9)	-	-		2	-	+ 2
Flatto-Sharon	35,049	(2.0)				1		+ 1
Independent Liberals	21,277	(1.2)	56,560	(3.6)	− 2.4	1	4	− 3
Citizens' Rights	20,621	(1.2)	35,023	(2.2)	− 1.0	1	3	− 2
United Arab List (Arab Lists)	24,185	(1.4)	39,012	(2.5)	− 1.1	1	3	− 2
Hofesh (Black Panthers)	2,498	(0.1)	13,312	(0.9)	− 0.8	0	0	
The New Generation	1,802	(0.1)				0		
Kach (Rabbi Kahane)	4,396	(0.2)	12,811	(0.8)	− 0.6	0	0	
Women's Party	5,674	(0.3)				0		
Arab Reform Movement	5,695	(0.3)				0		
Beit Yisrael (Yemenites)	9,505	(0.5)	3,195	(0.2)	+ 0.3	0	0	
Coexistence with Justice (Arab)	1,085	(0.1)				0		
Zionist Panthers	1,798	(0.1)	5,945	(0.4)	− 0.3	0	0	
Zionist and Socialist Renewal (Mordecai Ben Porat)	14,516	(0.8)	-	-		0	-	
Other Lists in 1973 (7 lists)			40,624	(2.8)				

Source: *Jerusalem Post: International Edition*, May 31, 1977, p. 9.

who had supported the Labor party for their entire lives were presented with an alternative that was unusually attractive: a party that was essentially of the same ideology as Labor, that had electoral reform as its major campaign platform, an issue that was bound to appeal to a population that was tired of what it perceived as an old, corrupt leadership. It is clear from Table 9.1 that of the 15 percent of the vote that Labor lost between the 1973 and 1977 elections, the Democratic Movement for Change (DMC) gained the lion's share—12 percent—whereas the Likud only gained 3 percent of the vote. This 3 percent increase was enough to give the Likud four extra seats in the Knesset and to put Likud in the position for the first time in Israel's history of being the party to form Israel's Government.[3]

The election returns were a surprise to all, and a shock to many. Virtually all of the Israeli press had been speculating the week prior to the election as to the coalition arrangement in a new—and further weakened—Labor cabinet. Stories appeared in the press about the intentions of the Likud leadership deciding not to be "a shadow cabinet," but instead to make every effort to be an effective opposition without handing out "portfolios."[4] Abba Eban forecast that the DMC and the NRP would both join the Labor party in a government coalition, and intimated "that the government might embrace 'those elements in the Likud who realize the futility of staying indefinitely in the opposition.'"[5] On the day of the election the Labor alignment was issuing ultimatums to the DMC that if the DMC did not modify its platform, it would not be admitted to the Government coalition.[6]

The problem that everyone was having was not entirely the result of inaccurate polls. Of the two polls the final weekend before the election, one predicted forty-four seats for the Labor alignment and thirty-eight or thirty-nine for the Likud, and the other predicted the Labor alignment and the Likud both with thirty-eight and thirty-nine seats. Both polls, however, found a very high percentage of the electorate still unwilling to commit itself, with "more than 20 percent" of the persons interviewed unwilling to indicate their preferences.[7]

Once the returns were in, and after the various actors had recovered from the surprise of the returns, there was no shortage of *post hoc* analysis. Peres attributed the Labor defeat "to a number of domestic and international trends" but also cited the "failure of demoralized party activists to push hard for victory," adding that "corruption hurt us the most."[8] The National Religious party was surprised to find that it had gained two seats in the new Knesset; the feeling had been that its two-seat loss in 1973 from the 1969 Knesset election results had been the start of an antireligious party trend, and it had been expecting to lose one or two more seats in 1977. In response to the electoral returns, party Secretary-General Zvi Bernstein indicated that the general public was "fed up with 'licentiousness and absence of values' in Israeli society and has come to see that the NRP stands for the values that are lacking."[9]

The task immediately before Menachem Begin was to find enough support to create a majority coalition. Immediately after the election, former General Ariel Sharon announced that his "Shlomozion" party (with two seats in the new Knesset) would merge with the Likud, bringing the Likud total to forty-five seats in the Knesset. Begin now needed to find another sixteen seats. After excluding the parties that were clearly incompatible with Likud, such as the Communists, Begin was left with a reasonably short shopping list of potential partners: the National Religious Party (twelve), Agudat Israel (four), Poale Agudat Israel (one), the Democratic Movement for Change (fifteen), Samuel Flatto-Sharon's one-man party, and the Labor alignment (thirty-two). Begin invited Peres to join in a "Government of National Unity," but Peres declined. Begin's options were thereby narrowed.

The Democratic Movement for Change, meanwhile, found itself in an interesting situation. Its electoral strategy had been to gather enough votes to make itself indispensable to a Labor coalition, at which point it would have been negotiating from a position of strength and could demand major electoral reform, one of its principal concerns. What the DMC found was that whereas its goal had been to be indispensable to a Labor government coalition, it had, in fact, killed its supposed partner and it was *still dispensable* to the Likud.

Begin invited Peres and "all loyal parties"[10] to join in a national unity government one more time. There was some concern within the Likud party about creating a coalition with the Agudat Israel/Poale Agudat Israel parties as part of the Government. Their extreme religious orthodoxy meant that on some political questions they simply could not be counted upon to vote with the Likud, and the Likud leaders were hoping that a coalition could be created that would not have to depend upon them.

Begin's first major controversial move was to invite Moshe Dayan—who had run for the Knesset in the number seven position on the Labor list—to join the Government as minister of foreign affairs. Dayan, after all, had a worldwide reputation, and Begin was hoping that this would add to the legitimacy of the new Government. The Labor party was in an uproar—mostly directed at Dayan for "selling out"—and the Likud party was mad as well; many Likud supporters argued that they had voted for the Likud because they wanted a *change* in leadership, and bringing Dayan on board as foreign minister was hardly that. The Likud executive board passed a compromise resolution that reaffirmed "Begin's right to make the nomination [as Prime Minister designate], but did not . . . endorse the nomination."[11] Because of this appointment the DMC temporarily broke off coalition negotiations with the Likud.

Meanwhile, it was beginning to look more and more as though the Likud (with forty-five seats) would have to depend on the religious parties, the National Religious party (twelve) and the two Agudah parties (five), to attain majority status and create a coalition. In spite of the DMC's refusal to negotiate, the Likud and the religious parties were continuing to discuss the details of their coalition agreements.[12]

The DMC was, in reality, eager to join the coalition for both positive and negative reasons. The leadership of the DMC felt that it could provide a crucial balance in influencing the thrust of the new Government's foreign policy if it were part of the cabinet; in the opposition its influence would be minimal, to say the least. The leaders of the DMC also felt that the party might well disintegrate as a cohesive political force if it were forced to spend four years as the junior party of the opposition. If the DMC was anxious to join the coalition, the Likud was just as anxious to have the DMC join. This was true primarily because the Likud wanted to "modify the image of a hawkish government, and to reduce its dependence on the religious parties."[13] This fear of dependence on the religious parties is very similar to the "uncertain information" factor that was suggested in discussing Israeli coalition formation in chapter 3. The DMC made two initial demands for entering the coalition: the Foreign Ministry for Yigal Yadin, the party leader, and major electoral reform within two years. These demands were not entirely satisfactory to the Likud, since it had already promised the Foreign Ministry to Dayan, and the Likud was not in a rush to undertake electoral reform, having just won its first plurality in thirty years.

As time went on, Likud leaders grew weary of the DMC's demands and indicated that the DMC leaders "had better make up their minds soon whether they want to join the Likud;"[14] the Likud leaders indicated that if the DMC did not start cooperating, they would go before the Knesset with a bare minimum winning coalition, if need be. On June 14, 1977, about a month after the election, Begin acted on this basis, and announced that he would go ahead with his cabinet, even without the DMC's support. Combining the Likud's forty-five seats with twelve of the NRP and four of the Agudat Israel party gave Begin sixty-one votes, a majority. An independent MK, Samuel Flatto-Sharon, indicated that he would vote with the Government, even though he was not formally a part of the coalition. There was also some hope that the one-seat Poale Agudat Israel party would later join the coalition, too. This brought the total to sixty-three seats, perhaps sixty-four if Moshe Dayan kept his Labor-won seat, and Begin felt confident that he could proceed, at least for the time being, on that basis. He did, however, leave the invitation to the DMC open: Yadin could have the posts of deputy prime minister and minister of social betterment, and the DMC could have two additional ministries, if the DMC were to join the coalition.

On June 21, the coalition agreement was signed by the three participating parties, and the agreement reflected the influence and the indispensability of the religious parties in the new government. The agreement included a proposed amendment to the Law of Return so that only conversions made according to the Halacha (religious laws) could be recognized, a position that had long been advocated by the religious parties. Also in the agreement was a proposed amendment to the Anatomy and Pathology Law to ban autopsies "without the family's written consent," since religious Israelis had objected to mandatory autopsies in the past. Legislation would also be introduced to ensure that Sabbath observers would not be discriminated against in their jobs for refusing to work on the Sabbath, stricter enforcement of the laws prohibiting publication and distribution of pornographic literature would be undertaken, and so on.[15]

Begin presented his coalition to the Knesset on June 20, 1977, and received a vote of confidence by a 63–57 margin. He indicated that he would keep the ministries of Social Betterment, Justice, Transport, and Communications open for the DMC for four or five weeks in case the party changed its mind. It took the DMC until October 24 to decide to join the coalition, and even then the vote of the DMC membership on the question of whether or not to join the coalition was 68–45.[16]

The final coalition contract between the DMC and the Government contained three major conditions. First, the DMC retained freedom of expression in the Knesset and the freedom to abstain (but not to vote against the Coalition) on all matters relating to Judea and Samaria. (The DMC position on this issue was one of favoring concessions, whereas the Likud position was clearly the opposite.) Second, the DMC retained a free vote on *all* religious matters. Third, the Coalition agreed to set up a committee of the four coalition parties (Likud, DMC, NRP, and AI) to take up the topic of electoral reform. This committee would decide upon the number of regions into which the country might be divided for district-based representation, if such were to be the case. The DMC retained freedom of vote on the proposed bill to come out of this committee.[17]

Menachem Begin thus found himself at the end of 1977 with the strongest coalition in Israeli politics in almost ten years, with seventy-eight Knesset seats represented in the cabinet, considerably larger than the "minimum winning coalition" size discussed in chapter 3. The reasons for Begin's desire to go beyond the minimum winning size have already been indicated: a

The Knesset in the Eighties

desire to appear to have a more moderate coalition and a desire to not be in the position of having to depend on the religious parties for the basis of a coalition.

Following his election in 1977, Begin had his ups and downs in the Knesset and in public opinion polls. The DMC splintered as a party and only a few of its seats remained in the Begin Government, lowering Begin's margin of safety. In early 1980, inflation in Israel was running at about 133 percent per year, unemployment was on the rise, and polls showed that if elections were held at that time the Likud under Begin would lose to the Labor Alignment by twenty-five Knesset seats (30–55). The polls also showed that if Ezer Weizman, who resigned as Defense Minister in June of 1980, were leading the Likud it would lose to the Alignment by only two seats (45–47).[18] Although no one can predict what the future holds in store for individuals or parties in the Israeli political arena, one point is clear: the fact that the Likud party finally penetrated the Labor party's monopoly on power makes the Likud a much more viable alternative to Labor in the future, and party turnover in office—the substituting of Labor governments for Likud and Likud governments for Labor—will very likely be much more frequent in the future than it has been in the past.

Reforms in the Knesset

To the surprise of no one, the DMC's proposals for electoral reform, which the DMC characterized as central to any reform of Israeli politics, have not received universal acclaim in the Knesset in the time since the DMC joined the Likud government in 1977. The leaders of the DMC knew when they signed the coalition agreement with the other parties that setting up a committee of the four coalition parties to "study" their reform proposal was comparable to putting a cat *in* a bird cage to protect the bird; Agudat Israel had openly condemned the proposal before the elections, and both Likud and the NRP were skeptical, at best. Although neither the Likud nor the NRP have openly officially supported the Agudat Israel desire to kill the DMC proposal, they certainly have not rushed into the fray to help the DMC, either.

What would the consequences of the DMC plan for electoral reform be? Although one cannot be positive, because the DMC has not unveiled its intentions down to the smallest detail, it is safe to say that the consequences of this *type* of change would be enormous. To change from an electoral system based upon proportional representation and a single national electoral list as we have described it, to *any* kind of district-based representation as suggested by the DMC—regardless of the actual number of districts to be decided by the cabinet committee and regardless of the number of MKs per district to be chosen—would have crucial consequences for party discipline in the legislature. Giving legislators a specific district and constituency to which they are to feel responsible should lessen the vulnerability of the individual MK to the party leadership to some degree, because of the absence of the single national party list. For this reason many of the non-DMC party leaders are opposed to the reform, which would reduce their control over who is elected to the legislature. The Likud's having won a plurality of the seats in the Knesset for the first time in thirty years is also not a great incentive for members of the Likud to demand change now.

Assuming that broad system-level structural changes do not take place, what trends in Israeli politics can be foreseen? There are four aspects in a response to this question: (a) preelectoral coalitions, (b) coalition governments, (c) Israeli voting behavior, and (d) the future of religious parties.

The trend toward preelection grand coalitions of several identifiable political parties that retain their individual identities is a practice we have discussed earlier. There is no reason to expect this practice to decline in the near future. Although the creation of new political parties continues to be a fairly common occurrence in Israeli politics, these parties often come to the conclusion that the way to maximize their electoral chances is to join in one of the preelection grand coalitions, either with the Likud or with the Alignment.

Similarly, there is no reason to expect a change in the pattern of Israel's coalition governments. This comment does not pretend to predict *which* parties will form future governmental coalitions, but rather addresses the need for coalitions themselves. No single party in Israeli history has ever won 50 percent of the seats in the Knesset—to a large degree because of the sheer number of parties involved in the contest for Knesset seats: the more parties involved in the struggle, the less seats are available for individual parties to win in the electoral process.

Having just indicated a likelihood that coalitions will continue to be a part of the Israeli political landscape, a word can be said about the parties that might belong to such coalitions, a function of voting behavior in Israel. The Begin victory in 1977 that led to the first Likud government in Israeli history, based upon Likud winning 33 percent of the votes, to a very large degree can be credited to the formation of the Democratic Movement for Change and the subsequent split in the Labor vote in Israel. Regardless of how or why Likud came into power, it seems clear that forming the Government has given the Likud a certain respectability that many Israelis felt it lacked prior to 1977, feeling that the Likud was only an opposition party.

Whether a Likud or a Labor alignment ends up winning a plurality in the 1981 election, it seems clear that another thirty-year period of Labor rule is extremely unlikely. Assuming that Labor is able to bring in the "new blood" and "fresh faces" that many feel it so desperately needs, and assuming that Labor loses the taint of corruption that apparently plagued it in the 1977 election for the Ninth Knesset, the Likud *could* find itself in the opposition again. The important point to note is that the Likud's new respectability makes this only a possibility, not a certain outcome. Many in Israel, who in the past would never have supported the Likud because it was perceived as an extremist party, perpetually in the opposition, have now decided that the Likud is a reasonable alternative to the Labor alignment, and having proven its ability to govern—regardless of policy outcomes—the Likud has become a much more viable alternative to Labor hegemony than it was before it had a chance to demonstrate its ability. One thing seems certain: future Israeli voting behavior will result in far greater party turnover in office than has been experienced in the past, regardless of DMC/Labor relations.

The religious parties have traditionally been the odd partners in coalitions; to a large degree their concerns have fallen outside much of the traditional "left-right" spectrum of political affairs. Their primary concerns include the role of Halacha (religious laws) in daily life, the "Jewish" character of the State of Israel, and Governmental policy toward occupied territory. This has made it possible for the religious parties to join in coalitions with both the Labor and Likud parties.

The religious parties have pretty consistently received from 10 to 15 percent of the popular vote in recent years. This consistency is to a large degree the result of the fact that their constituencies are fairly rigidly defined; as a general rule, the bulk of their electoral support comes from Orthodox groups, and the bulk of Orthodox Jews supports the religious parties. As the secular population in Israel increases or decreases (and trends point to the latter, not the former), we can expect to see slight shifts in support for the religious parties, but there is no reason to expect drastic change one way or the other.

Israel is, it might be recalled, still a very young nation with a short (modern) political history upon which it can draw. A great deal of time must pass before any of Israel's political structures or behaviors are as institutionalized as comparable structures and behaviors are in other Western democracies. Thirty years is a short time in which to build and develop a political infrastructure, especially given the fact that such a large proportion of the attention of both the Israeli government and the Israeli public in that period of time has been devoted to questions of governmental and systematic *survival*, not structural details.

Israel is a study in contrasts, that have been evident throughout this book. These contrasts, Western versus non-Western, developing versus developed, old versus new, religious versus secular, all have been seen to be reflected in politics, either in the political parties and the way they operate, in coalition agreements between and among parties, in electoral lists, or in some other manner, but they are present nonetheless.

A study of the Israeli Knesset, then, is undertaken from two different perspectives: as a study of a national legislature and as a study of political institutions of a particular nation-state. First, as a study of a national legislature the Knesset exhibits a fascinating combination of characteristics that are traditionally found in Western democratic legislatures, combined with a large number of characteristics that are idiosyncratic to Israel. Second, as a study of a democratic political system in a Middle Eastern setting in which democratic political systems do not customarily last a long time, the study of Israeli politics tells us a great deal about one particular nation's attempt to resolve societal problems in a democratic and peaceful way.

Many questions have yet to be resolved in the Israeli political system, constitutional questions, societal questions, and political questions. Although there undoubtedly will be moments of stress in Israeli politics in the future, our study of the Knesset has illustrated the firm commitment to democratic government and the positive approach to the future that are characteristic of both members of Knesset and the Israeli population at large.

Notes

1. For one comparative analysis, examining both the Israeli and the Canadian cases, see Gregory Mahler, "Political Consciousness and Political Events: A Study of Israeli and Canadian Members of Parliament," *Political Science* 31 (December 1979):89–107.
2. These data represent the combined returns of the parties that later merged to form Labor: Mapai, Ahdut HaAvodah, Rafi, and Mapam.
3. For an analysis of the election returns, see Don Peretz, "The Earthquake: Israel's Ninth Knesset Election," *Middle East Journal* 31 (1977):251–266.
4. *Jerusalem Post International Edition* (henceforth JPIE) April 19, 1977, p. 5.
5. JPIE, May 10, 1977, p. 1.
6. JPIE, May 17, 1977, p. 1.
7. Ibid.
8. JPIE, May 24, 1977, p. 6.
9. Ibid., p. 7.
10. Ibid., p. 10.
11. JPIE, May 31, 1977, p. 8.
12. Ibid., p. 3.
13. JPIE, June 7, 1977, p. 2.
14. Ibid., p. 1.
15. For a fuller discussion of this, see JPIE, June 21, 1977, p. 2.
16. This long-drawn-out process was covered in some depth by the press. See the following issues of JPIE: June 28, p. 6; July 5, pp. 1, 2, 10; July 12, p. 3; July 26, p. 3; August 9, p. 1; and September 12, p. 5.
17. JPIE, October 25, 1977, p. 1.
18. JPIE, February 3, 1980, p. 4.

Appendix 1

A Note on the Interviews

Meeting with members of any national legislature can be quite difficult, and this was the case in Israel, despite most legislators' perceptions of themselves as "citizen legislators," accessible to the public. This was true not so much because legislators refused to be interviewed, although a few (e.g., Prime Minister Rabin and Foreign Minister Allon) did indicate that an interview would not be possible, but primarily because legislators who agreed in principle to be interviewed had difficulty in finding time to speak with me.

Many strategies were employed to arrange interviews. The first approach involved face-to-face contact, when that was possible. I obtained a special photographic supplement to the *Jerusalem Post* that came out immediately after the elections for the Eighth Knesset, and tried, with picture galley in hand, to arrange appointments with members of Knesset by talking to them as they were entering the Knesset. Most of the backbenchers were so surprised that a foreigner would recognize them that they immediately consented to be interviewed.

A second approach involved the use of the telephone. I secured a list of the unlisted home telephone numbers of all the MKs (since they had no offices) from a sympathetic member of the Knesset staff, who asked to remain anonymous. Members of Knesset who were not available going to and from the Knesset were contacted by telephone and asked for an appointment. Most consented in principle to such a meeting.

A third approach involved the use of intermediaries. Three individuals were especially helpful in this regard. Two members of Knesset, Hillel Zeidel and Arie Eliav, were not only congenial and helpful in their own interviews, but went out of their way to help arrange interviews with other MKs—both in their parties and in other parties—who could not be contacted in other ways.

These were certainly not the only MKs who helped arrange interviews with their colleagues, but these two were especially helpful. The third principal intermediary was a Knesset page, Itzik Mazon, who had access to the inner reaches of the legislature and who was able to go after MKs when they were inaccessible to the public.

All counted, a very high percent (about 85 percent) of the MKs agreed in principle to be interviewed. Problems developed in applying principle to schedules, however. Appointments were forgotten by MKs, or, more often, emergency situations arose, and very often appointments had to be rescheduled or re-re-scheduled. One example is typical. The minister of transportation, Gad Yacobi, was a member of Prime Minister Rabin's "inner cabinet"; his influence in the Government was far greater than his position in the Ministry of Transportation would suggest. Yacobi was very willing to be interviewed, although he was quite busy, and an appointment had to be set up about four weeks ahead of the time of the interview. The day before the interview was to take place, Henry Kissinger flew into town (this was in the spring of 1975 when shuttle diplomacy was at its peak), requiring the rescheduling of the interview since Yacobi had to be available to the prime minister. The appointment was rescheduled for four weeks later. Four weeks later Kissinger would return. This happened a total of four times, and Mr. Yacobi never was interviewed.

The interviews themselves took from forty-five minutes to two hours, depending upon the MK involved and the degree to which he or she felt like expanding his or her comments (and telling stories). It was not permitted to take a tape recorder into the Knesset building, and since it immediately was apparent that MKs responded better to questions if I did not take notes, I followed the strategy explained by Matthews in *U.S. Senators and Their World* (p. 271). After asking questions from a prepared schedule I did not take notes but instead wrote up the interview immediately after it was finished.

Since the MKs did not have private offices, these interviews took place in a variety of settings, including the MKs' homes, the public cafeteria in the Knesset, the MKs' dining room, committee meeting rooms, party caucus rooms, and the Knesset's library. The interview was administered in four languages:

English, Hebrew (for MKs who either spoke no English or French or who preferred to do the interview in Hebrew), French (for the MKs who preferred French to English as a second language, or in the case of two MKs from Morocco, whose French was better than their Hebrew), and Arabic (for the Bedouin MK who spoke neither English, French, nor Hebrew). I did the translating for the French and Hebrew interviews, and the Knesset interpreter helped with the Arabic interview.

All of the information included in this book is derived from the highly structured interview schedule. A number of the MKs became interested in my work during the interview, and would stop and talk—sometimes at great length—whenever they would see me in the Knesset. These unstructured interviews provided a great deal of background material. A number of other individuals, either legislative staff or workers in party headquarters, were very helpful to me in filling in details when questions came up.

Appendix 2

The Interview Schedule

I. BACKGROUND

I would like to begin, if we can, by getting a little information about you.

1. Where were you born? When was this? Where were you raised?
2. [record sex] What is your religious affiliation?
3. [Only if not born in Israel] When did you come to Israel? With whom did you come?
4. How frequently do you attend religious services?
5. What was the last grade of school you completed?
6. Have you attended a university or college?
[if yes] Which one? Do you have a degree from a university or college?
Have you attended a graduate or professional school?
[if yes] Which one? Do you have a degree from a graduate or professional school?
7. What was the original national background of your family on your father's side? On your mother's side?
8. What was your father's usual occupation while you were growing up?
By and large, how would you describe your family's situation in your childhood by the standards of that time? Would you say you were (1) very badly off, (2) below average, (3) average, (4) above average, or (5) very well off?
9. Do you consider your position as an MK to be your principal occupation?
[if no] What do you regard as your principal source of income?

What was your occupation when you were elected to Knesset?

10. Can you name for me the two or three most important professional, civic, fraternal, or religious organizations to which you currently belong? Are you an officer in any of these organizations?

11. [Only if immigrant] With which, if any, Jewish/Zionist/Israeli organizations did you affiliate before you came to Israel? What positions, if any, did you hold in it/them?

II. POLITICAL SOCIALIZATION

Now I would like to move on and ask you to recall some of the events of your early childhood and school life that are concerned with politics.

12. Now, would you go back as far as you can remember to tell me two things. What is the first aspect of politics or public affairs that you were aware of? [If immigrant, this means before coming to Israel] How old were you at that time?

13. During this time would you say your father's/mother's interest in politics was very strong, quite strong, not very strong, weak, or parent had no interest? [record for each]

14. Was there ever discussion about politics in your home at this time? [if yes] Would you say there was a great deal of discussion, some discussion, or not much discussion?

Was your father ever active in politics at this time? Your mother? How were they active? [e.g., Did they hold elected public office, appointed public office, were they candidates for office, did they hold party office, etc.]

15. As a child in grade school or earlier, did you personally know any people who then held a public office, either elected or appointed?

During this same period of your life, were any of the people on this list that you might have been close to either active in politics or public affairs, or inactive but very interested in politics and public affairs? [List in-

Appendix 2

cludes: brother(s) and/or sister(s); more distant relatives; family friends; schoolmates; religious leaders; neighbors; neighborhood merchants; family doctor or lawyer; school teachers; youth group leader; other]

16. Thinking back now, how did you first become interested in politics? [Probe for *age*, *event*, and *circumstances* surrounding first interest.]

[*Note*: Questions 17-20 are to be asked only of new immigrants whose responses to questions 12-16 described non-Israeli events.]

17. Now could you tell me what was the first aspect of politics or public affairs relating to Israeli issues that you were aware of? How old were you at that time?

18. With whom did you live following your immigration to Israel?
Shortly after your arrival in Israel, can you remember which, if any, political party your ( ) preferred?
During this time would you say that your ( )'s interest in politics was very strong, strong, moderate, weak, or very weak?
Was there ever discussion about politics in your home at this time [if yes] How much discussion was there?
Was your ( ) active in politics during this time? [If yes] How was he/she active?

19. As a child in grade school or earlier, did you know personally any people who then held a public office, either elected or appointed?
During this same period of your life, were any of the people on this list that you might have been close to either active in politics or public affairs, or inactive but very interested in politics and public affairs? [see list Q. 15]

20. Thinking back now, how did you first become interested in Israeli politics? [Probe for *age*, *event*, and *circumstances* surrounding the interest.]

Now I would like to ask you a few questions about how you became attached to a particular political party.

21. When did you first begin to identify with a political

party? That is, a party you felt sympathetic, close, and loyal to? How old were you at this time, and where was this?

Which of the things on this list, if any, were important factors in the development of your sympathies for this party? [List includes: materials used for school courses; teachers; school friends and other schoolmates; immediate family members and other close relatives; friends, acquaintances, and neighbors; work experiences and co-workers; religious activities; recreational activities; examples set by public figures; important events that may have occurred; platform, policy of the party.]

Were your parents also supporting that party at the time?

[If party mentioned above is *not* an Israeli party, ask:] Did you ever identify in this way with another party before coming to Israel?

[If party mentioned above is *not* an Israeli party, ask:] When did you first begin to identify with an Israeli political party? How old were you at the time? What party was this? Which of the things on this list [see above] were important factors in the development of your sympathies for this party?

Have you ever identified in this way with another Israeli party? [if yes] How old were you when you changed allegiances, and which, if any, of the items on the list were important factors in changing your sympathies and identifications?

When did you begin to identify with your current party? [If Respondent immigrated to Israel with parents] And what was your father's/mother's Israeli party identification?

22. When you were growing up, did you belong to any political groups or organizations in school—that is, while you were in high school? In University?

23. And how about your friends? Were most of them interested in politics, were some of them interested, or were most not interested?

24. Now let's consider the whole period from when you

Appendix 2

first became aware of politics until you first became active in politics. In general, how closely did you follow politics and public affairs during this period? Did you follow them very closely, somewhat closely, or very little or not at all?

25. How well informed would you say you were compared to most people your age during this same period? Were you better informed than average, about average, or less informed than average?

26. How important were such matters to you during that same period? That is, if you followed politics and public affairs closely, would it have mattered to you if you couldn't have?

27. Of all the experiences, influences, and events between the time you first became aware of politics and the time you first became active in politics, which were particularly important in moving you in the direction of being active in politics?

III. POLITICAL RECRUITMENT

That question leads to my next topic, how you actually began a career in public life.

28. Had you ever been elected to a public office before becoming a candidate for a Knesset seat, or had you ever been appointed to a public or semipublic office? [if yes] What were these offices, and when did you hold them?

   Had you ever been a candidate for public office even before you held your first office? [if yes] What was/were the(se) office(s) for which you were a candidate? [get dates]

   Can you recall how it happened that you first became a candidate for the office? [Repeat the name of the first office for which he was a candidate and then the date; probe for circumstances, agents involved, whether he volunteered or was recruited, whether he had any opposition to his nomination, and what his motives were.]

29. Were you already a regular, active, and committed party

worker at the time you first became a candidate for public office? [if yes] How old were you when you became an active party worker? [if yes] What kind of activities did you perform?

[if no] Did you become an active and committee party worker before you became a candidate for a Knesset seat? [if yes] How old were you at that time, and what kind of activities did you perform?

30. Speaking of parties, have you ever held a formal party office? [if yes] What was this office?

31. Legislators in this country and in other Western democracies have given a variety of reasons to explain why they became active in politics initially. What do you think are the most important reasons people have for getting into politics? What about in your case?

Was there any particular person or group who encouraged you to enter public life, or was this pretty well a decision you made on your own?

32. Thinking now of how you were nominated for a Knesset seat, had you ever tried to secure a nomination for a Knesset seat before, but been unsuccessful? [if yes, record when]

Can you recall what things were important in making you try again to get a nomination?

What, in your opinion, were the reasons that you received the party's nomination at that time? That is, what were the important factors, people, and organizations that were instrumental in your nomination?

Can you recall why you decided to make the race for a Knesset seat?

33. In how many Knessot have you been a member?

Before this Knesset, had you been on your party's list for election, but not been successful? [if yes] Was your success a result of your name being moved up on the party's list? What do you think were the factors responsible for your name's being moved up on your party's list between elections?

[if elected to a previous Knesset] Did your position on the party list change between elections? Why do you think this happened?

Appendix 2

What activities do you currently perform for your party?

34. Do you think that today it is important for MKs to represent specific groups?
Which groups do you consider most important, local groups, occupational groups, ethnic groups, or some other kind of group?
Do you feel that you represent any group(s)? [if yes] Which one(s)?

35. What group, if any, played the most important role in your name being placed on the party list? [e.g., Central party headquarters, local party committees, a kibbutz movement, an ethnic or occupational group]

36. Do you expect to run for the Knesset again?

37. Are there any other public offices, elected or appointed, that you would like to hold sometime in the future?

IV. PERCEPTIONS

38. I've been told that every legislature has its unofficial rules of the game, certain things that members must do and certain things they must not do if they want the respect and cooperation of their legislative colleagues. What are some of the rules that a member must observe if he wants to have the respect and cooperation of his follow members?
Would you name four or five of your fellow members, regardless of party or position, who are most widely respected for following these "rules of the game"—I mean people that a new member should look up to when he's just learning the ropes.
Some members don't seem to have the respect and cooperation of their fellow members because they don't follow the "rules of the game." What are some of the things that may cause a member to lose the respect and cooperation of his fellow members? How do other members make things difficult for these people when they don't follow the "rules of the game." How did you hear of these rules? That is, was there someone who talked to you after the election but

before you took office, or did people talk to you after you took office, or did you just learn about them on your own.

In general, how do you feel about these informal rules? Do you strongly like them, like them, dislike them, strongly dislike them, or are you indifferent to them? Do you feel that your ability to accomplish your goals in the Knesset is greatly increased, increased, unaffected, decreased, or greatly decreased by these informal rules?

In regard to action designated to accomplish your goals in the Knesset, because of these informal rules are you much more likely to act, somewhat more likely to act, somewhat less likely to act, or much less likely to act in effort to reach you goals—or is your likelihood of action unaffected by the existence of these rules?

39. Just before you took office, did you have any ideas about what the job of being an MK entailed? [if yes] What were they?

[if yes] And during your first year as an MK, did things work out just about the way you expected them to, or were they somewhat different?

Of all the things you did during that first year, which did you find were the most gratifying? The most burdensome?

[if in the Knesset more than one term] Have these gratifying and burdensome acts changed over the years?

40. Did becoming an MK require you to make any adjustments from your previous life? [if yes] What were some of the major adjustments you had to make?

41. What are the most important things you have tried to accomplish as an MK?

42. What are the most important things you want to accomplish in the future?

43. Are there any changes in procedure or in the way the Knesset operates that you think would make it easier for MKs to accomplish their goals?

44. Do you feel there are differences between what you want to accomplish and what your party colleagues in the Knesset want? What?
45. Is there any particular area of work in the Knesset that you feel you have become an expert in? What?
How did you acquire your expertise in the(se) area(s)? Is there any particular area that you would like to become an expert in? Why?
46. What would you say are your chances of becoming a member of the Cabinet in the future, if you were reelected and your party were a part of the Government?
Why do you think this is so?
Are there any specific actions on your part that you feel could improve these chances?
From your own experience and based on the experience of others, what do you think are the principal criteria applied in selected Cabinet members?
47. To whom do you consider yourself accountable for what you do as an MK? [if more than one] Which of these is most important to you?
48. Could you rank the items on this list for me in terms of their usefulness in providing good advice or information? [List includes: editorial opinions; party leaders; business leaders; union leaders; religious leaders; leaders of ethnic groups; personal friends; friends in the Knesset; people with expertise on issues; people who write in; one's own common sense]

V. BEHAVIOR

[*Note*: Questions 49 and 50 are not asked of ministers. Question 51 is asked only of ministers.]
Let's talk about ministers for a moment.
49. How often do you contact a minister during an average month?
How do you usually contact a minister?
Which ministers do you contact most often—that is, the ministers of which departments? [record up to 5]

Is the occasion for such contacts usually constituency matters, interest groups matters, or in regard to the policy of the department?

How successful would you say you have been in getting what you have asked for or in getting your points across?

How do you determine how successful you have been?

Has it been your experience that there generally is little contact between ministers and other members? [if yes] Why do you think there have not been more contacts?

50. And how about deputy ministers, how often do you contact deputy ministers or other high ranking civil servants in an average month?

How do you generally contact a deputy minister or senior civil servant?

Which departmental deputies or civil servants do you contact most often? [record up to 5]

Is the occasion for such contacts usually constituency matters or in regard to the policies of the departments?

How successful would you say you are in getting what you have asked for, or in getting your points across?

How do you determine how successful you have been?

Has it been your experience that there is little contact between members and deputy ministers or other high-ranking civil servants? [if yes] Why do you think there have not been more contacts?

51. [*only* cabinet members] How often do members of your own and the opposition parties contact you during an average month?

How do they usually contact you?

Do members of your own or the opposition parties contact you most?

Is the occasion for such contacts usually matters having to do with the member's constituency or the policies of your department?

How successful would you say members are in getting what they ask for or in getting their points across?

Has it been your experience that there is little contact

Appendix 2

between ministers and other members? [if yes] Why do you think there haven't been more contacts?

52. Let's turn for a moment to Knesset committees. How many committees are you currently a member of? Which ones?
Which committees are you most interested in?
How often do you attend meetings of the (   ) committee? Do you generally stay for the whole meeting of a committee, or do you generally leave early? Which aspects of the committee's work especially interest you? Why?
How do you generally prepare for a committee meeting?
Do you think the principal function of committees is one of shaping the substance of legislation, of providing an opportunity to present party positions on substantive issues, or of giving the individual MK an opportunity to participate in a meaningful way in the policy process, or what?

53. Has your own work on committees led you to suggest policy changes or additions in any area?

54. How could the influence of the individual MK on a committee be increased?

55. What role ought a committee chairman to play in order to be most effective in his job?

56. Are there other ways, other than committees, that individual members of the Knesset could influence the work of the Knesset?

57. How much would you say that you participate in committee hearings? How do you participate?

58. How much would you say that you participate in debate on the floor of the Knesset? What do you do?

59. In comparison to other members of your party, did you have to do much campaigning in the last election?
What do you think is the most effective way of campaigning?
Generally speaking, what are the major items or areas on which campaign funds must be spent?
What percent of the Israeli electorate do you feel votes

according to traditional party loyalties rather than according to party issues positions?
60. Do you get much mail? What is the mail that you get generally about?
Do people communicate with you in other ways, such as personal visits or telephoning? What are these other types of communication usually about?
61. Generally, what type of people communicate with you? Are they average citizens, your friends and acquaintances, business associates, local political leaders, community leaders, spokesman for interest groups, or what?
62. Let's suppose that next week for some reason you had to give up being an MK. What would you miss most, not continuing in office? Are these the things that keep you in the Knesset? [if no] What are the things that keep you in the Knesset?
63. All in all, what aspects of an MK's job do you think deserve more of his time and attention? Less of his time and attention?
64. One finds, particularly through political biographies of Israel's leaders, that some MKs are mentioned consistently as being more influential in the Knesset than others, despite the fact that a number of these were never in the Cabinet, or even in the front benches of their parties. Who, in your mind, are the *ten* most influential members of this Knesset—regardless of party?
65. What things would you say contribute most to the influence that each of these men has in the Knesset? [record a factor for each "influential"]
66. Who are the three men, whether in your party or in another party, whose advice, opinions, and good judgment you especially value?
67. What, in your opinion, are the five most important Ministries? The five most important Knesset committees?

VI. POLITICAL PARTIES

68. Could you place the political parties in the Knesset for me on a scale, and then label the scale?

Appendix 2

69. Do you think there can be too much party competition in a country? [if yes] Under what circumstances?
70. How about the situation here in Israel? Would you say there is too much party competition, the proper amount of party competition, or not enough party competition? Why?
71. What role ought party leaders to play in order to be most effective in their jobs?
72. What in your opinion is the motivation behind the choice of coalition partners in the formation of a Government?

VII. LEGISLATIVE FREEDOM

73. How much influence do you feel individual MKs have in the formation of Government policies?
74. How much freedom are individual MKs allowed in their actions, generally? [e.g., voting, debating] Does this vary from party to party?
75. Do you think individual MKs should have more or less opportunity to act on an individual basis? Why?
76. Are there any circumstances when you feel it is not necessary to vote with your party? What are these?
77. How many times have you gone against a party whip since the start of this Knesset?
    What were the issues involved on the(se) occasion(s)?
78. What were the results of these actions on your part?

Bibliography

Akzin, Benjamin. "The Role of Parties in Israeli Democracy." *Journal of Politics* 17 (1955):507–45.

Albert, J. "Constitutional Adjudication without a Constitution: The Case of Israel." *Harvard Law Review* 82 (1969):1245–65.

Almond, Gabriel. "Introduction: A Functional Approach to Comparative Politics." In *The Politics of the Developing Areas*, edited by Gabriel Almond and James Coleman. Princeton, N.J.: Princeton University Press, 1960.

Arian, Alan. Ideological Change in Israel. Cleveland: Press of Case Western Reserve University, 1968.

———. *The Choosing People: Voting Behavior in Israel*. Cleveland: Press of Case Western Reserve University, 1977.

———. "Were the 1973 Elections in Israel Critical?" *Comparative Politics* 8 (1975):152–65.

———. "Stability and Change in Israeli Public Opinion." *Public Opinion Quarterly* 35 (1971):19–35.

———, and Weiss, Sheva. "Split Ticket Voting in Israel." *Western Political Quarterly* 22 (1969):375–89.

Axelrod, R. *Conflict of Interest*. Chicago: Markham, 1970.

Badi, Joseph. *The Government of the State of Israel*. New York: Twayne, 1963.

Ben-Dor, Lea. Jerusalem Post Editor. Jerusalem, Israel. Interview, March 21, 1975.

Ben-Gurion, David. *Israel: A Personal History*. New York: Funk and Wagnalls, 1971.

Blondel, Jean. *Comparative Legislatures*. Englewood Cliffs, N.J.: Prentice-Hall, 1973.

Brams, Steven, and Riker, William. "Models of Coalition Formation in Voting Bodies." In *Mathematical Applications in Political Science VI*, edited by J. Herndon and J. Bernd. Charlottesville, Va.: University Press of Virginia, 1972.

Brichta, Abraham. "Women in the Knesset." *Parliamentary Affairs* 28 (1974–75):31–50.

Brinker, Menachem. "A Battle of Intepretation: The Last Campaign in the Israeli Elections." *Dissent* 24 (1977):356–58.

Browne, Eric. "Testing Theories of Coalition Formation in the European Context." *Comparative Political Studies* 3 (1971):391–412.

———, and Franklin, Michael. "Aspects of Coalition Payoffs in European Parliamentary Democracies." *American Political Science Review* 67 (1973):453–69.

Burstein, Paul. "Social Cleavages and Party Choice in Israel: A Log-Linear Analysis." *American Political Science Review* 72 (1978): 96–109.

———. "Political Patronage and Party Choice among Israeli Voters." *Journal of Politics* 38 (1976):1024–32.

Campbell, Angus, et al. *The Voter Decides*. Evanston, Ill.: Peterson and Co., 1954.

Clarke, Harold, and Price, Richard, eds. *Recruitment and Leadership Selection in Canada*. Toronto: Holt, Rinehart and Winston, 1977.

Cormack, M. "The Australian Senate." *Parliamentarian* 53 (1972): 175–85.

Czudnowski, Moshe. "Legislative Recruitment under Proportional Representation in Israel: A Model and a Case Study." *Midwest Journal of Political Science* 14 (1970):216–48.

———. "Socio-Cultural Variables and Legislative Recruitment." *Comparative Politics* 4 (1972):561–87.

Dawson, Richard, and Prewitt, Kenneth. *Political Socialization*. Boston: Little, Brown and Co., 1969.

DeSwann, Abraham. *Coalition Theories and Cabinet Formations*. San Francisco: Jossey-Bass, 1973.

DeVine, Donna. "The Modernization of Israeli Administration." *International Journal of Middle Eastern Studies* 5 (1974):295–313.

Duverger, Maurice. *Political Parties*. New York: John Wiley, 1963.

Easton, David. "A Re-assessment of the Concept of Political Support." *British Journal of Political Science* 5 (1975):435–57.

———, and Dennis, Jack. "The Child's Image of Government." *The Annals of the American Academy of Political and Social Science* 261 (1965):40–57.

Etzioni, A. "Kulturkampf ou Coalition: Le Cas de Israel." *Revue Francais de Science Politique* 8 (1958):311–31.

Etzioni-Halevy, Eva. "Protest Politics in the Israeli Democracy." *Political Science Quarterly* 90 (1975):497–520.

Fein, Leonard. *Israel: Politics and People*. Boston: Little, Brown and Co., 1966.

Freudenheim, Yehuda. *Government in Israel*. New York: Oceana, 1967.

Froman, Lewis, and Skipper, James. "An Approach to the Learning of Party Identification." *Public Opinion Quarterly* 27 (1963):473–80.

Gamson, William. "A Theory of Coalition Formation." *American Sociological Review* 26 (1961):373–82.

Goodland, Thomas. "A Mathematical Presentation of Israel's Political Parties." *British Journal of Sociology* 8 (1957):263–66.

Gottschalk, Rudolf. "The Jurisdiction of the Courts of Israel in Maritime Law." *International and Comparative Law Quarterly* 23 (1974):873–79.

Greenberg, Edward. *Political Socialization*. New York: Atherton, 1970.

Greenstein, Fred. *Children and Politics*. New Haven: Yale University Press, 1965.

Gutmann, Emanuel. "Israel." *Journal of Politics* 25 (1963):703–17.

———. "Some Observations on Politics and Parties in Israel." *India Quarterly* 17 (1961):3–29.

———, and Landau, Haim. "The Political Elite and National Leadership in Israel." In *Political Elites in the Middle East*, edited by George Lenczwoski. Washington, D.C.: American Enterprise Institute, 1975.

Herman, Valerie, and Pope, John. "Minority Governments in Western Democracies." *British Journal of Political Science* 3 (1973):185–97.

Hopkins, Raymond. "The Role of the MP in Tanzania." *American Political Science Review* 64 (1970):754–71.

Israel Government Yearbook. Jerusalem, 1974.

Jacob, Herbert. "Initial Recruitment of Elected Officials in the United States." *Journal of Politics* 24 (1962):705–18.

Jerusalem Post (Jerusalem, Israel): January 16, 21, 1974.

Jerusalem Post International Edition (Jerusalem, Israel): April 19, May 10, 17, 24, 31; June 7, 21, 28; July 5, 12, 26; August 9; September 12, 1977.

Jewell, Malcolm. "Linkages between Legislative Parties and External Parties." In *Legislatures in Comparative Perspective* pp. 203–34, edited by Allan Kornberg. New York: David McKay, 1973.

———, and Patterson, Samuel. *The Legislative Process in the United States*. New York: Random House, 1973.

Johnston, Scott. "Politics of the Right in Israel." *Social Science* 40 (1965):104–13.

———. "Party Politics and Coalition Cabinets in the Knesset." *Middle Eastern Affairs* 13 (1962):130–38.

Kadashai, Yechiel. Likud Party Secretary. Jerusalem, Israel. Interview, April 3, 1975.

Katzover, Israel. Secretary-General of Jerusalem Branch of Agudat Israel Party. Jerusalem, Israel. Interview, February 15, 1975.

Kornberg, Allan. *Canadian Legislative Behavior*. New York: Holt, Rinehart and Winston, Inc., 1967.

———; Clarke, Harold; and Watson, George. "Toward a Model of Parliamentary Recruitment in Canada." In *Legislatures in Comparative Perspective*, edited by Allan Kornberg, pp. 250–81. New York: David McKay, 1973.

Labovitz, Sanford. "Statistical Usage in Sociology: Sacred Cows and Ritual." *Sociological Methods and Research* 1 (1972):13–38.

Langton, Kenneth. *Political Socialization*. New York; Oxford University Press, 1969.

LaPalombara, Joseph. *Politics within Nations*. Englewood Cliffs, N.J.: Prentice-Hall, 1974.

Leiserson, Michael. "Factions and Coalitions in One-Party Japan." *American Political Science Review* 62 (1968):770–87.

Ley, J. "Strengthening the Position of the Backbencher in Papua, New Guinea." *Parliamentarian* 53 (1972):303–8.

Likhovski, Emmanuel. *Israel's Parliament*. Oxford: Clarendon Press, 1971.

Limaye, M. "On Private Members' Bills." *Journal of Constitutional and Parliamentary Studies* 3 (1969):110–13.

Loewenberg, Gerhard. *Modern Parliaments: Change or Decline?* Chicago: Atherton, 1971.

Lynsky, J. "The Role of the British Backbenchers in the Modification of Government Policy." *Western Political Quarterly* 23 (1970): 333–47.

Mahler, Gregory. "Political Socialization and Political Interest in Israeli and Canadian Legislators—A Comparative Examination." *Political Science Review* 19, no. 2 (August 1980):1–27.

———. "Political Consciousness and Political Events: A Study of

Israeli and Canadian Members of Parliament." *Political Science* 31 (December 1979): 89–107.

———, and Trilling, Richard. "Coalition Behavior and Cabinet Formation: The Case of Israel." *Comparative Political Studies* 8 (1975): 200–233.

Matthews, Donald. *U.S. Senators and Their World*. New York: Vintage, 1960.

McMullin, A. "Proposed New and Permanent Parliament Houses for the Australian Parliament." *Parliamentarian* 51 (1970):263–69.

Mezey, Michael. "The Functions of a Minimal Legislature: Role Perceptions of Thai Legislators." *Western Political Quarterly* 25 (1972): 686–701.

Mosca, Gaetano. *The Ruling Class*. Edited and revised by Arthur Livingston. Translated by Hannah Kahn. New York: McGraw-Hill, 1939.

Nachmias, David. "A Temporal Sequence of Adolescent Political Participation." *British Journal of Political Science* 7 (1977): 71–84.

———. "The Right Wing Opposition in Israel." *Political Studies* 24 (1976):268–80.

———. "Coalition Politics in Israel." *Comparative Political Studies* 7 (1974):316–33.

Nie, Norman, et al. *Statistical Package for the Social Sciences*. New York: McGraw-Hill, 1975.

Oren, S. "Continuity and Change in Israel's Religious Parties." *Middle East Journal* 27 (1973):36–54.

Paltiel, K. Z. "The Israeli Coalition System." *Government and Opposition* 10 (1975):397–414.

Parenti, Michael. "Ethnic Politics and the Persistence of Ethnic Identification." *American Political Science Review* 61 (1967):717–26.

Patterson, Samuel, and Boynton, G. Robert. "Legislative Recruitment in a Civic Culture." *Social Science Quarterly* 50 (1969):260–75.

Patterson, Samuel, and Wahlke, John. *Comparative Legislative Behavior: Frontiers of Research*. New York: John Wiley, 1972.

Peretz, Don. "The Earthquake: Israel's Ninth Knesset Election." *Middle East Journal* 31 (1977):251–66.

———. "The War Election and Israel's Eighth Knesset." *Middle East Journal* 28 (1974):111–25.

Pettifer, J. "Privilege in the Parliament of the Commonwealth of Australia." *Parliamentarian* 53 (1972):280–91.

Piaget, Jean, and Weil, Anne-Marie. "The Development in Children of the Idea of the Homeland." *International Social Science Bulletin* 3 (1951):561–78.

Raphaeli, N. "The Senior Civil Service in Israel." *Public Administration* 48 (1970):169–78.

Riggs, Fred. "Legislative Structures: Some Thoughts on Elected National Assemblies." In *Legislatures in Comparative Perspective*, edited by Allan Kornberg, pp. 39–93. New York: David Mc Kay, 1973.

Riker, William. *Theory of Political Coalitions*. New Haven: Yale University Press, 1962.

———, and Ordeshook, Peter. *Introduction to Positive Political Theory*. Englewood Cliffs, N.J.: Prentice-Hall, 1973.

Robinson, J. "Staffing the Legislature." In *Legislatures in Developmental Perspective*, edited by Allan Kornberg and Lloyd Musolf, pp. 367–90. Durham, N.C.: Duke University Press, 1970.

Rossetti, Michael. "Israel's Parliament." *Parliamentary Affairs* 8 (1955):450–58.

Sager, Samuel. "Israel's Provisional State Council and Government." *Middle Eastern Studies* 14 (1978):91–101.

———. "Pre-State Influences on Israel's Parliamentary System." *Parliamentary Affairs* 25 (1972):29–49.

Singhvi, Laxmi. "Parliament in the Indian Political System." In *Legislatures in Developmental Perspective*, edited by Allan Kornberg and Lloyd Musolf, pp. 179–227. Durham, N.C.: Duke University Press, 1970.

Sisson, Richard. "Comparative Legislative Institutionalization: A Theoretical Explanation." In *Legislatures in Comparative Perspective*, edited by Allan Kornberg, pp. 17–38. New York: David McKay, 1973.

Swanson, W. "Voting Behavior in a Nonpartisan Legislative Setting." *Western Political Quarterly* 25 (1972):39–50.

Tufte, Edward. "Improving Data Analysis in Political Science." World Politics 21 (1969):641–54.

Von Neumann, John, and Morgenstern, Oscar. *Theory of Games and Economic Behavior*. Princeton, N.J.: Princeton University Press, 1944.

Wahlke, John, et al. *The Legislative System*. New York: John Wiley, 1962.

Weiss, Sheva, and Brichta, Abraham. "Private Members' Bills in Israel's Parliament." *Parliamentary Affairs* 23 (1969):21–33.

Wences, R. "Electoral Participation and the Occupational Composition of Cabinets and Parliaments." *American Journal of Sociology* 75 (1969):181–92.

Wheare, Kenneth. *Legislatures*. New York: Oxford University Press, 1968.

Wolf-Phillips, Leslie. "The Westminster Model in Israel." *Parliamentary Affairs* 26 (1973):415–39.

Zidon, Asher. *Knesset: The Parliament of Israel*. New York: Herzl Press, 1967.

Index

Accountability of MKs, 102-3, 177
Acquisition of expertise, 172-74
Ages of MKs, 106
Agriculture Ministry, 190; as a coalition payoff, 74
Agudat Israel party, 39, 48, 61, 217, 218, 220; organization of, 42
Ahdut HaAvodah party, 39, 44, 66, 67
Akzin, Benjamin, 39
Allon, Yigal, 226
Almond, Gabriel, 138
Aloni, Shulamit, 101, 168
Anatomy and Pathology Law, 220
Anti-Semitism and political awareness, 123
Arbelli, Shoshana, 168
Attendance in Knesset, 171, 202
Attractive committees in Knesset, 195
Axelrod, Robert, 69

Bader, Yosef, 168
Balfour Doctrine, 118
Begin cabinet of 1977, 58; creation of, 213-21
Begin, Menachem, 29, 68, 167, 168, 179, 211, 214, 217-21
Ben-Dor, Lea, 101
Bernstein, Zvi, 217
Boynton, G. Robert, 139
Browne, Eric, 75
Burdensome characteristics of MKs' job, 165-66

Cabinet: formation of, 36; membership in, 174; party seniority in, 175-77; payoffs to coalition partners, 75

Cabinet supremacy and party discipline, 55
Candidacy of MKs, 155-57
Changes in Knesset procedures suggested by MKs, 170-72
Childhood environment: party activity and, 148; political recruitment and, 145
Citizens' Rights party, 43, 214
Coalition formation, 54-82, 222-23
Coalitions, cabinet: causes of, 57-58; history of, 58, 60-69; in Israel, 212; legislative behavior and, 55; party membership in, 57, 74-80; payoffs to parties for, 75; size of, 69-71; theories of, 56-57; winning, 56
Coalitions, preelection, 39, 58-60, 222-23
Commerce and Industry Ministry, 190
Committee chairmen: functions of, 199-200; selection of, 88-89
Committees: assignments on, 88-89, 194-95; attractive, 195; frequency of meetings in, 196; functions of, 196-99; important, 182; legislative expertise on, 172-74; legislators and, 194-200; powers of, 89; role of, 89-90; seat assignments on, 90; work in Knesset of, 195-98
Communist party, 217
Constituency work of MKs, 202-6
Constitution, Israeli, 34-38
Constitution Committee, 182
Contact between Government and MKs, 189-94
Continuity of Government, principle

249

of, 37
Contracts Law, 35
Courts Law, 35
Culture as an influence on socialization, 116
Czudnowski, Moshe, 46

Data used in this analysis, 31
Dayan, Moshe, 80, 168, 218, 219
Debate in Knesset, 94-95
Defense Ministry, 182; as a coalition payoff, 74
Democratic Movement for Change party, 214, 216-22
Deputy Speaker of Knesset, selection of, 88-89
Development Ministry and coalition payoffs, 74

Eban, Abba, 168, 216
Education and Culture Committee important, 74, 182
Education and Culture Ministry, 182
Education of MKs, 111-13
Election of 1977, 213-21
Elections and Knesset behavior, 172
Electoral lists, 43; group and symbolic candidates on, 46-47; importance of, 44; order of candidates on, 44-47; recruiting with, 51; zones on, 45
Electoral reforms, 221-22
Electoral system, 43-47
Eliav, Arie, 226
Elites in the Knesset, 178-83
Equal Rights for Women Law, 35
Eshkol, Levi, 66
Expectations of job of MKs, 164-65
Expertise in the Knesset, 172-78

Family environment and socialization, 119-20
Finance Committee, 182; attraction of, 195; power of, 89
Finance Ministry, 182; as coalition payoff, 74
Flatto-Sharon, Samuel, 217, 219

Foreign Affairs and Security Committee, 89, 182, 195
Foreign Affairs Ministry, 190; as coalition payoff, 74; important, 182
Franklin, Mark, 75
Free Center party, 39, 44, 45, 214
Functions of committees in Knesset, 197-99
Fundamental Law, 34-38; Fundamental Law Human Rights, 35; Fundamental Law The Army, 35; Fundamental Law The Economy, 35; Fundamental Law The Government, 35-36; Fundamental Law Israel Lands, 35; Fundamental Law The Knesset, 35-36, 90-91; Fundamental Law The President of the State, 35

Gahal alignment, 66, 67, 69, 75, 80
General Zionist party, 61, 66
Geographic origin and socialization, 118-19, 128-29
Goodland, Thomas, 48
Government (cabinet), formation of, 36
Government, relation to Knesset, 37-38, 187-94
Gratifying characteristics of MKs' job, 164-65
Greater Israel Movement party, 39, 44
Greenstein, Fred, 114
Group candidates on electoral lists, 47
Group membership and political recruitment, 142-47
Gutmann, Emmanuel, 42

Hammer, Zevulon, 168
Health Ministry, 190
Herman, Valerie, 56, 60
Herut party, 39, 44, 66, 214
Histadrut, 151
History: impact on coalitions, 58; influence on socialization, 116, 124-25
Home political environment: and

Index

party identification, 131–34; and political awareness, 120; and political interest, 127; and political recruitment, 145–47
Housing Ministry, 74, 190

Ideology, 47; and coalition formation, 58, 69; and party platforms, 48
Immigrant composition of Knesset, 108–11
Immigration and Absorption Ministry, 190–91
Immunity, Rights, and Duties of Members of Knesset Law, 86
Imperfect information and coalitions, 69
Important committees, 182
Important ministries, 182
Influence, sources for MKs, 201–2
Influentials in the Knesset, 178–83
Informal rules of the Knesset, 166–70
Interior Ministry, 182

Jacob, Herbert, 139
Jerusalem Women's Association, 47
Judges Law, 35
Judicial Review, 35
Justice Ministry, 182; as a coalition payoff, 74

Kargman, Israel, 168
Keys, electoral (distribution of Knesset seats), 43
Keys to cabinet, 72–80
Knesset: areas of influence for MKs, 201–2; Building Law of 1952, 87; distribution of seats in, 43; immunity of building, 87; party membership in, 59; parliamentary structure of, 85; physical organization of, 97–98
Knesset Committee, 182
Kornberg, Allan, 166

Labor alignment, 29, 39, 44, 67, 68, 80, 213, 214, 216–18, 221
Labor Committee, 88, 182

Labor Ministry, 182
Landau, Haim, 42
Langton, Kenneth, 114
Law and Administration Ordinance of 1948, 35
Law of Return, 35, 219
Legislative behavior, 99–103, 170–72
Legislative process in the Knesset, 95–97
Legislative roles, 28–29, 166–70
Legislative supremacy, 54
Legislators and legislative output, 28
Legislatures: approaches to, 24; functions of, 25–28; reasons for study, 23, 28
Leiserson, Michael, 56, 61, 70
Levels of offices held by MKs, 152–53
Liberal party, 39, 44
Library of Knesset, 99
Likud alignment, 39, 44, 45, 68, 69, 103, 213, 214, 216–19
Lists, electoral, 43–47
Location of birth: impact upon political awareness, 119; impact upon political interest, 128

Mail to MKs, 204–5
Mapai party, 39, 41, 44, 61, 64–67, 69, 70, 71, 74, 75; forming cabinets, 60; reasons for decline of, 41
Mapam party, 39, 44, 65, 66, 67, 68, 71
Matthews, Donald, 166, 227
Mazon, Itzhak, 227
Meir, Golda, 66, 68–69
Mezey, Michael, 28
Migration of MKs, 109–10
Minimal winning coalition: defined, 56; inhibitors of, 69–71; theories of, 57
Ministers, contacts between MKs and, 189–94
Ministry of Interior and the National Religious Party, 75
Ministry of Justice, 74
Ministry of Police, 190

Mosca, Gaetano, 178
Motion to add to the agenda, 92–93

Namir, Ora, 47
National backgrounds of MKs, 109–10
National Religious party, 38, 48, 61, 67–70, 75, 80, 216–18, 220; coalition payoffs and, 64, 70; committee assignments of, 88; electoral reforms and, 221–22; Ministry of Interior and, 75; Ministry of Religious Affairs and, 74–75; Ministry of Social Welfare and, 74–75
Nationality Law, 35
Navon, Itzak, 168
NRP. See National Religious Party

Occupations of MKs prior to Knesset, 113
Offices held by MKs prior to Knesset, 149–54
Ombudsman behavior of MKs, 102, 190–91

Parental politics: and initial party identification, 132; and political awareness, 120; and political interest, 124–25; and political recruitment, 145–47
Parliamentary government, 50, 54
Parliamentary immunity, 85–87
Parliamentary inviolability, 85
Parties, political: activities of, 57; as socializing agents, 42; decline in numbers of, 41; functions of, 39, 42, 50; impact on legislative process, 51; importance of, 212–13; in government coalitions, 60–62; numbers of, 38, 43, 50, 57; quotas for bills in Knesset, 95
Party activity: childhood environment and, 148; of MKs, 147–48, 154–55; political group membership and, 147; political recruitment and, 147–48
Party allowance for MKs, 98
Party control of debate, 94

Party control of legislation, 95–96
Party discipline, 50, 55, 170, 186, 201, 213; and cabinet supremacy, 55; and legislative behavior, 50–51, 95–96, 101; and questions to Ministers, 93–94
Party identification: defined, 131; importance of, 131; of MKs, 130–36, 142–45; political group membership and, 142–45; reasons for, 135; religious parties and, 134
Party impact on coalition formation, 57
Party lists. See Electoral lists
Party membership in Knesset, 59
Party officeholding by MKs, 149–54
Party organizations, 42
Party seniority and cabinet membership, 175–77
Pathways to parliament, 140
Patterson, Samuel, 139
Payoffs, cabinet positions as, 60–69, 72–80
Perceptions of MKs: of Knesset procedure, 170–72; of MK job, 164–66
Peres, Shimon, 168, 214, 217
Place of birth of MKs, 110–11
Poale Agudat Israel party, 217–18
Police Ministry, 74, 190
Policy outcomes and coalition payoffs, 61
Political awareness of MKs as children, 116–24
Political group membership, 142–45, 147
Political interest of MKs as children, 124–30
Political party system, 38–43
Political recruitment: defined, 138–39; group membership and, 142–47; party activity and, 147–48, 155; political interest and, 144; political socialization and, 139; reasons for study, 156–57
Political socialization: effects of stimuli, 115; defined, 113–15; political awareness and, 116–24; political

Index

interest and, 124–30; theories of, 115
Pope, John, 56, 60
Position on party electoral list, 44
Preelectoral coalitions, 58–60, 222–23
Prime minister, selection of, 36–37
Prime Minister's Office, 182; as a coalition payoff, 74; as important, 182
Procedures of Knesset, 90–91; and legislative behavior, 170–72; reforms of, 221–25
Professional backgrounds of MKs, 113
Progressive party, 65, 71, 74
Proportional representation, 43–47, 212
Provisional Council of Government, 35
Public offices held by MKs, 150–54

Question time in Knesset, 91–92, 171
Quorum of Knesset, 91

Rabin, Itzhak, 168, 179, 214, 226
Rafi party, 39, 44, 66, 67, 75, 80
Reasons for recruitment of MKs, 156–57
Recruitment, political. *See* Political recruitment
Recruitment to candidacy of MKs, 155–57
Reforms in Knesset, 221–25
Relationship between legislators and the Government, 187–94
Religious Affairs Ministry, 74
Religious characteristics of MKs, 108
Religious parties and party identification, 134
Riker, William, 69
Roles, legislative, 28–29. *See* Legislative roles
Rules of the game, 166–70

Sanctions for violations of informal rules, 168–69
Sapir, Pinhas, 168

Seats in Knesset, assignment of, 44
Sex of MKs, 106
Sharon, Ariel, 217
Shlomozion party, 217
Social Welfare Ministry, 74, 190
Socialization of MKs. *See* Political socialization
Speaker of Knesset, 86–87; election of, 87–88; legislators' immunity and, 86–87; procedures and, 90–93; question time and, 91
State Controller Committee, 88
State List Movement party, 39, 44–45
Subjects of initial political awareness, 121–23
Subjects of initial political interest, 129–30
Suggestions for change in Knesset, 170–71
Symbolic candidates on electoral lists, 47

Tamir, Shmuel, 168
Tel-Aviv Women's Association, 47
Term of the Knesset, 91
Tourism Ministry, 74
Transportation Ministry, 74
Types of offices held by MKs, 151–53

Urgent motion to add to the agenda, 92–93

Warhaftig, Zerah, 168
Weizman, Ezer, 221
Westminster model of government, 34–35, 54, 211–12
When MKs were born, 107
"Who is a Jew?" question, 64, 68

Yacobi, Gad, 226
Yadin, Yigal, 219
Yadlin, Aharon, 68
Year of birth: impact upon political awareness, 117; impact upon political interest, 125

Zadok, Haim, 168
Zeidel, Hillel, 226
Zidon, Asher, 87

Zionism: influence on socialization, 117–18; party identification and, 134; party platforms and, 48; political awareness and, 123